CYBERPUNK AND CYBERCULTURE

SCIENCE FICTION AND THE WORK OF WILLIAM GIBSON

DANI CAVALLARO

THE ATHLONE PRESS
London & New Brunswick NJ

First published in 2000 by
THE ATHLONE PRESS
1 Park Drive, London NW11 7SG
and New Brunswick, New Jersey

British Library Cataloguing in Publication Data
*A catalogue record for this book is available
from the British Library*

ISBN 0 485 00412 7 HB
0 485 00607 3 PB

Library of Congress Cataloging in Publication Data
A catalog record for this book has been requested

Distributed in the United States, Canada and South America by
Transaction Publishers
390 Campus Drive
Somerset, New Jersey 08873

Typeset by RefineCatch Limited, Bungay, Suffolk
Printed in Great Britain by
Athenaeum Press Ltd, Gateshead

To Paddy, with love

To Patty, with love

CONTENTS

CONTENTS

PREFACE

In contemporary western and westernized cultures, people are surrounded by an increasingly wide range of tangible products that seem to impart a sense of solidity to their lives. Objects such as mobile phones, computers, portable physiotherapy units, personal stereos, microwave ovens, video recorders and fax machines (to mention but a few examples) are integral components of many people's everyday existence. Often, they are regarded not merely as useful tools for the accomplishment of practical tasks but actually as defining aspects of people's identities, lifestyles and value systems.

They thus become comparable to *prostheses*, the artificial supports used by medical technology to complete otherwise lacking physical organisms. However, the aura of solidity surrounding those commodities and their human users is something of an illusion. Indeed, technologically mass-produced objects and their consumers are incessantly caught in cultural operations – centred on advertising, the media and the information industry – that are not so much concerned with tangible products as with images, fashions and styles. The material CD player or laptop PC one happens to own, for example, is far less significant than the immaterial images or ideas of such objects promoted by designers and advertisers. Moreover, those images and ideas keep shifting, being constantly modified by the introduction of minimal differences that rapidly consign even the most attractive products to obsolescence. It would therefore be preposterous to view the sense of solidity conveyed by certain products as anything more than a fantasy.

William Gibson's classic definition of cyberspace quoted above highlights the fantastic quality of many of our quotidian experiences. The solidity of many of the products we consume is, by and large, a *hallucination* – something delusory, illusory, mirage-like. Yet Gibson's definition also suggests that our illusions and mirages form the basis of a kind of *consensus* by being continuously shared by large groups of people. This sharing is achieved by transforming individual experiences into collective representations. Advertising, the media and the information industry capitalize on the translation of people's subjective desires, emotions and fantasies into images of ideal and desirable products. Such images bypass individual tastes and preferences by being presented as universally appealing. They thus create a curious notion of commonality, based on the assumption that belonging to a culture amounts to desiring the same commodities desired by virtually any other individual inhabiting that culture. In this illusory community, people are often little more than anonymous strangers to one another: all that connects them is an abstract network of representations. They are characters in a narrative, or actors in a play, who roughly know the plot without being familiar with the rest of the cast.

The consensus produced by contemporary technoculture is always a product of contingent trends and is accordingly open to ongoing redefinition. It is clearly not founded upon the values of the Enlightenment. In its western conception, that philosophy grounds the possibility of intellectual and ethical agreement among humans in the principles of reason, progress and common sense, supported by the idealization of science and technology as unproblematically rational discourses, by the demonization of the body as inferior matter, and by the discrediting of myth as superstition. Cyberpunk foregrounds the provisional status of all definitions of value, rationality and truth in a radical rejection of the Enlightenment ethos. It amalgamates in often baffling ways the rational and the irrational, the new and the old, the mind and the body, by integrating the hyperefficient structures of high technology with the anarchy of street subcultures.

This book explores the issues outlined in the preceding paragraphs in two ways. First, it assesses the impact of postmodern science and digital technology in terms of both their current relevance and their relationship with older structures of meaning, such as mythology. Second, it investigates the interplay between specialized forms of technological expertise and everyday discourses pertaining to the urban setting, the fashion and health industries, approaches to sexuality and gender, education, and entertainment. As to the choice of Gibson's work as a lens through which these issues may be examined, the following rationale obtains: Gibson is referred to in legion articles, essays, chapters in books and websites. However, analyses of his work tend to be cursory, often superficial and almost invariably repetitive. If Gibson has, as many argue, indeed become a cult figure or guru, it would seem worth investigating in depth both his work and the reasons behind his gaining such a status. At the same time, it is necessary to study Gibson's cyberpunk in relation to other authors who have likewise engaged with the fate of advanced technocultures and directly or indirectly helped to shape cyberpunk as a genre.

Cyberculture, an environment saturated by electronic technology, and its fictional representation in cyberpunk compel us to reassess drastically ideas of time, reality, materiality, community and space. The gap between the present and the future becomes narrower and narrower, as the futuristic fantasies of classic science fiction turn out to be integral parts of the here-and-now. As Bruce Sterling has observed, 'The cyberpunks are perhaps the first SF generation to grow up not only within the literary tradition of science fiction, but in a truly science-fictional world.'[4] The here-and-now, moreover, can hardly be called real, since it is more a product of media-based images and simulations than a tangible state of affairs. It is the transient effect of an abstract play of data that insistently blurs the distinction between human memory and electronic memory, material space and virtual space. The reassessment of conventional notions of reality is fundamentally brought about by cultural changes initiated by technology. However, the rhetoric through which these changes are narrated and charted reverberates with images drawn from older traditions and belief systems. Classical mythology, voodoo, spiritualism, neo-Christian cults and a whole theology of artificial intelligences constantly interact with modern and postmodern technologies. Cyberpunk has not only redefined current understandings of science fiction. It has actually forged a new language and image repertoire to describe and negotiate contemporary culture in relation to both the future and the past, and by stressing the enduring hold of mythology and fantasy.

As philosophers and historians talk of the end of history and the end of art, religious and spiritualist movements (such as angelmania) proliferate, as do books and films about mysterious occurrences, monstrosity and weird sexualities, websites devoted to the esoteric and the occult, and legion fashions inspired by magic and the supernatural. As Jenny Dyson points out:

> In uptown Manhattan, a twentysomething fashion PR straight out of *Sex and the City* is 'smudging' her apartment with a bundle of smouldering sage leaves (a Native American ritual thought to rid spaces of 'dead energy'). In Paris, a model is thoughtfully carving a wish onto a candle before lighting it and watching it burn. In Auckland, a successful television producer is addressing a letter to the angels of real estate, requesting ... the specific dimensions of the new home she is hoping for. In London, pop stars and career girls are having their tarot cards read at Mysteries, the capital's best known New Age store. As if by magic, magic has become mainstream.[5]

Central to this trend is an increasing emphasis on the body, as demonstrated, for example, by contemporary cinema. From Greenaway's hyperbolically grotesque imagery to Lynch's inscription of the grotesque into familiar structures, from Fincher's and Bigelow's satanic urbanscapes to the *X-Files'* dramatizations of the inexplicable and Cronenberg's postmodern pastiches of paranoid haunting, we detect a trajectory of incremental corporealization. According to

Istvan Csicsery-Ronay, this is marked by the shift from a logic of 'expansion' where 'projectiles of human consciousness fly giddily into "outer space"' to a focus on the 'destruction of liberal ideology by autonomous technology. . . . Where there was uncontrolled expansion, the *afflatus* of an expanding technicist ego hallucinating cosmic humanism, now there is implosion.'[6] Moreover, if in the 1960s and 1970s fantastic texts tended to depict squeaky-clean and decontaminated worlds in which human *minds* were controlled by machines, in the 1980s and 1990s the emphasis falls on the eternal night of apocalyptic megalopolises wherein abjection and monstrosity are *written on the body*. *Alien*, for example, could be read as an allegory of the body's colonization by the economic and political imperatives of late capitalism (for example, downsizing and permanent unemployment). The monster feeding on and tearing apart defenceless human anatomies replicates the Company's pitiless exploitation of its workers. Bret Easton Ellis's *American Psycho* (1988), as a further example, dramatizes the body's subjugation to aesthetic and stylistic addictions typical of consumer society and distorts the material world in a darkly parodic form. As Charlotte Raven observes:

> [A]ll his novels are full of it – the suits and the CD cases, the sushi and Phil Collins compilations – the detritus of modern life. From his first book . . . to . . . *American Psycho*, Ellis has been preoccupied with more or less similar themes: our society's obsession with surfaces, the extent to which contemporary culture deprives us of the will (or the ability) to be human, the commodification of everything.[7]

Furthermore the novel, through its chilling suppression of the dividing line between fact and fantasy, embodies the supreme fear that behind every powerful and successful person may lie a deranged creature and that anybody may be his next victim. It records the dual status of the serial killer, as both the obverse of the respectable citizen and the personification of the latter's own tabooed desires.

The ravaged bodies presented in the fictions just mentioned illustrate a typically Gothic sensibility. The term Gothic is here used to designate not simply a style but rather a whole cultural discourse that emphasizes images of psychological and physical devastation and a pervasive sense of alienation, fragmentation and decay.

Cyberpunk is indebted to this discourse on several levels. Gothic connotations are evident in cyberpunk's settings, in its characters' psychological make-up, in its attitudes to the body and in its narrative techniques. Like Gothic *spaces and places*, cyberpunk's settings often capitalize on a sense of the sublime, on fantastical proliferations of structures and ornamental detail, on unrestorable ruins, on calculated ugliness and inversion. These locations are psychological maps traversed by secrets and traumas that their labyrinthine geography may disperse but never exorcize. *Historically*, the Gothic often refers to archaic, anti-classical and mediaeval epochs. These temporal associations are frequently invested with ethical and moral significance to suggest the barbaric, the savage and the primitive. These connotations are also evident in cyberpunk's exposure of the violent, brutal and anarchic core of cyberculture at large. On the *psychological plane*, the Gothic refers primarily to tropes of transgression and haunting. In this respect, some of the key words shared by cyberpunk and the Gothic are: decay, decomposition, disorder, helplessness, horror, irresolution, madness, paranoia, persecution, secrecy, unease, terror. Moreover, the Gothic *body* exemplifies the phenomenon of 'abjection' by standing out as an object of both fascination and revulsion.[8] What makes it simultaneously attractive and repulsive is the fact that its identity and boundaries are unstable: it is always on the verge of becoming something else. The outcome of its metamorphosis is unpredictable, as it may disclose beauty or, equally well, spawn monsters. Cyberpunk's bodies are likewise fluid and permeable: their integrity is continually challenged and violated. Pollution, contagion, disease, bestiality and monstrosity are some of the most harrowing aspects of the body that recur in both the Gothic and cyberpunk. *Stylistically*, cyberpunk often shares with the Gothic a penchant for exaggeration, the accumulation of details, the proliferation of rhetorical figures and narrative layers, which could be read as a parody of classic realism and its claims to descriptive accuracy and authorial control.

Whichever way we look at it, the Gothic emphasizes everything that points towards or symbolizes death: crumbling, decaying, fractured and partial forms. This fascination with death and corruption is central to many aspects of contemporary culture, as testified by the texts mentioned earlier and many related others, and requires us to confront certain crucial questions. Is the death-wish located at the heart of the Gothic a morbid obsession or an invitation to confront humanity's most deep-seated fears? Could the Gothic be read as an attempt to give shape to those irrational extremes beyond our control that haunt us all the time? Could it be read, more specifically, as a reminder that what we fear most is ourselves – that is, the alien *in* us? If so, the Gothic could be said to dramatize the breakdown of personal and social structures, in order to compel us to face up to a nightmare we continually repress, yet continually re-experience, in a world in which our ability to hold ourselves together is slipping away.

Cyberculture highlights these issues with a focus on the complex relationship between technology and mythology. Technology and mythology are primarily brought together by their shared attitudes to the body as the object of alternately magnifying and minimizing practices. Mythology empowers the body through figures such as gods, titans and giants and simultaneously dwarfs it through figures such as invisible spirits and diminutive goblins. Technology likewise enhances the body's faculties, by means of cosmetic surgery, genetic engineering and prosthetics, and concurrently swamps it in a deluge of abstract information, representations and data. Drawing on both mythology and technology, cyberpunk emphasizes the body's centrality. Pivotal to the genre is the notion that cultural transformations are performed first and foremost on the stage of the human body. Gibson offers contrasting readings of this state of affairs. On the one hand, the fusion of the biological and the technological signals the disappearance of the body, its reduction to lifeless meat. On the other, it opens up fresh opportunities for experiment, recombination and play. Cyberpunk presents a bleak vision of a future in which people are subjected to ruthless communications networks, are totally disconnected from one another and long to leave the body behind, yet are trapped in a physical maze of junk. At the same time, it dissolves conventional notions of corporeality, inaugurates novel forms of intersubjectivity and alternative ways of figuring space. Though the physical dimension is often marginalized by digital technology, both the biological body and the body of the posturban megalopolis go on presenting eminently material traits, intensified by their lacerations and vulnerabilities. The bodies generated by cyberpunk are simultaneously mythological, as products of imagination and fantasy, technological, as products of science and ideology, and Gothic, as products of psychotic and fragmented environments, of physical and mental disarray, of deviance and transgression.

In compelling us to reassess the concept of embodiment, cyberculture also asks to reconsider the meanings of story-telling, of science and of the relationship between the two within a cultural scenario of permanent irresolution. At the same time, cyberculture encourages us to recognize that the structures of power and knowledge that define any historically embedded society are never transparent or indeed plainly visible; that the relationship between what we know and what we see is always unsettled; and that understanding the present requires grappling with the tension between what we think we understand and what may be imagined beyond the limits of the understandable. Gibson's fiction, in particular, stresses the failure of teleologies based on notions of evolution, emancipation and progress and throws into relief the brutal demolition of traditional concepts of culture, community, individual agency and hope itself. It concurrently foregrounds the complex ways in which computer technology both draws us towards a novel understanding of our relationship with ourselves and myriad – often faceless – others, and destabilizes conventional forms of communication and interaction. It does so by imagining the future but also, perhaps more importantly, by finding the grounds of the future in the present and intimations of the not-yet in the now. However, the picture painted by cyberpunk is not univocally bleak. In fact, Gibson's narratives also alert us, through jocular incursions into the tenebrous realms of exploitation and decay, to those fleeting disturbances in the fabric of the given that, like dying yet dazzling supernovas, prick the dark expanse of postcapitalist dispensations. On this basis, *Cyberpunk and Cyberculture: Science Fiction and the Work of William Gibson* argues that provocative forms of knowledge can be deduced from cyberculture and, in particular, from Gibson's dystopian narratives, and that these may help us situate ourselves both as individuals and as collectivities.

A BRIEF GUIDE TO THE BOOK

INTRODUCTION: SCIENCE FICTION AND CYBERPUNK

This provides a brief 'history' of science fiction, meant to contextualize cyberpunk in relation to the broader genre from which it derives. It shows that although science fiction is often seen as an essentially twentieth-century phenomenon, science-fictional motifs can be traced much further back. Examples of early science-fiction writers are supplied, ranging from Classical times, through the late Renaissance, to the eighteenth and nineteenth centuries. By looking at science fiction's precursors, at the Pulp Era, at the New Wave and finally at contemporary science fiction, the Introduction outlines changing themes, approaches and techniques. The relationship between science fiction and classic detective stories, utopian/dystopian narratives and postmodernist fiction is also discussed. The main features of cyberpunk are then outlined with an emphasis on its shift from classic science fiction's robots and spaceships to cybernetics and biotechnology. The genre is examined in terms of its combination of technoscientific themes and urban subcultures inspired by a punk sensibility, its focus on invasive technologies and its dystopian depiction of a junk-infested world of losers and loonies.

I CYBERPUNK AND VIRTUAL TECHNOLOGIES

This is a 'bridge' chapter designed to help the reader place cyberpunk in the context of growing electronic technologies. Drawing on a wide range of critics that have examined the phenomena of virtual reality and cyberspace, this chapter looks at the principal debates about the impact of technology on notions of time, space, community and embodiment. It contrasts optimistic interpretations of cybertechnology as a kind of 'brave new world' and negative assessments of its repercussions. It also discusses the etymology of the term 'virtual', the politics of interactive programmes (MOOs and MUDs), and virtual reality's intermingling of the real and the imaginary in relation to relevant philosophical and psychoanalytical positions.

2 CYBERPUNK, TECHNOLOGY AND MYTHOLOGY

This chapter shows that cyberpunk combines technological images and issues with themes derived from myth, legend and mystical traditions. It examines the relationship between technology and mythology with reference to their linguistic origins in words such as *mythos*, *techne*, *poesis* and *ars* and demonstrates that there are interesting similarities between mythology's and technology's approaches to the body. This idea is illustrated with reference to various uses of the cybernetic organism in the military, medical, philosophical and fictional arenas and to cyborgs popularized by cinema. Cyberpunk's use of heterodox religions, preternatural figures and spiritualistic trends is also assessed and various reasons are adduced for the fusion of technoscience and fantasy in cyberpunk. The final section of this chapter contextualizes cyberpunk's amalgamation of technology and mythology with reference to the development of the discipline of 'Science Studies' and to the appropriation by philosophers, theorists and fiction writers of scientific terminologies.

3 CYBERPUNK AND THE BODY

This chapter argues that in spite of several critics' claim that technology has erased the body, this is not really the case. Technology has transformed the body (at times by empowering it, at others by attenuating it) but it has not taken it away. Technological transformations of the body are crucial tools through which contemporary cultures define themselves, their beliefs and their desires. Cyberpunk enhances the body through biotechnology and futuristic surgery but simultaneously exposes it to environmental threats, corporational greed and sexual exploitation. Developing some of the ideas discussed in the previous chapter, this section examines cyberpunk's construction of hybrid bodies that blur the distinction between tech-noscience and mysticism. Special attention is paid to three main figures: that of the 'ghost', used by cyberpunk as a means of showing that people's bodies are constantly haunted by the spaces they inhabit, by other people, by machines and by their own obsessions; that of the 'stranger', employed to stress the difficulty of living with the ghosts and aliens that are *inside* us; and that of the 'doll' as an intriguing admixture of the natural and the artificial. Close readings of a selection of texts show how cyberpunk utilizes images of the technological body as a way of commenting on the commodification of knowledge, health, beauty and personal identity.

4 CYBERPUNK, GENDER AND SEXUALITY

This chapter opens with a general assessment of the relationship between cyberpunk and issues of gender and sexuality and shows how cyberculture compels us to rethink traditional gender roles and erotic experiences. It then focuses on technological constructions of gender (through practices such as body-building, cosmetic surgery and the electronic control of reproduction and birth) and contextual-izes these issues in relation to a wide range of perspectives on the relationship between gender, technology and ecology. Subsequently, this chapter looks at cyberpunk's ambivalent approach to gender stereotypes: its perpetuation of images such as the tough dame and the femme fatale, on the one hand, and its introduction of alternative types suggesting female strength and independence, on the other. The closing part examines the phenomenon of computerized intercourse ('virtual sex' or 'cybereroticism') in terms of various interpretations that alternately read it as a clean and safe form of sexuality or as the ultimate collapse of the human—machine bound-ary. Ambivalent attitudes to the relationship between machines and human sexuality are traced back to the nineteenth century and to the dawn of the industrial age.

5 CYBERPUNK AND THE CITY

This chapter develops some of the ideas discussed in the previous one, with a focus on the 'body' of the dystopian cybercity. The city organized by digital technology is, apparently, a rational and clean environment. Yet cyberpunk shows that the posthuman megalopolis is a dirty and messy 'Sprawl', full of crime and disease. The opening section explores some of the ways in which geometry, astronomy, genetics and physics have used 'maps' as a means of lending order and stability to physical worlds that are actually chaotic and caught in processes of constant change. It is then suggested that the cyber-city could be understood in terms of the computer's most basic operations: its binary ON/OFF options, and the gates (AND, OR, NOT) through which various data are arranged. These operations can be seen as metaphors for organizations of space based on prin-ciples of presence and absence, order and disorder, that have con-cerned both traditional and postmodern geographers. Emphasis is placed on representations of the city of Venice as a symbol of the fluidity of cyberspace and of the boundless worlds depicted by cyberpunk. The final section compares cyberpunk's fragmentation of space with scientific approaches to ideas of chaos, crisis and catastrophe, and shows, by means of close textual analysis, how cyberpunk's narrative structures articulate these ideas through their formal features.

6 CYBERPUNK AND THE GOTHIC

This chapter argues that cyberpunk displays eminently Gothic traits – obsession, monstrosity, transgression, social unrest, psychological disorder – and assesses the Gothic legacy from the eighteenth cen-tury to the present. It examines some of the ways in which cyber-punk defamiliarizes familiar situations through the Gothic uncanny and relates this theme to Faustian imagery. It then focuses on cyber-punk's appropriation of architectural motifs of Gothic derivation, based on the principles of proliferation and accretion, and argues that the image of the multilayered Gothic building is used primarily to convey a deep sense of confusion, uncertainty and excess. The relationship between Gothic buildings and the nature of the families that inhabit them is then assessed to suggest that in traditional Goth-ic literature and cyberpunk alike the mysterious shape of the Gothic building reflects the secrets and obsessions of their owners and that these impact, specifically, on trapped female characters. This chapter also examines the idea of the Gothic as a fashion or style by relating cyberpunk's attraction to clothes and accessories of Gothic origin to the creations of contemporary designers, as well as to the sym-bolic use of clothing in classic Gothic fictions. The final section concentrates on the relationship between cyberpunk and the Gothic with a focus on the concept of time and particularly on their inter-weaving of present, past and future dimensions. By exploring these issues, this section also constitutes a link between Chapter 6 and the Epilogue, where notions of history and memory are addressed.

EPILOGUE: CYBERPUNK AND MEMORY

This closing section sums up the main themes and issues explored in the body of the book, using as a leading thread the idea that cyber-punk and cyberculture reconfigure radically our grasp of history and time, with profound repercussions on both individual and collective memories. In both cyberculture generally and cyberpunk specifically, memories tend to take an increasingly prosthetic form, as images that do not result from personal experience but are actually implanted in our brains by the constant flow of mass information. Cyberpunk articulates a postmodern conception of time and history that radically disrupts linearity. Human memories are palimpsests in which different levels of experience are superimposed on one another. Much of the time it is hard to tell to whom both the experi-ences and the memories actually 'belong'.

FURTHER READING AND BIBLIOGRAPHY

The guide to further reading lists a selection of critical texts dealing with various aspects of cyberpunk and cyberculture, and briefly out-lines the contents and approaches presented by each. Its aim is two-fold: to familiarize the reader with the principal ideas and debates addressed by contemporary writers and theorists concerned with the impact of technoscience on our lives; and to contextualize cyber-punk as a fictional genre in relation to broad cultural issues. The bibliography is divided into primary and secondary sources.

INTRODUCTION

SCIENCE FICTION AND CYBERPUNK

The future is unwritten. There are best-case scenarios.
There are worst-case scenarios. Both of them are great
fun to write about if you're a science fiction novelist, but
neither of them ever happens in the real world. What
happens in the real world is always a sideways-case scenario. World-changing marvels to us, are only wallpaper to
our children.

(Bruce Sterling)[1]

We [science-fiction writers] are sort of charlatans: we
come up with a few ideas and we make a living out of
that.

(William Gibson)[2]

Science fiction is hard to define to any reader's or critic's satisfaction.
This is largely due to the often puzzling variety of themes,
approaches and techniques exhibited by the genre, as well as to the
difficulty of situating historically the origins of science fiction. In
some of its most popular interpretations, science fiction is considered a fundamentally twentieth-century phenomenon, rooted in a
predominantly western experience of technological growth. Yet the
genesis of science fiction could be traced back to much earlier
periods. Indeed, in as early as the year AD 150, Lucian of Samosata
was already experimenting with the themes of interplanetary travel
and warfare in his *Vera Historia* ('True History'), a parodic
reinterpretation of the official truths recorded by previous histori-
ographers. More recent evidence for the existence of science-fictional
narratives that well predate the twentieth century can be found in
Cyrano de Bergerac's seventeenth-century stories, such as *Voyage to*

the Moon (1661). According to Italo Calvino, Cyrano is 'the first true forerunner of science fiction'. Calvino also highlights the poetic and philosophical qualities of Cyrano's narratives:

> Cyrano extols the unity of all things, animate or inanimate, the combinatoria of elementary figures that determine the variety of living forms; and above all he conveys the sense of the precariousness of the processes behind them. That is, how nearly man missed being man, and life, life, and the world, the world.[3]

Recognizing the speculative approach and metaphysical preoccupations of this early writer of science fiction is important, considering the negative reputation later acquired by the genre as a form of pulp incapable of serious intellectual commitment. Such a reputation is based on specifically twentieth-century prejudices spawned by the popularization of science fiction. Yet if we look further back in time we find that the precursors of modern science fiction are literary and philosophical texts commonly held in high esteem.

Indeed, a wide range of texts, now regarded as classics, that deal with imaginary journeys, dream visions, supernatural explorations and metaphysical tasks could be classified as science fiction. A number of narratives produced over as broad a period as the one that spans ancient Greek civilization to the nineteenth century would make likely candidates for inclusion in a potential canon of proto-science fiction: Homer's *Odyssey*, Dante's *Divina Commedia*, Ariosto's *Orlando Furioso*, Rabelais's *Gargantua and Pantagruel*, More's *Utopia*, Swift's *Gulliver's Travels*, Voltaire's *Candide*, Rousseau's *Emile* and Goethe's *Faust*, for example.

Mary Shelley's *Frankenstein* (1818) is arguably the best-known predecessor of modern science fiction. What makes it a classic in the field is its focus on the question of what constitutes humanity in a world that both promises opportunities for the enhancement of human powers via science and dehumanizes people through technology. Frankenstein, a student of natural philosophy, is able to create an artificial being with the aid of technology. He is guided by benevolent intentions, yet he is dragged into a whirlpool of fear, loathing and violence, since his creature comes to symbolize everything that humanity deems most threatening about technology. *Frankenstein* could be read as a variation of the Faust myth in that it capitalizes on the topos of the overreaching scholar daring to challenge nature's most fundamental laws. This theme will prove hugely popular among subsequent science-fiction writers and film-makers. Yet it is important to remember that the novel does not merely pave the path to a wayward generation of mad scientists, sadistic doctors and self-deluded researchers. In fact, it also introduces an issue of tremendous ideological significance for science fiction, that of monstrosity, and thus articulates a deep sense of trepidation surrounding anything *other*. The monster and the alien (both variations on the theme of the non-human) are used by science fiction, as by the Gothic novel, to give form to inchoate fears and prejudices. The dread of the non-human encapsulates legion cultural anxieties about the contamination of dominant social classes, privileged sexualities, national values and whole empires by a putatively deviant and evil *alter ego*. Frankenstein's creature combines all the disturbing markers of alterity that Shelley's culture would have readily associated with the *illegitimate* members of society: foreigners, women, the disenfranchised, the poor and the disabled. Concurrently, the novel shows that true monstrosity does not lie with the creature's repulsive appearance but with power structures and institutions capable of transforming an initially benevolent being into an evil-doer. Shelley also bequeaths to later science fiction the idea of the other's *physical* difference, an idea amply documented by scores of green little people, by ET and by the monstrous creatures of *Leviathan*, *The Fly* and the *Alien* series.

Beside Shelley, the best known precursors of modern science fiction are Jules Verne and H.G. Wells. Written in the mid- and late nineteenth century, their stories anticipate later developments in the genre by attempting to present fantastic adventures as scientifically plausible and, particularly in Wells's case, to ground fantasy in a thorough knowledge of scientific issues. Wells's *The Time Machine* (1895) introduces several themes destined to become prominent in later science fiction, the main ones being those of travel through time, the prospect of world annihilation and the encounter between the human and the alien. *The War of the Worlds* (1898) develops the theme of alien invasion. These texts could not possibly be regarded as mere fantasies, for they actually articulate in uncompromising ways deep-seated anxieties about cultural degeneration, the confusion of traditional boundaries, the potentially destructive consequences of technological progress and, above all, the erosion of Victorian certitudes in a declining imperial culture. Wells has influenced many subsequent British writers of science fiction, such as John Wyndham, whose *The Day of the Triffids* (1951) deals with the predicament of the last man or woman left on earth after terminal catastrophe, and conveys a nostalgic desire to rebuild the world from the available fragments and leftovers. This kind of science fiction shows that the genre is not monolithically concerned with a hard, glossy and thoroughly mechanized future. Much of the time, in fact, it focuses on visions of cultural breakdown and disorder that are already palpably evident in the present.

For many critics and readers, the crucial moment in the development of modern science fiction is the year 1926, the date that witnesses the publication of the first issue of the American magazine *Amazing Stories*, edited by Hugo Gernsback. This publication proved immensely popular and, although it indubitably inspired some of the most successful science-fiction writers to come, it also spawned a half-hatched progeny of pulp fictions and films that detrimentally contributed to the berating of the genre. Gernsback, who was himself an occasional writer and amateur scientist, had a somewhat paradoxical understanding of what a science-fiction story should consist of and accomplish. On the one hand, he expected it to be based on science and to be of topical interest to young men engaged in scientific careers. On the other, he wanted it to be 'a charming romance intermingled with scientific fact and prophetic vision'.[4] The outcome of Gernsback's aesthetic was a series of space operas that have come to be associated with the Pulp Era of science fiction. Produced by 'experienced pulp-magazine authors', these stories were, according to the *Grolier Multimedia Encyclopedia*, 'hackneyed adventure tales in which heroes outfitted in dubious space metal wrecked alien worlds and rescued space maidens'.[5]

Wells himself had tagged his science-fiction narratives *scientific romances*, the term romance referring not so much (as it would today) to a popular fiction with sentimental connotations as to an imaginative work uniting the natural and the supernatural. This interpretation of the romance partly derives from the tradition of the Gothic novel, where real situations are explored by means of fantastic and prodigious distortions. As will be argued later in some depth, the Gothic novel is itself a potential precursor of science fiction and especially of contemporary cyberpunk.

Despite (or maybe because of) its paradoxical aesthetic, Gernsback's *Amazing Stories* proved so popular that it was followed in rapid succession by *Science Wonder Stories*, *Wonder Stories* and *Astounding Stories* in the late 1920s and in the 1930s. The magazine *Astounding Stories*, founded by John W. Campbell in 1930, turned out to be an especially valiant competitor for Gernsback's own enterprise. Its founder's aesthetic was based on a notion of science fiction as a credible representation of the impact of technology on both individuals and whole cultures achieved through high levels of literary expertise, sophisticated narrative techniques and a rigorous approach to subject matter. Campbell's venture witnessed the flourishing of science-fiction writers such as Isaac Asimov, Robert A. Heinlein, Theodore Sturgeon and Arthur C. Clarke, whose works have come to be regarded by many as the Golden Age of science fiction. It was in this context that some of science fiction's major themes developed, which *Grolier* lists as: 'robots, alternate worlds, faster-than-light travel, the seeding of the galaxies by human or alien cultures, the meeting of humans and aliens and its many astonishing consequences, and, in the later 1940s, the full range of possibilities presented by nuclear power'.[6]

From the 1950s onwards, science fiction became more and more concerned with the impact of technology on everyday lives and on the fate of the planet. A particularly important development was the New Wave, a phase associated with authors such as Brian Aldiss and J.G. Ballard and with the British publication *New Worlds* (1946–70), edited by Michael Moorcock. The New Wave's focus was on topical issues such as environmental depletion, urban overcrowding and the relationship between technology, crime, drug addiction and sexuality. Thus, the New Wave in some ways preludes to cyberpunk's preoccupation with the impact of technology on the present no less than on the future, the crucial element added to the picture by Gibson and his contemporaries being, of course, computer technology.

The intermingling of reality and fantasy highlighted by Wells, Gernsback, the Gothic, the New Wave and contemporary science fiction repeatedly suggests that speculative fiction is not an escape from cultural reality but rather a means of sharpening people's awareness of this reality by defamiliarizing it through fantasy. As Kingsley Amis argues in *New Maps of Hell*, the fantasy worlds of science fiction do not merely ask us to address the part played by science in our lives but also to evaluate the role of *pseudo-sciences* such as sociology, anthropology, linguistics, psychology and theology.[7] Arguably, both the hard sciences (physics, biology, chemistry) and the pseudo-sciences combine fact and fiction in their programmes, for the main function of both is to *speculate* about people's destinies. They do not give us knowledge as a fully packaged commodity. Rather, they invite us to question what knowledge *is*. This is partly the thrust of Darko Suvin's argument when he states that in examining science fiction, 'cognition' is a more relevant term than 'science'.[8]

The work of J.G. Ballard provides an emblematic example of science fiction's defamiliarizing effects with an emphasis on the instability of knowledge in contemporary technoculture. Scarcely concerned with conventional science-fictional themes such as interplanetary travel or indeed with the representation of a distant future, Ballard's narratives focus on the catastrophic side of science fiction to intimate that catastrophe is not a destiny that awaits humans but rather something that has already happened. Furthermore, as the writer states in his introduction to *Crash*: 'the future is ceasing to exist, devoured by the all-voracious present. We have annexed the future into the present, as merely one of those manifold alternatives open to us.'[9] *Crash* (1973) corroborates this idea by foregrounding disturbing images of junk-strewn urban scenes and horribly mutilated bodies that convey, in a surrealist fashion, a distinctively Gothic sense of loss. As Fred Botting observes:

> The loss of human identity and the alienation of self from both itself and the social bearings in which a sense of reality is secured are presented in the threatening shapes of increasingly dehumanized environments, machinic doubles and violent, psychotic fragmentation.[10]

David Punter concurs: 'the principal subject at issue' in Ballard's writings 'is the conflict between the individual and a dehumanized environment'.[11] 'The world of assassinations and high-speed car crashes which he depicts has ceased to be amenable to interpretation in terms of natural laws, and individuals have ceased to hold themselves together either literally or metaphorically.'[12]

Thus, at the same time as grounding science fiction in the here-and-now, Ballard also suggests that the ultimate journey is not into outer space but into the uncertainties of a tenuous and estranged self. This self is caught between the hard technology of traffic lanes jammed with 'cellulosed bodies' and the soft technology of human bodies and faces that resemble 'rows of the dead looking down at us from the galleries of a columbarium'.[13] The motor car plays a central role in Ballard's fiction and, as Stephen Metcalf observes, is instrumental to the construction of 'a terminal eroticism of technology as it collides with the human body and shatters it into fragments, violently hollowing out a subjectivity which is deposited as waste'.[14] Bodies and machines map themselves upon each other, as demonstrated by pictures of 'breasts of teenage girls deformed by instrument binnacles', 'mutilated penises, sectioned vulvas and crushed testicles', annotated by clear indications of the 'portion of the car which had caused the injury'. By emphasizing the sexual nature of crash-inflicted injuries, Ballard portrays 'a new currency of pain and desire',[15] a taxonomy of subtle variations of 'sex within the automobile'.[16]

Like Ballard, Doris Lessing and Angela Carter have turned to science-fictional motifs to paint scenes of social decline and cultural depletion. In both writers, moreover, issues of gender and sexuality are seen to play a key role in the never-ending debate about the future of humankind and its planet. Incorporating elements of mysticism and concepts derived from Jungian psychoanalysis, Lessing's science-fiction series *Canopus in Argos: Archives* (1979–83) speculates about an evolutionary development of both human history and the universe as a whole in which psychic powers and metaphysical hypotheses on the relationship between good and evil play a more prominent role than science as such. In books such as *Heroes and Villains* (1969) and *The Passion of New Eve* (1977), Carter portrays post-catastrophe scenarios akin to Ballard's. The futuristic dimension of science fiction is interwoven with a satirical debunking of cultural binaries such as good/evil, love/hate, reality/fantasy and masculinity/femininity, set against a macabre background of Gothic inspiration.

As these texts indicate, defining science fiction often proves arduous for the reasons that its generic boundaries are fluid and that, as a result, scientific and technological motifs are frequently interwoven with themes and issues that are not overtly science-fictional. Let us consider a couple of examples of cross-pollination between science fiction and other genres. C.S. Lewis's 'cosmic trilogy' comprising *Out of the Silent Planet* (1938), *Perelandra* (1943) and *That Hideous Strength* (1945) is regarded by many critics as a work of science fiction. Others, however, stress that Lewis's trilogy has more to do with the supernatural, with the angelic realm and with Christian mysticism than with science. Significantly, mysticism will come to play an important part in subsequent adaptations of the genre, not least in cyberpunk. Another interesting example is supplied by Aldous Huxley's and George Orwell's dystopian satires – *Brave New World* (1932) and *Nineteen Eighty-Four* (1949) respectively – and by the paradigmatic anti-utopia that prefigured and influenced them both – Yevgeny Zamyatin's *We* (1922). In their delineation of future worlds, these texts exhibit many features that a reader could readily associate with science fiction. At the same time, they engage with sociological and political issues of great complexity in ways that run counter to the view of science fiction as a purely entertaining genre (a view, as already noted, that stems from biased assumptions about science fiction's inferior literary credentials). Margaret Atwood's *The Handmaid's Tale* (1986) could likewise be described as science fiction and as a dystopian critique of religious fundamentalism that draws attention to the broad ideological themes of nationalism and political tyranny. Technoscience is the primary means of constructing useful, productive and thoroughly disciplined bodies – particularly female ones – through the systematic repression of both biological drives and cultural desires. The connection between science fiction and dystopian interpretations of both present and future worlds will gain fresh resonance through cyberpunk.

While it is necessary to contextualize cyberpunk in terms of its place in the internal development of science fiction as a genre, it should be noted that cyberpunk has also been influenced by authors other than science-fiction ones. A major influence behind cyberpunk's characters and settings is the hard-boiled detective fiction that developed in America in the late 1920s and 1930s. In the history of crime fiction, the hard-boiled school represents a radical break with the tradition of the Golden Age: the post-Sherlock-Holmes narratives most commonly associated with writers such as Agatha Christie and G.K. Chesterton (among many others). While Golden Age writers tended to concentrate on the solution of enigmas in closed settings, such as country houses or villages, and on the detective's flair for working towards the solution in a logical, deductive and orderly fashion, hard-boiled authors take us into an open and formless urban scene. They question notions of rationality, community and stability and, concomitantly, the very concept of a tradition based on fundamentally British values. As Ian Ousby writes:

Their heroes embark on journeys through the city, taking in its extremes of glamour and sleaze. Though they need to solve mysteries, they usually do so by stirring up trouble and being tough enough to handle the consequences. Hard-boiled endings, rather than returning society to order or vindicating the power of reason, affirm their heroes' ability to survive against the odds.[17]

Dashiell Hammett's *Red Harvest* (1929) is a classic of hard-boiled detective fiction that anticipates important aspects of cyberpunk. Its hero is a loner (like Gibson's Case, Turner and Laney, for example) who has to face up to an amorphous world of corruption and violence and juggle with his toughness as both a physical attribute and an intellectual faculty. The figure of the tough guy, responsible for solving puzzles in a surreal setting of urban brutality, deprived of any real sense of belonging and forced to do the sorting out single-handedly, is consolidated by another hard-boiled classic: Raymond Chandler's *The Big Sleep* (1939). Chandler emphasizes the isolation and rootlessness of his hero, Marlowe, by hinting at an analogy between the modern detective and the knight errant of the mediaeval chivalric tradition. This idea anticipates cyberpunk in two ways. First, the ordeals undergone by several cyberpunk heroes and heroines (such as in Gibson's *Count Zero*, *Virtual Light* and *Idoru*) are redolent of traditional quests. Of course, the conventional dragon is replaced by another monster, the greedy corporational economy, and the stereotypical maiden in distress by a commodified victim. Second, cyberpunk echoes Chandler's appropriation of medieval motifs in its articulation of a markedly Gothic sensibility.

Dystopian narratives are also important precursors of cyberpunk. Bernard Wolfe's *Limbo* (1952), for instance, foreshadows cyberpunk in its depiction of a North America emerging from nuclear destruction, in which invasive technologies of the body, including lobotomy, play a significant part. The theme of body transformation – bound to become central to cyberpunk in its treatment of biotechnology – also features prominently in Alfred Bester's *The Stars My Destination* (1955). This novel also heralds cyberpunk through its anarchic emphasis on the collapse of intelligible boundaries between acceptable and criminal forms of conduct. The link between dystopian visions of the future and criminal behaviour is central to another classic that in some ways looks forward to cyberpunk: Anthony Burgess's *A Clockwork Orange* (1962). The tests and brain modifications inflicted on cyberpunk characters (such as Gibson's Case, Angie Mitchell, Laney and Slick) are vividly reminiscent of the mind-control experiments to which Burgess's Alex is subjected. As in Bester's novel, the dividing line between good and evil is blurred: while Alex's exposure to EST and filmic displays of the most appalling Nazi horrors may turn him away from crime, it also annihilates his aesthetic values and ability to experience harmless pleasures. Burgess's elaboration of a complex language (Nadsat) that combines in pastiche fashion Latin, Russian, Cockney rhyming slang and other idioms and registers could also be read as an anticipation of cyberpunk's neologisms, idiosyncratic vocabularies and jargons. Above all, *A Clockwork Orange*'s gang-infested and nocturnal world of mindless violence, peopled by pathologically fashion-conscious young men, foreshadows cyberpunk's Gothic dimension, with an emphasis on the destiny of the individual in a callous technological society that has reached a state of advanced urban decay.

Moreover, cyberpunk bears many points of contact with postmodernist fiction. Indeed, cyberpunk novels and films are often taught on courses on Postmodernism. It would not be realistic, in this context, to try to relate cyberpunk to all the forms of postmodernist fiction developed in the latter part of the twentieth century. A few examples seem worth mentioning, however. William S. Burroughs's *Naked Lunch* (1959) is arguably a vital influence behind cyberpunk. Gory, raw and, for some readers, downright nauseating, *Naked Lunch* uses the theme of 'the junk virus' – drug addiction – as the starting point for a heady journey into the realm of abjection: the state of body and mind that renders certain objects and experiences simultaneously attractive and repulsive. This idea, taken in conjunction with the novel's consistent fusion of reality and fantasy, humour and horror, crooked medical theories and erotic dreams, paves the way for subsequent cyberpunk speculations about related themes. Thomas Pynchon's *The Crying of Lot 49* (1966) is not even remotely as disturbing as *Naked Lunch* in physical terms. Nevertheless, it is deeply unsettling in its presentation of a world in which there are no certainties for people to cling on to. There are only hints, clues, guesses and hypotheses to guide Pynchon's heroine, Oedipa Maas, though a labyrinth of conspiracies that may but equally well may not be real. The novel's radical questioning of the credibility of reality has provided fertile ground for the growth of cyberpunk. So has its interweaving of high and mass cultures, its use of technological metaphors and its portrayal of obsessive and alienated characters. The principal aspect of Pynchon's work inherited by cyberpunk is, as Brian McHale points out, his 'paranoid vision of a world controlled by multinational corporations, who are controlled, in turn, by the self-actuating technologies upon which their power depends'.[18]

Another postmodernist narrative that in some ways anticipates cyberpunk is Don DeLillo's *White Noise* (1984). This novel comments on the dystopian connotations of late capitalism by highlighting the precariousness of the apparently safe and idyllic life of small-town North America. The material security of consumer society is punctured through DeLillo's introduction of two disturbing events: an industrial accident leading to the possibility of large-scale toxic contamination; and unlicensed drug experiments meant to cure the fear of death, which lead to violence and psychological mayhem. Like cyberpunk, DeLillo's fiction combines humour and drama in what ultimately amounts to an absurd world, juxtaposing the false certainties and dreams of white suburban communities and the cynical reality of a thoroughly commodified and TV-saturated society. DeLillo also addresses, in a satirical fashion, the effects of information overload. The protagonist, at one point, is hugely fascinated by one of his daughters' sleep-talk and almost mesmerized by its incantational poetry – until it turns out that what she is muttering in her dreams are words repeated by TV commercials to the point of nausea.

The theme of overload features frequently in cyberpunk and is often described in a darkly humorous vein. Ted Mooney, for example, comments on the psychosomatic effects of excessive exposure to the media in *Easy Travel to Other Planets* (1981) through the description of '. . . a woman harmed by information excess. All the symptoms are present: bleeding from the nose and ears, vomiting, deliriously disconnected speech, apparent disorientation, and the desire to touch everything', allied to a surrealistically 'complicated monologue: Birds of Prey Cards, sunspot soufflé, Antarctic unemployment'.[19]

The image of a society totally immersed in electronic means of communication and surveillance is vividly conveyed by John Brunner's *Shockwave Rider* (1975), a work that straddles New Wave science fiction and cyberpunk. Looking back at the hard-boiled crime tradition through the character of the fugitive Nickie Heflinger and forward to cyberpunk's dystopian settings through the city of

Precipice, *Shockwave Rider* questions the meaning of humanity in a world where humans are increasingly encoded as bytes in a sprawling flow of data controlled by government agencies.

The roots of cyberpunk are not, of course, purely literary. The 'cyber' in cyberpunk refers to science and, in particular, to the revolutionary redefinition of the relationship between humans and machines brought about by the science of cybernetics. The word cybernetics was introduced in 1948 by the mathematician Norbert Wiener (1894–1964) in a book titled *Cybernetics, or Control and Communication in the Animal and the Machine*. Cybernetics derives from the Greek word *kibernetes*, which means 'steersman', to imply that control should be a form of 'steersmanship', not of 'dictatorship'. Wiener believed that biological bodies and mechanical bodies are self-regulating systems connected by the basic fact that both work in terms of control and communication. Moreover, Wiener divided the history of machines into four stages: the golemic age (a pre-technological world), the age of clocks (seventeenth and eighteenth centuries), the age of steam (late eighteenth and nineteenth centuries) and the age of communication and control (the era of cybernetics). To each of these stages corresponds a different model of the physical organism: the body as a magical clay shape, as a clockwork mechanism, as a heat engine and, finally, as an electronic system. The notion of the body as an electronic system proceeds from its equation to a communications network capable of absorbing information through the senses and of subsequently acting upon the information received. Central to research in the field of cybernetics is the idea that, if the human body can be conceived of as a machine, it is also possible to design machines that simulate the human organism. This is effected by using as a working model the nervous apparatus, a graded system of control governed by the brain. A machine so designed is a *cybernetic organism*, a technological construct that replicates the human body on the basis of an understanding of the structural similarities between machines and living organisms.

The virtual interchangeability of human bodies and machines is a recurring theme in cyberpunk and intrinsic to its representations of cyborgs. If Wiener's theories are of vital relevance to an understanding of cyberpunk's scientific background, equally important is the development of digital technology in the course of the twentieth century. The dawn of computer-based artificial intelligence is the

Turing machine, designed by the British mathematician Alan Mathison Turing (1912–54). The machine consisted of a long tape of squares, some with numbers on them, others blank. It could read one square at a time and could move the tape backwards and forwards to read other squares. In Turing's system, the machine's physical construction was irrelevant; what mattered was its ability to carry out particular instructions in order to solve specific problems.

Moving from cyberpunk's literary and scientific forebears to its genesis as a genre in its own right, it is noteworthy that the years 1983 and 1984 are of particular significance. Indeed, the term 'cyberpunk' was introduced by Bruce Bethke in a short story bearing this title that he wrote in the spring of 1980 and that was published in *Amazing Science Fiction Stories* in November 1983. In an article that appeared in the *Washington Post* about a year later (December 1984), the term was employed by Gardner Dozois to describe the fiction of authors such as Sterling, Cadigan and, of course, Gibson, whose epoch-making *Neuromancer* appeared in the same year. According to David Porush, a major concern linking these various writers is the question: 'What aspect of humanity makes us human?'[20]

This question is undoubtedly central to cyberpunk and crops up repeatedly as so-called *real* humans interact with Artificial Intelligences, androids, cyborgs, computer-simulated bodies, mutants and replicants and are required to establish what exactly distinguishes the natural from the artificial. Much of the time, this distinction is very hard to draw. This is clearly exemplified by Philip K. Dick's *Do Androids Dream of Electric Sheep?* (1972), a novel that anticipates cyberpunk in important ways. Its hero, Rick Deccard, is recruited to destroy replicants and is asked to identify his targets by means of a test supposed to recognize non-human creatures. Yet the test is fallible, according to Kevin McCarron:

> The Voigt-Kampff test is designed to demonstrate levels of empathy, the one quality which it is believed the androids cannot fake. However, the novel makes it quite clear that intelligence can find out a way of simulating empathy, and that people who cannot empathize are not necessarily replicants. On several occasions the author points up Deccard's own inability to empathize with the replicants.[21]

This suggests that artificial beings may be capable of deeper emotions than humans. The point is brought home by *Blade Runner* (1982), Ridley Scott's cinematic adaptation of Dick's novel, where the replicant Rachel implies that if the hero Deccard were to be subjected to the test he would not demonstrate the expected levels of empathy.

As indicated earlier, the 'cyber' component in the term cyberpunk alludes to the fact that the point of reference of this branch of science fiction is cybernetics rather than spaceships and robots. The 'punk' element, for its part, hints at a defiant attitude based in urban street culture. Cyberpunk's characters are people on the fringe of society: outsiders, misfits and psychopaths, struggling for survival on a garbage-strewn planet which, resorting to Rudy Rucker's image, is always on the verge of dissolving into a quagmire of 'muddy dreams . . . just brown mud all night long'.[22] Cyberpunk presents visions of the future based on the extensive application of the idea of cyberspace, a term that first appeared in William Gibson's novel *Neuromancer* (1984). This is the story of 'computer cowboy' Case (a computer cowboy is an illicit operator in the Net), of the 'Matrix' (a global representation of the databanks of all the computers in the human system) and of the deceptions, crimes and power struggles associated with its users. Biotechnology plays a crucial role in *Neuromancer*. Flesh can be 'vat-grown' and any organ can be lifted out of the body and replaced with a brand new one. A huge black-market network incessantly trades body parts and genetic materials, and surgery can enhance the body's powers in countless ways. Molly, one of the main characters, has mirror-shade implants over her eyes which allow her to see in the dark, as well as lethal retractable blades inserted under each of her fingernails.

If reality is a difficult concept to define in science fiction generally, this is particularly true of cyberpunk. According to Vivian Sobchack, science fiction is the 'cognitive mapping and poetic figuration of social relations as these are constituted by new technological modes of "being-in-the-world"'.[23] Larry McCaffery argues that the kind of 'cognitive mapping' specifically supplied by cyberpunk is an effort 'to find a suitable means for displaying the powerful and troubling technological logic that underlies the postmodern condition'. Concocted out of 'equal measures of anger and bitter humour, technological know-how and formal inventiveness', cyberpunk 'systematically distorts our sense of who or where we are, of what is "real" at all, of what is most valuable about human life'.[24] Reality and identity are rendered unstable by their reduction to the status of commodities, namely interchangeable and disposable products doomed to a fate of planned and rapid obsolescence.

In some cyberpunk texts, people actually change their identities as easily as we would change our clothes. The computer scientist and roboticist Hans Moravec believes that in the not too distant future it will indeed be possible to transfer mental functions to computer software.[25] This process, which Moravec calls 'transmigration', may take some time to materialize in practice, but it has already found expression in the world of fiction. In G.A. Effinger's trilogy *When Gravity Fails* (1987), *A Fire in the Sun* (1990), and *The Exile Kiss* (1991), for example, all the characters need to do in order to acquire alternative identities is to chip software directly into their wired brains. The software consists of personality patterns (*moddies*) which can be purchased from *modshops*. In his treatment of the theme of identity change, Effinger also shows that the advantages of technology are not evenly distributed in cyberculture. The trilogy depicts a brutally hierarchical society in which poor people are routinely killed for their organs. A black market of body parts is thus constituted for the benefit of the fabulously wealthy. The identities acquired by Effinger's characters as they plug software into their brains are by and large fictional. Yet the trilogy indicates that software modules can also be fashioned out of the brain of a real person through a kind of mental rape. Effinger's protagonist, for example, is subjected to torture, and in the process his emotions are downloaded onto a moddie.

A variation on this theme is offered by Kathryn Bigelow's *Strange Days* (1996). In this film, any event (actual, imagined, wished for, feared) can be translated into portable software. People can then relive it with the aid of a wired contraption placed on the head like a cap. What they re-experience, however, is not simply the superficial appearance of facts that have already taken place, but also the feelings, thoughts and emotions that accompanied the occurrence. They can thus enter other people's brains and their future projections. W.J. Williams's novel *Hardwired* (1986) likewise explores the theme of personality modification. His characters are able to alter their identities, including sexual ones, through a formidably powerful programme named Project Black Mind which 'sets up a mind in crystal. Then goes into another mind, a live mind, and prints the first mind on top of it. Imposes the first personality on the second. Backs up the program' and thus totally erases the initial character of the invaded mind.[26] Like *Hardwired*, Pat Cadigan's *Mindplayers* (1987) also explores the theme of mind invasion, replacement and obliteration. Here, people are able to relinquish their original identities and purchase artificial ones from the Power People company. However, there are limits to the players' freedom which elliptically underscore technology's duplicity as a concurrently liberating and disciplining force. Indeed, forms of mindplay deemed illegal by the Brain Police are punished through *mindsuck*, a strategy that wipes out completely the player's personality.

In Rudy Rucker's novel *Software* (1982), an elderly scientist agrees to have his brain functions taken out of his body by powerful automata, in exchange for an immortal robot body of his own. He then finds out, much to his disappointment, that immortality doesn't give him absolute power; his mental patterns have been appropriated and stored in a Mr. Frostee ice-cream truck. Rucker also focuses on the relationship between the theme of personality change and drug addiction, a phenomenon bound to gain considerable importance in subsequent cyberpunk fiction. Consider the following passage as a classic illustration of the interweaving of hallucinatory and technological images:

> Riding his hydrogen-cycle home from work Friday afternoon, Sta-Hi began to feel sick. It was the acid coming on. He'd taken some Black Star before turning in his cab for the weekend. That was an hour? Or two hours ago? The digits on his watch winked at him, meaningless little sticks. He had to keep moving or he'd fall through the crust.[27]

Bruce Sterling's fiction develops the motif of physical transformation through the deployment of intrusive technologies and indeed views 'the theme of body invasion: prosthetic limbs, implanted circuitry, cosmetic surgery, genetic alteration' as one of cyberpunk's keynotes.[28]

In some of his work, Sterling takes the idea of body invasion so far as to present worlds in which human beings have become obsolete and their bodies have been replaced by 'a variety of posthuman species'. In *Schismatrix* (1985) and in 'Twenty Evocations' (1988), the Earth and humankind are remote vestiges of bygone ages. Central to these narratives are the posthuman Shapers and Mechanists:

the former, as Claudia Springer notes, 'use genetic engineering to design their organic bodies and extend their lives', while the latter 'become increasingly mechanical as they incorporate technology into their cyborg bodies'.[29] 'Twenty Evocations' traces the life trajectory of Nikolai Leng from childhood to death, through twenty brief passages containing snippets of dialogue and descriptive detail. From these, we learn that the human species has long been extinct: 'The first true settlers in space were born on Earth – produced by sexual means. Of course, hundreds of years have passed since then.' The place once occupied by humans is now the battleground on which Shapers and Mechanists vie for supremacy. Shapers pride themselves on never being born. The corollary of this is that they may never die. Mechanists sometimes appear more vulnerable than Shapers due to their reliance on technologies that may well prove 'malfunctioning' and go 'click-whirr, click-whirr'. Yet they regard the Shapers as inferior, flimsy chattel. A Mechanist declares to an audience of Shaper kids: 'Genelines . . . I can buy you, grow you, sell you, cut you into bits. Your screams: my music.'[30] The society presented by Sterling is decidedly schizophrenic and accordingly capable of spawning schizophrenic personalities. This is clearly documented by Nikolai's experiences. A Shaper, he gets involved with a Mechanist woman in the context of a complex game of contraband and piracy. As a result, he has a number of prosthetic devices implanted in his body by Mechanist technicians: miniaturized 'visual mechanisms', a 'bio-feedback monitor' and 'a television screen', among others.[31] However, Nikolai retains a strong connection with his Shaper mentality. When his Mechanist wife is murdered, he has her posthumously cloned, the result being a woman who could, in principle, be regarded as his *daughter*. But parental and filial terms do not hold much significance in this web of genetic and mechanical manipulations, and Nikolai and the clone woman end up husband and wife. This is described as 'bigamy', although the word *incest* springs as readily to mind. By now, Nikolai is 'a hundred and ten or so' and proud of his 'choice of longevity programs' but also aware that he no longer has either the flexibility or the daring he once had. Opting for retirement, he dies, triumphantly announcing: 'Futility is Freedom!'.[32]

The power of this short, apparently fragmentary yet poetically coherent narrative cannot be ascribed purely to its content. The picture of a split identity (both personal and cultural) is graphically conveyed by its language and structural orchestration, as well as by its subject matter. The reader is faced with a world of conflicting values that, on the surface, may seem mutually exclusive but are actually interdependent. The dividing line between Shapers and Mechanists is all too easily violated. So is the distinction between humans and their posthuman successors, for the latter often display emotions and attitudes that are very familiar indeed. *Schismatrix* also conveys this idea by showing that beneath the cyborgian façade of biotechnologically and mechanically engineered bodies still linger the same old longings. These may have to be voiced through new vocabularies so as to be intelligible but their physical import remains virtually the same. Take this exchange between Kitsune and Lindsay (both products of the Shapers in different ways):

> 'Give me what's real,' she said.
> She undid her obi sash. Her kimono was printed in a design of irises and violets. The skin beneath it was like a dying man's dream of skin.
> 'Come here,' she said. 'Put your mouth on my mouth.'
> Lindsay scrambled forward and threw his arms around her. She slipped her warm tongue deep into his mouth. It tasted of spice. It was narcotic. The glands of her mouth oozed drugs.
> . . .
> She slipped her hands inside his loose kimono. 'Shaper,' she said, 'I want your genetics. All over me.'
> Her warm hand caressed his groin. He did what she said.[33]

The reorientation of science fiction occasioned by cyberpunk, especially through its treatment of the themes of identity and body metamorphosis, may best be understood in relation to its representatives' cultural milieu and generational make-up. As McCaffery observes:

> [T]he cyberpunks were the first generation of artists for whom the technologies of satellite dishes, video and audio players and recorders, computers and video games (both of particular importance), digital watches, and MTV were not exoticisms, but part of a daily 'reality matrix'. They were also the first generation of writers who were reading Thomas Pynchon, Ballard, and Burroughs as teenagers, who had grown up immersed in technology

but also in pop culture, in the values and aesthetics of the coun-
terculture associated with drug culture, punk rock, video games,
Heavy Metal comic books, and the gore-and-spatter SF/horror
films of George Romero, David Cronenberg, and Ridley Scott.[34]

Cyberpunk writers and artists have actually witnessed the birth and
growth of technologies that earlier generations of science-fiction
authors could only fantasize or speculate about. As Steve Brown
points out, instead of having to invent visions of the future practically from scratch, they have been in a position to collect 'bits and
pieces of what was actually coming true, and feed it back to the
readers who were already living in Gibson's Sprawl, whether they
knew it or not'.[35]

The final pages of this Introduction will be devoted to an examination of the relationship between cyberpunk and the subculture of
punk. The coupling of cybernetics and punk may well seem an
unholy marriage, given certain popular tendencies to associate the
former with control, order and logic and the latter with anarchy,
chaos and unrest. However, that pairing should not come as a total
surprise, for what writers like Gibson needed – in order to represent a
paradoxical culture riven by conflict and contradiction – was precisely a figure that could bring together apparently incompatible
aspects of contemporary life. Moreover, cybernetics and punk are
not as diametrically opposed as they may at first seem to be.
Cybernetics does supply the means of organizing social existence
according to abstract principles that can be represented as data and
translated into tangible products for public consumption. Yet, as was
argued in the Preface, these products are valued less for their materiality than for their symbolic significance as desirable adjuncts to the
human body and even as defining markers of identity. Hence,
embedded in cyberculture is a sense of instability; as long as the
abstract formulae of cybernetics are translated into commodities
which, in the logic of capitalism, are required to undergo constant (if
minimal) transformations, there can be no real permanence. At the
same time, cybernetics is rendered unstable by its openness to diverse
readings: as a philosophy based on precise calculations about the
nature of organisms and mechanical constructs; as an esoteric form
of knowledge comparable (in the eyes of non-experts) to black
magic; as the technological underpinning of corporational economies and their value systems. According to Istvan Csicsery-Ronay

Jr., 'Cybernetics is . . . a paradox: simultaneously a sublime vision of human power over chance and a dreary augmentation of multi-national capitalism's mechanical process of expansion. . . . Cybernetics is, thus, part natural philosophy, part necromancy, part ideology.' Cyberpunk couches the ambiguity of cybernetics in explicitly popular terms by associating it with punk: a subculture that, in undermining all accepted values, was also willing to undermine itself through 'a self-stupefying and self-mutilating refusal to dignify or trust anything that has brought about the present world'.[36]

Punk constructed a whole aesthetic out of a reality of socioeconomic alienation and discrimination. This aesthetic did not merely show how and why dominant ideologies marginalize dispossessed strata of the population. In fact, it cultivated and magnified anything that mainstream culture would deem least savoury; it deliberately exaggerated the features that would make it the object of revulsion and aversion and intensify the establishment's desire to outlaw it. Punk sought rejection with a self-destructive determination by defiantly constructing a simultaneously desecrated and self-desecrating subculture. Murky, earthy, scruffy, rough, hollow-cheeked and chain-laden, versed in gutter-snipe registers and punctuated with symbolic ornaments replete with horrific connotations (such as the swastika), the average punk figure would instantly stand out as a *sinister* counterpart to the glamorous and ostentatiously elegant rock stars of previous generations. Moreover, as Dick Hebdige observes, 'the punk look was essentially undernourished: emaciation standing as a sign of Refusal. The prose of the fanzines was littered with references to "fat businessmen" and "lard-ass capitalists".'[37]

Punks also aimed at developing a rhetoric of self-conscious alienation by associating themselves with ethnic groups often branded as peripheral to British culture. As Hebdige points out: 'the punk aesthetic can be read in part as a white "translation" of black "ethnicity"'.[38] Punk found certain 'basic models' in West Indian cultures and subcultures and in the Rastafarian aesthetic. (Gibson hints at this in *Neuromancer*, where he introduces Rastafarian value systems and alludes to the Rastafarian belief in the imminent collapse of white colonialism, defined as 'Babylon'.) Punk associated itself with reggae, contributed to 'the Rock against Racism campaign', developed hair-styles that 'approximated to the black "natty" or dreadlock styles' and 'some punks' even 'wore Ethiopian colours'.[39]

However, although both marginalized ethnic groups and punks shared the same drab and violent slum culture, the former could lay claim to *roots* whereas the latter could not. Punk grew out of 'the recognizable locales of Britain's inner cities. It spoke in city accents.' Nevertheless, 'it was predicated upon a denial of place. It issued out of nameless housing estates, anonymous dole queues, slums-in-the-abstract. It was blank, expressionless, rootless.'[40] Urban black groups, conversely, could situate themselves in relation to historical origins, identities and places, such as the West Indies and Africa. Their 'exile' had 'a specific meaning' and entailed 'a specific (albeit magical) solution in the context of Rastafarianism and Negro history'.[41] While there were indubitably important points of contact between punks and blacks, punks were marked by a rootless condition that, in lacking a past, could hardly afford a future. It is on this condition that cyberpunk writers place consistent emphasis.

Furthermore, as Larry McCaffery has argued, cyberpunk exhibits telling affinities with punk music. Cyberpunks and punk musicians share an urge 'to use technology as a weapon against itself, and to seize the control of its form from the banalizing effects of the media industry and reestablish a sense of menace, intensity'.[42] There has been a widespread tendency to associate punk music with vulgarity, lack of refinement and a cheap addiction to shocking effects. Yet punk music did have a distinctive language of its own, and many of its formal attributes and themes are echoed by those of Gibson and his contemporaries. Among the most prominent features shared by punk music and literary cyberpunk is the 'reliance on collage and cut-up methods' reminiscent of some of the techniques deployed by artistic avant-gardes such as Dada and Surrealism, where artworks would often be produced by pasting together *found objects* supplied by consumer culture. Indeed, Gibson describes himself as 'a kind of literary collage artist' and 'SF as a marketing framework' that enables him 'to gleefully ransack the whole fat supermarket of twentieth-century cultural works'. Other features common to punk music and cyberpunk are the use of 'highly idiomatic lingoes, drawn primarily from subcultures of drug and crime'; 'a willingness to use obscenity, "noise", sensory overload'; and an emphasis on paranoia and 'sexual and psychic violation'.[43]

At times, musical and literary cultures literally come together in cyberpunk. This meeting is best exemplified, according to some commentators, by John Shirley. Often dubbed 'the Lou Reed of

Cyberpunk',[44] Shirley is not only known as a cyberpunk novelist and essayist but also as the lead singer of the San Francisco rock band the Panther Moderns (a denomination, incidentally, appropriated by Gibson in *Neuromancer* to describe a subversive network). The punk component of Shirley's fiction emerges in the depiction of political dystopias, particularly in the trilogy comprising *Eclipse* (1985), *Eclipse Penumbra* (1987) and *Total Eclipse* (1989), where fascist totalitarianism resurges as a powerful system. Shirley's cyberpunk also portrays societies in which human identities are routinely pulverized by illegal practices. These include the trade and consumption of *sink* (synthetic cocaine), a substance so addictive that rehabilitation leaves the user feeling 'like a processor with a glitch'; the installation of brain chips for the augmentation of mental and physical powers, which often turn out to be '*busted*'; the transformation of people into zombie-like creatures by means of obnoxious products concocted by mixing 'organic stuff' with polymers and plastics gleaned from 'the trash heap'. Mutations of people's DNA code also play a key role, as do the disorienting effects of various addictions. One of the most disturbing is the hallucinatory impression that other people form 'a network of distorted self-images, caricatures of grotesque ambitions'.[45]

Cyberpunk also portrays punk culture in opposition to 'hippie', as one of the main twentieth-century subcultures that attained to the status of a dominant culture and that for the punk generation could therefore easily equate to parental domination. Lewis Shiner's 'Stoked' (1988) contrasts hippie and punk in the form of a generational conflict involving a hippie father and a punk son:

> I'm into the music when my dad starts pounding at the door. It's Suicidal Tendencies doing 'Possessed to Skate'. I unlock the door and he goes over first thing to turn it down.
>
> My dad is like losing all his hair in front so he lets it grow out over his collar in back. He has to do it, see, because he wants everybody to know that even though he's a lawyer and has a Mercedes and everything he didn't sell out. As if anybody cared. A hippie is still a hippie, even if he wears ties and drives a Mercedes. Even if he's your dad.
>
> So he says did you take your skateboard to school again.
>
> I tell him NO.
>
> Don't lie to me Bobby, he says. Mister Woodrow called me

today and said you and some of those other skate punks were fighting at lunch.

I don't think he's ever called me a skate punk before. I kind of like it. I say we weren't fighting we were thrashing.[46]

It is in its treatment of the theme of addiction that cyberpunk exhibits one of its most explicitly 'punk' dimensions. On one level, cyberpunk's junkies are utterly nonchalant about their dependence on an unimaginably broad range of illegal substances. Drug consumption is just a game, as monotonous and ultimately meaningless as any other activity on which their directionless society hinges. At the same time, however, there are indications that the consumption of drugs is the age-old way of anaesthetizing troubling emotions and memories. A good example of the ambivalent character of addiction in cyberpunk is supplied by James O'Barr's comics sequence 'Frame 137'. Its female protagonist is concurrently scary and seductive, lethal and vulnerable, self-confident and dangerously isolated. These ambiguities are borne out by her attitude to drugs. When we first encounter her she seems quite in control, aware of what she is consuming and why: 'I dry sucked four or five percs and half a dozen white crosses; let the barbiturates and amphetamines fight it out in my system. Leave me pumped and calm.' Next we discover that she is not quite so firmly in control, for she is actually the object of patronizing judgments and not all the substances she consumes are necessarily of her own choice:

The bar tender, Richo, saw me chewing the caps and set up a gin for me with a 'never learn' look on his rice paper face like he was my dad or something. The gin tasted like petrol and urine in equal amounts.[47]

Shortly after, we realize that this ostensibly tough lady's use of drugs is also a means of numbing unbearable images and that her hard shell encases a painfully sensitive being:

Last summer I saw my sister Kay for the first time in four years. On a screen. In a holo porn shop. She was nine years old. Thinking about Kay made my gut churn so I ate two more percs and something purple, finishing the gin and whatever kerosene extract Richo had diluted with it.[48]

Cyberpunk also comments on the ambiguous connotations of drugs by intimating that in a culture saturated with artificial substances (be they legal or illegal), the notion of what is 'good' for you is bound to become increasingly hazy. This is thrown into relief, in a darkly jocular tone, by Mark Leyner in 'I Was an Infinitely Hot and Dense Dot' (1990), where the protagonist's dietary options suggest that counterbalancing damaging addictions through the consumption of putatively wholesome food is not as easy as one may expect:

> I'd been habitually abusing an illegal hormone extracted from the pituitary glands of human corpses and I felt as if I were drowning in excremental filthiness but the prospect of having something good to eat cheered me up. I asked the waitress about the soup du jour and she said that it was primordial soup – which is ammonia and methane mixed with ocean water in the presence of lightning.[49]

Moreover, drug addiction becomes somewhat marginal in an organism so thoroughly reshaped by biotechnology as to contain 'a miniature shotgun that blasts the cells of living organisms, altering their genetic matrices'.[50]

Leyner's narrative exemplifies cyberpunk at its most surreal through the association of the themes of addiction and biotechnological transformation with a monstrously distorted world picture. This picture does not merely reflect any one individual's *habits* but also a collective *habitat* dominated by bewildering accumulations of disconnected and fragmentary images.

The texts cited in the preceding pages illustrate some of the ways in which the 'cyber' and the 'punk' components of cyberpunk constantly interact to produce varying constellations of the relationship between the glossy world of high technology and the murky world of addiction and crime. What is arguably most distinctive about cyberpunk is that neither of these two elements ever gains priority over the other, the genre's effectiveness actually depending on their dynamic interplay. At the same time, cyberpunk is required to record and adjust to ongoing changes in both the realm of cybertechnology and the realm of urban culture. The term 'cybertechnology' goes on gaining fresh connotations as research and industry expand the scope of its applications. The term 'punk' is also, obviously, open to redefinition, as contemporary writers, artists, musicians and critics continue evaluating its historical impact. What must be stressed is that 'punk' is not always used literally by cyberpunk writers as a context-bound and context-specific subculture. Were this the case, cyberpunk would now be outdated. In fact, punk has become a metaphor for rootlessness, alienation and cultural dislocation in the context of contemporary society. In cyberpunk, 'punk' tends to refer to virtually any form of subcultural disruption of the cultural fabric played out among the debris of sprawling urban conglomerates.

CHAPTER I

CYBERPUNK AND VIRTUAL TECHNOLOGIES

Cyberpunk has been described as 'hip, poetic, and posthuman' (Targowsky); as 'a postmodern literary-cultural style that projects a computerized future' (Heim); as a 'ubiquitous datasphere of computerized information' (Person); as 'a return to roots' (Sterling); as the 'supreme literary expression if not of postmodernism, then of late capitalism itself' (Jameson); as 'a new form of existence, loosed from the bonds of the physical body' (Jeschke); and as the 'collision of punk sensibility – the unrest, the rebellion – with desk-top computers' (Cadigan). The multi-accentuality of cyberpunk is paralleled by that of the related phenomena of cyberspace and virtual reality. Disparaged by some critics for fostering individualism and depersonalized forms of intercourse and by some for perpetuating illusions of mastery and stereotypical power structures, cyberspace and virtual reality are celebrated by others as a means of establishing new communities unhampered by traditional prejudices.[1]

Complex information and communication networks are not exclusive to modern technology, since they were already operational in the power structures of ancient empires, and indeed vital to their preservation. Yet modern understandings of information and communication were modified by a crucial shift that took place in the western Renaissance, whereby those concepts came to be predicated on the differentiation between 'normality' and 'abnormality'. The segregation of the insane (typified by Sebastian Brant's *The Ship of Fools* of 1494), in particular, served to systematize information and communication structures on the basis of a discriminatory map. It was now possible to distinguish so-called valuable and legitimate data from so-called nonsense and aberration and, accordingly, to exclude the so-called deviant from either the production or the dissemination of valid information. In *Gut Symmetries*, Jeanette Winterson compares imaginary and mystical enterprises, such as the one undertaken by the Ship, with the projects of modern physics, especially the GUTs or Grand Unifying Theories. These aim at establishing harmonizing systems and structures able to account for the relationship between matter and energy throughout the cosmos. In her novel, Winterson intimates that the GUTs' objectives and the Ship's project are analogous, for both deal with a universe in which the search for meaning is always a pursuit of the unfathomable:

> SHIP OF FOOLS: A mediaeval conceit.
> Lunatics/Saints sailing after that
> which cannot be found.[2]

There may, paradoxically, be a modicum of sanity in a quest that knows its object to be unattainable. There is also a sense in which the Ship's legendary destiny could be read as a reward for its foolish undertakings. After all, it is the Ship of Fools that roams the heavens and cruises through the galaxies, while the so-called real vessels of both the present and the past are either tied to the surface of the ocean, like the *QE2*, or 'ghostly and abandoned beneath' it, like the *Titanic*.[3] The shaman boat of disreality, by contrast, floats eternally above the sublunary domain: 'Legend has it that the Ship, while seeking the Holy Grail, sailed off the end of the world and continued forever . . . chasing that which has neither beginning nor end.'[4] The analogy proposed by *Gut Symmetries* between physics and the 'medieval conceit' of terminal madness raises interesting questions about the relationship between present-day scientific practices and notions of rationality and irrationality. Cyberculture, particularly in its fictional interpretation by cyberpunk, lends urgency to these issues against the backdrop of pervasive forms of electronic mediation, such as virtual reality.

'Virtual reality', a phrase coined by the computer scientist, composer and visual artist Jaron Lanier in the late 1980s, refers to an environment in which reality is simulated through computers and in which the body can experience artificially generated data as though they were coming from the real world. People immersed in a virtual environment can actually experience the realistic feeling of inhabiting that world. People could move through a computer-generated house in which they might wish to live even before the house is built, or visit simulated holiday resorts before actually booking the holiday. These experiences are not the same as watching a film, because people can interact with their environment in ways that cinema and video cannot offer. The user of virtual reality receives images and impressions from various mechanical devices attached to the user's body, to provide the impressions of sight, sound and touch. Stereo headphones supply sounds; head-mounted goggles (eyephones) supply computer-generated images; wired gloves (datagloves) and computerized suits (datasuits) supply the sense of touch. These devices are also able to monitor the body's movements, so that what users see or feel changes according to their movements. In addition, different people may experience the same virtual spaces simultaneously without physically occupying the same location, since information can be communicated across a broad network via modems. A recent development in virtual technology is the *cave* (a term redolent of Plato's philosophy): a system that uses a pointer, worn by a guide for a small group of people, in a dome wherein virtual images are projected.

Gibson's cyberpunk takes virtual technology several steps further by positing the possibility of a direct neural connection between the human brain and the computer. This connection is effected by means of electrodes or sockets, situated behind the ear, that can receive chips and thus give access to digital memory. Once these gadgets are in place, human bodies and minds are not only in a position to enter an intimate relationship with computers. They also become able to access the ultimate virtual space, cyberspace, and interact with other bodies and minds in the construction of whole worlds out of data. As Katherine Hayles observes, 'Cyberspace is created by transforming a data matrix into a landscape in which narratives can happen.'[5]

The human body immersed in a virtual environment is made harder and shinier by its fusion with technology. Yet it also crosses over into the domain of the hybrid, for its humanity is indissolubly linked to non-human apparatuses. The responses elicited by such an interpenetration of the organic and the inorganic are ambivalent; on the one hand, technology is viewed as a kind of magical mirror capable of multiplying human powers *ad infinitum* and of reflecting humanity in an idealized form; on the other, technology is associated with the engulfment of the human by the non-human. Either way, the 'hyper-texted' body constructed via technology, 'with its micro-flesh, multi-media channelled ports, cybernetic fingers, and bubbling neuro-brain', displaces the binary opposition between wired corporeality and organic corporeality. The hyper-texted body is both: it is, according to Arthur Kroker and Michael Weinstein, 'a wired nervous system embedded in living (dedicated) flesh'. In cyberculture, our bodies are not simply 'interfaced to the Net through modems and external software'. In fact, they become *nets* in their own right, for in cruising cyberspace we are physically involved with oceans of data and images that impact directly on our sensorium.[6]

It is practically commonplace to observe that computer technology has had a profound impact on traditional notions of community and space. Some writers have even questioned the appropriateness of the term 'space' to define the forms of interaction enabled by computer technology. Brenda Laurel, for example, proposes 'telepresence' as a preferable alternative, for it suggests a medium rather than a site.[7] Others have argued that cyberspace is not really a space because it does not pre-exist the individuals who inhabit it but is rather brought about by them and their interactivity. Its status as space is potential, not given. Moreover, it is conceptual rather than geographical because the physical positioning of the machines we use to enter it is quite irrelevant to the communications networks that result from them. Critics and scientists are by no means in agreement over the exact nature of the impact of cyberculture on our lives. Does it provide a realm of fluid and global interaction or a prison-house of atomized individualism? Some maintain that the substitution of an abstract mode of interpersonal integration for face-to-face communication and intimacy represents the peak of a process of depersonalization fostered by capitalism since its inception. These critics blame technology-saturated environments for alienating the individual on two levels. First, computerized worklife increasingly fashions the worker as a workstation and an entry in a database. Second, the Internet reduces the user to an anonymous cell in a homogenized system, where pluralism really amounts to the erasure of differences and hence of the possibility of progressive politics. Sean Cubitt supplies a vivid commentary on this state of affairs:

> At the same time as glamorizing through clean technology, bureaucratic capital deskills its labour force, and while offering the appearance of naturalness and emancipation from onerous chores, introduces new orders of supervision and surveillance. . . . The progressive technologization of the workplace cannot disguise

the fact that the knowledge professions are engaged in vital labours of information inputting, filing and management, distribution and exchange, billing and banking, as they have been since *A Christmas Carol*.[8]

Embracing what could be termed a brand of neo-Luddism, critics such as Howard Besser and Iain Boal challenge the celebratory responses common in early theorizations of the Internet – for example, Michael Benedikt's *Cyberspace: First Steps*, where cyberspace is presented as akin to a Brave New World – by warning us against the perils of digital technology. Besser, in particular, ominously portrays the Information Superhighway as 'a ten-lane highway coming into the home, with only a tiny path leading back out – just wide enough to take a credit card number or to answer multiple-choice questions'.[9] A.L. Shapiro, for his part, deplores cyberspace's denial of dialectical tension and vibrancy, and views it as an anonymous place where 'you can shape your route so that you interact only with people of your choosing and with information tailored to your desires'.[10] There are also those who argue that there is the danger of turning cyberspace into a transcendental signified, a grand unifying agent akin to God or Fatherland. Concomitantly, there is a risk of idealizing the Information Superhighway as a total conquest of space, which perpetuates conventional illusions of mastery. At its most sinister, this fantasy of absolute control threatens to reinforce stereotypical power structures by advancing the interests of dominant groups: what Stephen Pfohl calls a 'male-minded and fantastic preservation of the narcissistic ego WITHOUT END'.[11] The conquest topos is explicitly brought out by the Electronic Frontier Foundation's positioning of computer networks 'as some kind of electronic equivalent of the American West', as Chris Chesher puts it, and a 'vista of a new frontier' predicated upon the 'myth' of 'white male Americans' as the quintessential colonizers.[12]

There are, however, writers who invest cyberspace with the power to restore a sense of belonging in a society where people increasingly feel both physically and intellectually lost. Bruce Sterling, for example, has stressed the educational potential of cyberspace for the younger generations, its ability to provide alternative communities and stimulate forms of communication uninhibited by traditional approaches to learning:

Kids need places where they can talk to each other, talk back and forth naturally. They need media that they can fingerpaint with, where they can jump up and down and breathe hard, where they don't have to worry about Mr. Science showing up in his mandarin white labcoat to scold them for doing things not in the rulebook.[13]

Amy Bruckman, for her part, argues that there is a risk of overinflating the divisive elements of Net culture when, in fact, user identification, interactivity and participation in admissions policies may produce a novel atmosphere of commonality.[14] Without embracing a utopian ideology, Nicholas Negroponte presents the new communities and forms of ownership and distribution fostered by cyberspace as inevitable phenomena in a cultural trajectory we might as well accept and capitalize upon, for 'the change from atoms to bits is irrevocable and unstoppable'.[15] The critics who interpret cyberspace in the most positive terms are those who believe that it allows for forms of communication and community unburdened by conventional assumptions about social status, sexuality and racial identities. But what does the term *community* actually connote in a simulated environment? Arguably, community is less and less a nuclear structure and more and more a multilayered apparatus. As Rob Shields points out, the collapse of traditional boundaries generated by Net culture results from a history of incremental decentralization of both policy issues and of conceptions of history and locality.[16]

Virtual technologies decentre conventional notions of knowledge and its relationship with ethical issues. Ambivalent responses to virtual reality show an inclination to polarize technology as either liberating or repressive. Arguably, these contradictions could be related to the problematic genealogy of the word 'virtual'. Etymologically linked to the Latin root *virtus*, the virtual would seem to stand on the side of moral excellence for, as John Wood notes, the Latin word 'combined the semantic idea of "truth" with the ethical idea of "worth"'.[17] What this assessment leaves out, however, is a supplementary – yet no less momentous – encoding of *virtus*, which gained fame and indeed notoriety in the Renaissance at the behest of political philosophers such as Machiavelli. Here 'virtue' is practically synonymous with expediency, opportunism, dissimulation and secretiveness. Although he does not focus on this particular semantic and ethical shift, Wood adduces other key developments in the history of western thought to explain the deterioration of the word 'virtue' into a distressingly equivocal signifier – particularly, Plato's association of the virtual with the ideal realm of Pure Forms, in contrast with the actual as the natural domain of the copy. If the virtual, in Platonic terms, is imperceptible and eternal, how are human beings to grasp it, let alone fulfil it, in *this* world? And in what sense is cybernetic imagery virtual, in this context? Does it host Platonic Ideas of a superior order of being? Nobody has any evidence for this and, in fact, the only *spiritual* forms to be found in cyberspace to date are Gibsonian vampires, voodoo gods and spectres that would no doubt cause Plato to turn in his grave. If cybernetic imagery is not virtual in Plato's sense, in what ways *is* it virtual then? Arguably, the virtuality of cybersystems lies primarily with their penchant for blurring the divide between presence and absence, by capitalizing on images that are simultaneously real and unreal – just as mirror images are virtual, uncannily reversed counterparts of the objects they reflect. The distinction between presence and absence is also questioned by the operations of computer memory. When we use a computer, we can work *as though* we possessed a substantially larger store of information than is actually present. Decisions as to what moves from the main store to contingent texts depend on a *heuristic*, a mechanism which, however thoroughly programmed, none the less works by incremental exploration towards an *unknown* goal.

Virtual technologies also decentre conventional notions of space and locality. The question of whether the spaces produced by virtual reality and computer technology generally are likely to lead to democratic emancipation or, in fact, to a perpetuation of hierarchical structures is still unanswered among the many critics concerned with the ideological implications of the digital body politic. Mark Poster offers a balanced account of Internet politics which considers the viability of both options and indeed the possibility of their coexistence. He states that 'the salient characteristic of Internet community is the diminution of prevailing hierarchies of race, class, age, status and especially gender'. At the same time, however, he alerts us to the 'asymmetries' of cybernetic communities 'which could be termed "political inequalities"'. As an example, Poster cites the interactive features of MOOs (Multi-User Dimensions, Object Oriented) which 'divide into adventure games and social types' and encompass different ways of constructing both identities and spaces:

On the MOOs of the social variety, advanced possibilities of postmodern identities are enacted. Here identities are invented and changeable; elaborate self-descriptions are composed; domiciles are depicted in textual form and individuals interact purely for the sake of doing so. MOO inhabitants, however, do not enjoy a democratic utopia. There exist hierarchies specific to this form of cyberspace: the site administrators who initiate and maintain the MOO are able to change the rules and procedures in ways which most regular players cannot.[18]

Issues of creativity and hierarchy are also raised by the interactive programmes known as MUDs, the acronym for Multi-User Dungeons. This phrase derives from Dungeons and Dragons, the immensely popular role-playing game invented in the 1970s and later adapted as a series of computer programmes. In the original game, the players constructed roles for themselves and played them out in an imaginary world organized by the 'dungeon Master'. In digital MUDs, already in vogue in the early 1990s, people likewise create characters and adventures within a virtual context. All MUDs pivot on the possibility of interaction among Net users. Where particular MUDs differ, as Sherry Turkle has observed, is in the degree of openness of the worlds they present. The world of a MUD:

... can be built around a mediaeval fantasy landscape in which there are dragons to slay and gold coins and magical amulets to collect, or it can be a relatively open space in which you can play at whatever captures your imagination, both by playing a role and by participating in building a world.[19]

Turkle's observations highlight the MUD's ability to loosen spatial and temporal boundaries and hence to question the stability of anything we may call a world. The MUD's ontological status is postmodern, in that it concurrently amalgamates diverse time-scales, locations and identities into new wholes and shatters any vision of wholeness:

There are parallel narratives in the different rooms of the MUD; one can move forward or backward in time. The cultures of Tolkien, Gibson, and Madonna coexist and interact. Authorship is not only displaced from a solitary voice, it is exploded.[20]

The cultural pastiches produced by a MUD also problematize the notion of personal identity. If all role-playing activities allow people to explore alternative selves, this is especially the case with digital role-playing games. The user is a creature of the border, suspended between a reality that often feels unreal and a fantasy world that often feels almost *too* real. Cyberpunk narratives foreground this issue by intimating that in computer-saturated environments everything may ultimately amount to role-playing, that roles may not always be of one's own choice and that various roles may never converge but rather carry on indefinitely as parallel lives.

Arguably, cyberspace is rendered particularly ambiguous by the character of the *fantasies* that its users live out within its datasphere. On the one hand, these are salutary ways of expanding one's horizons in imaginative form and of acknowledging the vital role played by fictions in our day-to-day existence. According to Sherry Turkle:

> The Internet allows people to express, learn and play out aspects of themselves on-line. When that happens, there is a kind of 'play space' – a consequence-free zone which enables people to learn to know themselves in different ways.[21]

There are critics, however, such as Vic Seidler, who find the arenas released by cyberspace potentially perilous due to the possibility of the playing out of one's fantasies degenerating into obsessional addictions, and of the stigmas conventionally associated with shameful or taboo fantasies being exacerbated:

> The very privacy of the Net, which can be a release, can also bind us into structures of shame and can intensify fantasies which never have to be brought into contact with the reality of everyday life. . . . Hence virtual space becomes as much a refuge, into which we withdraw, as a space of freedom.[22]

Ideally, cybertechnological sites should offer not a hiding place but a forum for the exchange of ideas and opportunities. In Lisa M. Blackman's words, such a domain may constitute 'a world beyond dichotomies' capable of exposing 'the embeddedness of subjectivity in different spaces and places' and of foregrounding not only 'the fluid and contextual nature of identity' but also 'the mechanisms of those power/discursive relations through which we are constructed and construct ourselves'.[23]

Moreover, virtual technologies highlight some of the processes through which people are culturally constructed as both minds and bodies. Some theorists have adopted the rationalist approach that posits the mind as superior to the body and regarded virtual reality as a means of transcending the body's flaws. Jaron Lanier appears to follow this line.[24] His seminal writings on virtual reality suggest that digital technology allows the mind to pursue its objectives unencumbered by physical burdens. In this scenario, it seems both possible and desirable to leave behind the flesh imprinted by the defining stamps of social existence: race, class, gender and status. The virtual reality user becomes a universal and homogeneous creature, scarcely affected by contingent cultural circumstances. However, other critics stress that the user is not an abstract entity divorced from culture and specific markers of cultural identity. Concomitantly, they argue that it is important to acknowledge the heterogeneity of virtual users. Differences – physical ones included – should not be flattened and homogenized in the name of the cult of a wholly intellectual self. In fact, they should be cultivated in a spirit of heightened mobility. Whether this is ultimately conducive to emancipatory politics or to an intensification of consumerist mechanisms whereby identities are put on and discarded as easily as garments remains something of a moot point, at least for the time being. It is, however, undeniable that virtual reality has the potential of inaugurating configurations of identity characterized by unprecedented fluidity.

This fluidity is emphasized in Michael Heim's assessment of virtual reality and explicitly associated with a Gothic sensibility, by reference to the relationship between cyberspace and the discourse of the *sublime*:

> [T]he ultimate VR experience is a philosophical experience, probably an experience of the sublime or awesome . . . the final point of a virtual world is to dissolve the constraints of the anchored world so that we can lift anchor – not to drift aimlessly without point, but so we can explore anchorage in ever new places.[25]

If this picture comes across as somewhat idealistic, it is worth bearing in mind that in cyberculture, as in the Gothic, utopias and dystopias are inextricable. This is explicitly borne out by Gibson's work: while expecting the matrix to deliver boundless playing fields, Gibson's characters approach jacking in with the same desperate single-mindedness of drug addicts keen only on throwing themselves 'into a highspeed drift and skid, totally engaged but set apart from it all'.[26] In cyberculture, we encounter an eminently postmodern culturescape wherein technoscience challenges the western tendency to conceive of the real as fixed and of science as the means of quantifying and representing it. The real is now liable to be remade over and over. Science does not reflect the real but produces it according to human perceptions and projections. It is no longer a matter of adapting the ideal to the real but rather of making the real conform to the ideal. Neither is reality reliable nor is any available epistemology trusted with the power to grasp its essence. Reality is a hall of mirrors. We may bring it to us in virtually any guise we fancy and what we fancy may, paradoxically, coincide with what we most deeply abhor.

It could be argued that reality may ultimately be describable purely in terms of *design*, design practices and design principles. But what could be meant by 'design' in a culturescape that increasingly blurs the distinction between the natural and the artificial? Where does design stand in relation to both of these ubiquitous categories? According to Victor Margolin, 'Until recent years, the distinction between nature and culture appeared to be clear, with design, of course, belonging to the realm of culture.' Drawing on the theorizations of design practice initiated in the nineteenth century by the like of Henry Cole, and perpetuated in the twentieth by theoreticians and practitioners such as Charles Eastlake and Adolf Loos, Margolin argues that the modernist approach to design insistently stresses principles of 'simplicity' antagonistic to expressive – let alone excessive – ornamentation:

> In the discourse of the modernists ... objects were considered to be signs of value with uncontested referents such as clarity, beauty, integrity, simplicity, economy of means and function. The reductive slogan 'form follows function' assumed that use was an explicit, unambiguous term. Thus, the meaning of objects was to be found in their relation to a value that was grounded in belief.[27]

Poststructuralism and postmodernism have undermined this

ethos, largely by challenging the opposition between the natural and the artificial, as well as that between the essential and the decorative. This has had important repercussions for current understandings of design. Design is not a cultural means of encoding natural values in simple and functional objects. Nor is it the artificial counterpart of the organic processes at work in the physical world. In so far as constructedness pervades all forms of being and signification, design bears upon the natural no less pertinently than on the fabricated. Reality is not the stable ground on which value may be accorded to either objects or people. Reality is context-bound, tied to the specific circumstances in which the term 'reality' is used. Design can no longer be placed on the side of culture as the antonym of nature because the nature/culture binary has lost its credibility.

In certain brands of postmodernist speculation, this has led to drastic redefinitions of the very concept of value. It would be preposterous to claim that postmodernism totally negates value. In fact, what many a theorist proposes is a world densely populated, indeed overpopulated, by values of all kinds. These, however, do not grow organically and do not retain permanent identities for their most salient features, as Gianni Vattimo points out, are 'transformability' and 'convertibility'.[28] According to Margolin, Gibson's *Neuromancer* typifies this state of affairs by depicting a world in which 'being is convertible into infinite forms, and values of identity are constituted primarily through the manipulation of technology', thereby making 'design . . . victorious at the expense of reality' and 'meaning' a contingent effect of 'operational rather than semantic concerns'.[29] The gap opened by the demise of the real as a reliable reference point is filled by an endless circulation of data and by unceasing data-processing. Heim argues that this scenario offers mixed blessings:

> [W]hat technology gives with one hand, it often takes away with the other. . . . [T]he computer network . . . brackets the physical presence of the participants, by either omitting or simulating corporeal immediacy. In one sense, this frees us from the restrictions imposed by our physical identity; . . . in another sense, the quality of the human encounter narrows. The secondary or stand-in body reveals only as much of ourselves as we mentally wish to reveal.[30]

Cyberpunk comments on the conflicting perspectives examined in the preceding paragraphs by emphasizing the idea that reality is always up for grabs. The future does not signal an *escape* from but actually an *amplification* of the drab, messy, bruised texture of the everyday as we know it. In taking the logic of post-capitalism to its direst conclusions, Gibson's writings juxtapose physical and mental decomposition and high technology, just as cyberpunk cinematic classic *Blade Runner* combines the conventions of *film noir* with those of postmodern science fiction. Whereas the parameters by which reality and the willing suspension of disbelief are measured in classic science fiction are technological, those within which Gibson's characters operate are fundamentally economic. The overcrowding and hyperpollution of collapsing urban wastelands become the landmarks of a bleak universe, and the apparently alternative land-scapes of orbital existence merely replicate the sloppiness and chaos of the derelict cybercity.

Blade Runner suggests that it still makes sense to speculate about the nature of the bodies that overpopulate the posturban maze (in an attempt to ascertain their status as humans or replicants) and that replicants themselves are assessable by recourse to human values, to afflictions spawned by mindless abuse on the part of their makers. Gibson's fictions intimate that all identities are artificial, *designed* or at least partially *edited*, that reality cannot be established by differen-tiating the synthetic from the natural, and that suffering is as inevit-able as life itself. The subject is always, even when it is not overtly assaulted by corporational greed, on the verge of metamorphosis, always open to reprogramming strategies whose ramifications are as unforeseeable as those unleashed by the dinosaurs' breach of their genetic coding in Spielberg's *Jurassic Park*. In Gibson's gritty world picture, speculations about the nature of the real collapse into hyper-reality: 'The sinister thing about a simstim construct, really, was that it carried the suggestion that *any* environment might be unreal.'[31] By contrast with the expanding ambitions of 1950s and 1960s science fiction, cyberpunk, according to Istvan Csicsery-Ronay, presents a scenario of 'implosion, a drastic, careening plunge toward some inconceivable centre of gravity that breaks up the categories of rationality by jamming them together'.[32] This is accomplished pri-marily through a radical interrogation of the relationship between the real and the imaginary.

The terms *real* and *imaginary* may seem unreconcilable. How can an imaginary space or concept be real? How can reality associate itself with the imaginary? These sorts of questions result from an ingrained tendency to situate reality on the side of things as they are and the imaginary on that of things as they might be or might have been. However, although the link between the imaginary and the imagination is historically and philosophically inevitable, other readings of the imaginary should also be taken into consideration. Particularly relevant to this context are interpretations of the imaginary carried out in the fields of psychoanalysis and political philosophy – most notably by Jacques Lacan and Louis Althusser, respectively. Here the imaginary does not merely refer to the construction of fantasies disassociated from reality. In fact, the imaginary is a *process*, embedded in reality and vital to its survival, through which images *of* the subject and *for* the subject are created.

In psychoanalytical terms, the imaginary coincides with the phases of development of our bodies and minds through which we form a sense of self, of our autonomous existence as *subjects*. These moves are imaginary to the extent that the versions of subjectivity we embrace do not reflect inviolable and material properties of our being but rather proceed from misrecognition: we identify with images of what we wish to be or are expected to be. In Lacan's famous mirror-stage parable, we take as our *reality* what is in fact an illusory ideal.[33] In the domain of ideology, an analogous state of affairs obtains. Central to Althusser's notion of interpellation is a prolonged moment of misrecognition whereby ideology, in hailing us into existence as autonomous authors of our choices and actions, endeavours to efface our subjection to values that have always already been elected on our behalf.[34] In this scenario, as in the psychoanalytic one, we are required to adopt mythological identities – those of encultured creatures validated by tradition and by power structures – which are simultaneously technological in so far as they are predicated upon disciplinary strategies of normalization. The imaginary, then, is not exclusively coterminous with the imagination as a denial, repression or transcendence of the real. In fact, the imaginary is that which supplies us with images: images of ourselves necessary to our sense of being as individual objects, and images for ourselves designed to ensure our conformity to what our culture deems legitimate.

In bringing the real and the imaginary together, virtuality intimates that structures and relations of power are never clearly present or visible. They can reach us through dull, routinized channels but are also capable of penetrating us through fictions and fantasies. Power structures and relations are diffuse and ambivalent. Virtuality emphasizes this state of affairs by inviting us to feel directly involved in the making of ourselves and of our environments by means of interactive technologies, and simultaneously retaining hierarchies and forms of discrimination. Gibson's fiction highlights these issues by showing that even in accessing the most exclusive and thoroughly protected fortresses of power by breaking ICE ('intrusion counter-measures electronics'[35]), his characters do not achieve total control over any set of data. They are at all times surrounded by unpredictable forces, including mythical ones. Power is hard to quantify or visualize. Indeed, it uncannily resembles a 'swollen ghost', only occasionally visible 'and then in sidelong glances'.[36] Power's spectral texture forces us to realize that the relationship between what we see and what we know is, almost by definition, unsettled and haunted by renegade phantoms.

CHAPTER 2

CYBERPUNK, TECHNOLOGY
AND MYTHOLOGY

The Dutch surgeon liked to joke about that, how an unspecified percentage of Turner hadn't made it out of Palam International on that first flight, and had to spend the night there in a shed, in a support vat. It took the Dutchman and his team three months to put Turner together again. They cloned a square metre of skin for him, grew it on slabs of collagen and shark-cartilage polysaccharides. They bought eyes and genitals on the open market. The eyes were green. . . . He was as good as new, How good was that? He didn't know.

(William Gibson)[1]

. . . false beliefs and superstitions are rejected by the critical side of the SF intellect, but on the other side SF writers and fans are attracted to magic because it presupposes *as yet unknown and unpredictable changes* in our reality system.

(Casey Fredericks)[2]

TECHNOLOGY AND MYTHOLOGY: ORIGINS

What do mythology and technology share? In keeping with its etymological root, *mythos* (meaning 'talk', 'story'), mythology is commonly associated with bodies of legends and fictions, often propagated by oral traditions. Given the eminently fantastic content of these stories, their affiliation with the supernatural, and their cultivation of mysticism and irrationality, mythology is frequently categorized as the antonym of technoscientific knowledge. This trend obviously proceeds from the association of technology with the mechanical, industrial and, increasingly, electronic application of scientific findings, with the new, and with rational and measurable environments. This somewhat stereotypical understanding of technology does not adequately take into consideration its etymology: the Greek word *techne*, meaning 'art'. Acknowledging this link means having to reassess the relationship between mythology and technology. First, if technology is in some ways 'art', it cannot be linked exclusively to the rational, the measurable and the demonstrable: elements of imagination and fantasy enter its equations and these relate it to mythological story-telling. Second, the 'art' underlying technology does not merely refer to the production of objects such as narratives, paintings or buildings. *Techne* alludes to production and construction in general: the *making* of something out of the raw materials supplied by either nature or the imagination or both. This reading of 'art' has profound repercussions for our grasp of mythology and shows that mythology is, in many ways, technological: it *produces* images of people and worlds (both material and incorporeal). Technology, in turn, refers not merely to an apparatus of scientific practices and applications but also to a set of discourses through which subjects are regimented and fashioned. As Michel Foucault has demonstrated, this productive process tends to serve the interests of specific ideologies. Production is more often than not the production of useful, disciplined beings, who may be harnessed to the pursuit of culturally dominant imperatives. Therefore, technology is informed by mythology, insofar as it is an *artistic* practice, and mythology is informed by technology because *construction* is its fundamental purpose.[3]

The ancient Greek language has another word for 'making', *poesis*, that is no less complex than *techne*. Originally, *poesis* referred to 'making' or 'construction' in general but eventually it came to be associated with one particular kind of construct, namely poetry. Poetry's close association with mythology, fantasy and the imagination is well documented throughout history. It is hence tempting to suggest that there is a constant overlap between 'making' as a functional and pragmatic operation and 'making' as the production of fictions. At the same time, *poesis* invokes a contrast between the constructed and the putatively natural. The poet/maker does not produce things under the guidance of natural instincts in the way a bird, bee or beaver would. 'Art' itself is a problematic term, in this respect. It derives from the Latin word *ars*, which denotes a practical and acquired (as opposed to natural) skill. Yet *ars* is etymologically related – probably through the Arian root *ar*, meaning to fit or join –

to words that refer to both nature and culture: *armus* (meaning 'shoulder-joint', later to become 'arm', the term used to define an anatomical limb) and *arma* (that is, 'weapons', 'arms' in the military sense of the word). Here again, we witness a conflation of apparently contrasting ideas. While *mythos* and *techne* coalesce in the concept of 'making', and *poesis* narrows down the concept of 'making' to the production of narratives, *ars* blurs the distinction between natural object and artefacts.

Mythology and technology collude primarily on the territory of corporeality. Mythobodies (bodies forged through the coalescence of the natural and the supernatural) and technobodies (bodies produced by the encounter of the biological and the artificial) are hybrid compounds which underscore the brindled character of embodied subjectivity. The interplay of reality and fantasy points to the mythobody's infiltration by technology and to the technobody's imbrication with mythology. While the hard and shiny technobody hardly contains the murky and spooky aspects of the mythological fantasies that inform it, the loose and opaque mythobody, for its part, is shaped by technologies of the subject that organize its polysemy into a discourse. Technologies and mythologies are inextricably intertwined. The technobody carries mythological connotations and the mythobody technological ones.

Moreover, mythological and technological discourses figure the body in analogous ways, their most salient similarity consisting of the simultaneous employment of strategies of magnification and strategies of minimization. Both mythological and technological bodies are inflated and attenuated, enhanced and etherealized, at one and the same time. Mythology and fantasy have, since time immemorial, figured the body by recourse to these strategies. In one scenario, mythical and fantastic bodies are larger than life: they are idealized and amplified in the forms of mighty deities, giants, heroes and supermen. In the other scenario, mythical and fantastic bodies are smaller than life: they are dwarfed and rarefied in the guises of ghosts, phantoms, pixies and sprites. These two modalities are not binarily opposed, for the preternatural body may be at once powerful and invisible, decorporealized and overwhelming. Technology ideates the body according to analogous mechanisms of enhancement and reduction; it simultaneously empowers the physical being and curtails its materiality, consolidates its boundaries and opens it to alien incursions. Besides, mythology and technology are brought together by their common fascination with the image of the body as an aggregate of disparate – and by no means organically harmonized – elements. Mythology teems with figures fashioned precisely on the basis of a body's ability to merge with, invade or metamorphose into, *other* bodies. The contemporary part-body fostered by techno-science could be read as a descendant of the ancient shaman, the Dionysian reveller, the vampire, the werewolf. It thus bears traces, for all its novelty, of remote and ritual identities.

What may specifically characterize our times, however, is a heightened concern with the part-body and with part objects, with computational aggregates and simulated compounds, promoted by strategies of technological reinvention of the human body. These cannot be confined to the realm of fiction as a distinct domain, for they capitalize on the infiltration of so-called reality by the virtual, the hyperreal and the simulated. According to Arthur Kroker, this culturescape is responsible for the emergence of a schizophrenic sense of embodied subjectivity: we are torn between our *new* identities, as 'techno-mutants in the name of an expanding freedom' and our *old* identities, as 'critics of technology as degeneration'. The tension between the old and the new is dramatized by the ascendancy of virtual reality as the 'mass emigration of genes from the old world of the human body to the new world of digital reality'.[4] The deluge of contemporary mechanisms of mediation constructed in terms of virtual spaces, cyberspaces and the electronic realm problematizes with unprecedented intensity the relationship between natural and artificial bodies. Cyborgology exemplifies this process by deploying simultaneously scientific and fictional discourses.

CYBORGS

The figure of the cyborg encapsulates many contemporary anxieties about the encounter of the natural and the artificial and the idea that there are no clear divisions between the non-human and the human, the technological and the biological, the original and the copy. In doing so, it simultaneously questions many conventional assumptions and boundaries. As Gary Lee Downey, Joseph Dumit and Sarah Williams point out, 'cyborg anthropology poses a serious challenge to the human-centered foundations of anthropological discourse' by 'examining the argument that human subjects and subjectivity are crucially as much a function of machines, machine relations, and information transfers as they are machine producers and operators'.[5]

The term *cyborg* (cybernetic organism) was put forward by Manfred E. Clynes and Nathan S. Kline in 1960 to describe a self-regulating man-machine system, supposed to be more flexible than the human organism thanks to the fusion of organic and mechanical parts. Clynes and Kline's cyborg is fundamentally an enhanced human, ideally capable of surviving in extraterrestrial worlds: 'Altering man's bodily functions to meet the requirements of extraterrestrial environments would be more logical than providing an earthly environment for him in space. . . . Artifact-organism systems which would extend man's unconscious, self-regulatory controls are one possibility.'[6] Clynes and Kline's project inspired the 'Cyborg Study' conducted on behalf of NASA in 1963. This project, observes Robert Driscoll:

> . . . concerns itself with the determination of man's capabilities and limitations under the unpredictable and often hostile conditions of space flight, and the theoretical possibility of incorporating artificial organs, drugs, and/or hypothermia as integral parts of the life support systems in space craft design of the future, and of reducing metabolic demands and the attendant life support requirements.[7]

Cyborg technologies have military origins but have also found useful applications in the medical arena, as well as in the realms of entertainment and industry. Chris Hables Gray, Steven Mentor and Heidi Figueroa-Sarriera have observed that not all cyborg technologies use the same strategies or indeed serve the same purposes:

> Cyborg technologies can be restorative, in that they restore lost functions and replace lost organs and limbs; they can be normalizing, in that they restore some creatures to indistinguishable normality; they can be ambiguously reconfiguring, creating posthuman creatures equal to but different from humans . . . and they can be enhancing, the aim of most military and industrial research, and what those with cyborg envy or even cyborg-philia fantasize.[8]

In examining the ideological, psychological and physiological attributes of the cyborg, the following points should be taken into consideration: (1) the cyborg is both a creature of myth and a creature of social reality; (2) the cyborg incarnates conflicting visions of power and powerlessness; (3) the cyborg embodies cultural fears and anxieties.

The cyborg is not simply a fantastic creature. Many people's bodies are cyborg-like to various degrees, as testified by ordinary bodies either supplemented by prostheses or immersed in cybernetic information systems. As Gray, Mentor and Figueroa-Sarriera point out: 'anyone with an artificial organ, limb or supplement (like a pacemaker), anyone reprogrammed to resist disease (immunized) or drugged to think/behave/feel better (psychopharmacology) is technically a cyborg'.[9] Katherine Hayles corroborates this point by stating that 'about 10% of the current U.S. population are estimated to be cyborgs in the technical sense, including people with electronic pacemakers, artificial joints, drug implant systems, implanted corneal lenses, and artificial skin'.[10] Cosmetic surgery, biotechnology, genetic engineering, and the replacement of organic functions by biochip implants show that there is simply no such thing as a *pure body*. The brain and nervous system are still exceptions, but for how long? As already mentioned, the computer scientist and roboticist Hans Moravec believes that in the not too distant future it will be possible to transfer mental functions to computer software.[11] A corollary of this process, according to Figueroa-Sarriera, is that the mind is not 'tied to a single body': mental activity may be configured in a 'infinite number of patterns', thereby 'rearticulating the ancient myth of Proteus, the sea-god who possesses the ability to change shape at will'.[12] The cyborg is the ultimate (at least to date) emblem of a hybrid subjectivity. A tangible body forged through the coupling of the biological and the mechanical (or the electronic, or both) the cybernetic organism is also a network of texts through which cultural identities and roles are negotiated. As a hypercrafted child of technology, the cyborg may seem to have little in common with the jumbled bodies of mythology and lore. However, its employment by ideological discourses and commercial operations devoted to fuelling the myth of invulnerability underscores the cyborg's mythological stature in iconographic and symbolic terms. In Anne Balsamo's words: 'From children's plastic action figures to cyberpunk mirrorshades, cyborgian artifacts will endure as relics of an age obsessed with the limits of human mortality and the possibilities of human replication. . . . [O]ur technological imagination imbues cyborgs with ancient anxieties.'[13]

The cyborg embodies two opposite fantasies: that of the pure body and that of the impure body. On one level, the cyborg presents a sealed, clean, hard, tight and uncontaminated body. It offers the ideal of a body that does not eat, drink, cry, sweat, urinate, defecate, menstruate, ejaculate: a body that does not suffer any illnesses and does not die. This Puritanical body without secretions and indiscretions incarnates a fantasy of omnipotence. The mechanical parts that replace ordinary anatomical parts are supposed to enhance the body's power potential and repudiate its association with *leaky* materiality. This point is underscored by Les Levidow and Kevin Robins: 'through a paranoid rationality, expressed in the machine-like self . . . we deny our dependency upon nature, upon our own nature, upon the "bloody mess" of organic nature'.[14]

Verhoeven's *Robocop* and Cameron's *The Terminator* and its sequel *Terminator 2: Judgment Day* are possibly the best known and most popular dramatizations of the cyborg theme. The cyborg body presented by these films is strong, hardly susceptible to injury and pain and able to self-repair very quickly. It is also a very *masculine* body: in western culture, it is the male shape that is conventionally seen as sealed and bounded, and the female one, by contrast, that is seen as leaky and unbounded. On another level, however, the cyborg is inevitably a hybrid and therefore *impure* being. It can only display its strength by putting on an armour. In both *Terminator* films, the Terminator makes his first appearance on this planet as a vulnerable and naked figure, folded up in a fetal position. He gains his phallic power and stereotypically masculine aggressiveness through the violent acquisition of leather gear and weapons. At the same time, this hypermasculinized figure is also endowed with benevolent dispositions. The Terminator in *Terminator 2*, in particular, operates as a kind of surrogate parent. As Cynthia Fuchs observes, 'Cyborgs incarnate two contradictions of masculine identity. First, they combine phallic masculinity and body permeability. Second, they contradict the sociobiological constructions of paternity and maternity.'[15] Phallic power, moreover, goes hand in hand with an implicit recognition of impotence for, as Jonathan Goldberg notes, 'Making every inch of the body hard, having erections everywhere, entails a massive denial of the adequacy of the penis.'[16] The cyborg's virility is also, to some extent, held in check by powerful female characters. In

The Terminator, Sarah Connor destroys the Terminator single-handedly, and in the sequel she features as a muscular and ruthless fighter. Her fate is associated essentially with motherhood, but she hardly fits into the nurturing woman stereotype. The model of the muscular angry woman could be seen as an embodiment of patri-archal values, as a fetish produced by male fears, especially the fear of the unbounded female body. Alternatively, it could be seen as an ideal to be aspired to by women who are still subjected to injustice. Yet a character like Sarah cannot be viewed unproblematically as *either* a male fetish *or* a feminist vision: she incorporates conflicting possibilities and, to this extent, reinforces the sense of ambiguity typical of cyborg narratives generally.

Though technologically constructed, the cyborg is *human* in so far as it symbolizes human cares and uncertainties. The *Terminator* films, for example, suggest that human beings need cyborgs in order to assert their humanity, to go on believing that they are *still* human, after all. In *Terminator 2*, in particular, we are faced with two differ-ent cyborg bodies: the old Cyberdine Systems Model 101, capable of many miraculous things but still, in some ways, stuck with its body, and the new T-1000, made exclusively of liquid metal and therefore able to reinvent its body endlessly. The old model is turned into a hero of sorts, while the new model is demonized. The new model is just too inhuman: its body happens to look human at times, but is equally convincing as an inanimate object. T-1000 cannot be seen as a friend because nothing about its structure and acts commits it finally to the human camp. Model 101, on the other hand, retains enough of a connection with real human bodies to count as a friend, to seem human even though it obviously is not. The cyborg is an intriguing metaphor for cultural and political preoccupations on a further level: its fundamental hybridity epitomizes the subversion of conventional notions of order, space, territory and identity by dras-tically challenging the tenability of both personal and collective boundaries. As Balsamo observes, 'Cyborg bodies are definitionally transgressive of a dominant cultural order, not so much because of their "constructed" nature, but rather because of the indeterminacy of their hybrid design.'[17]

The positive communicational potentialities of the boundless body are also noteworthy: a cyborg body, argues Gregory Bateson, 'is not bounded by the skin but includes all external pathways along which information can travel'.[18] The most enthusiastic assessment of the cyborg's association with transgressive politics is, arguably, to be found in Donna Haraway's 'A manifesto for cyborgs'. In this article, Haraway posits the cyborg body as a radical challenge to the myth of stable identities due to its emphasis on the interpenetration of self and other. By traversing the boundary between the human and the machine, the cyborg concurrently disrupts other binary opposites (culture/nature; reality/appearance; male/female) that have been 'systemic to the logics and practices of domination of women, people of color, nature, workers, animals'.[19] The transgressive cyborg body may be useful to feminism through its assault on essentialism and through its foregrounding of the interplay of biology and symbolism – namely, a strategy that has always been central to technological and mythological fabrications of the female body. The cyborg body inhabits a non-teleological and non-etiological universe which makes the fantasy of returning to an Edenic state of innocence quite irrelevant: 'it is not made of mud and cannot dream of returning to dust'.[20] Its ultimate political function lies with its ability to promote a world in which 'we can learn from our fusions with animals and machines how not to be Man, the embodiment of western logos'.[21] Furthermore: 'A cyborg world might be about lived social and bodily realities in which people are not afraid of their joint kinship with animals and machines, not afraid of permanently partial identities and contradictory standpoints.'[22] The cyborg, then, may offer an alternative configuration of the theory of the body politic to the orthodox Hobbesian version. In the latter, an analogy is proposed between organic and social bodies, the ruler signifying not merely the head but also the soul of the state, and the cybernetic version of the body politic displaces the very notions of both soul and centralized control, as Gray and Mentor point out: 'to offer a new map, a new way to conceive of power and identity'.[23]

One of the main structures of signification that cyborgology insistently challenges is the one that pivots on the relationship between *original* and *copy*. It might be tempting to explain the cybernetic organism away as a copy or simulation of the human mind—body continuum. Yet such an explanation is fraught with ambiguities, for the concept of copy is neither stable nor univocal. Some philosophical systems tend to envisage the copy as a second-rate replica of a worthy original. Others, however, idealize it as a perfect model or blueprint. Others still argue that the original only gains validity by virtue of its liability to reproduction. In Plato's universe, the copy is portrayed as incontrovertibly inferior to the Idea or Pure Form that is supposed to lie behind it. But this is by no means the only available perspective. Gilles Deleuze, for instance, maintains that notions of imitation, simulation and replication are differential and that it is therefore preposterous to speak of *the* copy as though this were a monolithic category. More specifically, Deleuze draws an important distinction between the *copy* and the *simulacrum*. The copy is associated with a hierarchical ethos. Though second-rate, it is invested with metaphysical significance by dint of its connection with an honourable original: it 'is far from a simple appearance, since it stands in an internal, spiritual, noological and ontological relation with the Idea or model'. In this scenario, the copy functions as something of a transparent envelope capable of enclosing the original as its own supreme source of meaning and being. It admits to the original's autonomous existence yet it also aspires, paradoxically, to eliminating all vestiges of difference between model and replica. The simulacrum, conversely, alludes to 'the state of free, oceanic differences, of nomadic distributions' and 'anarchy'.[24] It thrives on dislocation, multiplicity, errantry and heterogeneity. Moreover, the logic of the simulacrum challenges the Platonic belief in the original's superiority by making the very idea of originality conditional upon the possibility of simulation. The simulacrum undermines the notion of identity as a substance or essence and reinscribes it instead as a fleeting 'optical "effect"'.[25] In reading the cyborg as a *reproduction* of the human, it may be more apposite to think in terms of simulacra than in those of copies. In cyborgology, the 'primacy of original over copy, of model over image'[26] is negated. In simulating the human body, the cybernetic organism also compels us to reassess radically certain conventional ideas about embodiment. It cannot, therefore, be regarded as inferior or supplementary. The human may be designated as original only to the extent that it may be simulated, and that in the simulating process, the *original* itself is substantially reconfigured. The human body and its replica are mapped on each other.

The ambiguities surrounding the figure of the cyborg could be compared to the ambivalent feelings experienced by a person wearing a prosthesis. Prostheses enhance our bodies, but they also remind us of our failings, thus endowing us with a double identity: the better self and the failing self. Prostheses refine our capacities and alert us to our incapacities; they consolidate the edges of our bodies and simultaneously blur them. Indeed, by pointing to what is missing *in* and *from* the body, they question radically the body's integrity. Prostheses are there to remind us that we have always already slipped from the planes of completeness and self-sufficiency. We can never be totally sure where our edges are, where we begin and where we end. Furthermore, it should be emphasized that prosthetic devices do not simply encompass artificial limbs and implants but also the various technologies with which increasing numbers of people daily interact – from the Internet to fitness-club machinery. Is the person hooked into a computer and navigating through cyberspace, or the person developing his/her body schema through exercise equipment built with the latest technology *less* or *more* a cyborg than the person kept barely alive by machines in an intensive care unit, or the person connected by complex interfaces to a war craft? If all these people are cyborgs, do some retain a greater degree of humanness than others? If so, how is this humanness measured? Where does the human end and where does the technological begin?

In *Robocop*, the body is literally rebuilt through technology. The dominant concern is the violation of humanity by the machine. That Murphy is *more human* than machines (although it is by no means clear how much of his body has been salvaged besides his brain) is made clear by the fact that he goes on being haunted by human concerns even after he has been engulfed in a computerized existence. He is still able to experience deep emotional pain, particularly when he remembers his past life as a husband and father. He is also physically superior to the clumsy android Ed 209. OCP (Omni Consumer Products) believe that Murphy's personal identity can be erased through reprogramming. But Murphy retains the desire to break free because, somewhat magically, he has retained his will. The mechanical being Robocop remains human, in the logic of the series, as long as Murphy retains a mind as the *essence* of humanness. Yet the hero's conceptual superiority hardly makes him all-powerful. As Fuchs has indicated:

> Robocop is both too hard and too soft . . . repeatedly shot up, bloodied, exploded, and dismembered. . . . Murphy's self is irrecuperable when he is 'cyborged' into Robocop. His self-realization comes as he gazes at his reflection in a shard of mirror: he sees that he has no body, collective or individual, to be returned to him, only a bald head punctured by implants.[27]

As a scientific and technological experiment, the cyborg could be said to embody one of modernity's abiding dreams: the possibility of translating the unbounded organic body into a bounded inorganic artefact, produced according to the rules of mathematics and engineering. Within the parameters of modernity, the machine-like body is supposed to encapsulate principles of rationality, objectivity and abstraction. It is a means of turning the tumultuous harlequinade of images unleashed by modern life (typified by the accelerating tempo of the metropolis) into orderly patterns. However, the cybernetic organism also embodies a postmodern outlook that does not idealize technology as either rational or orderly but actually emphasizes its penchant for breaking down traditional boundaries: most importantly, the dividing line between the human and the non-human. From a postmodern point of view, the cyborg-body closely resembles Gibson's cyberspace. Indeed, both the cybernetic organism and the matrix are constructs apparently capable of *containing* an array of disparate elements and of *organizing* them into sophisticated networks. At the same time, both show that compartments and divisions are precarious. The instability of the elements they contain and organize insistently shuns any clear demarcations.

MYTH AND RELIGION IN CYBERPUNK

speculative science and myth-making interact: the concepts, world-views, and images . . . are located at various points along a myth-science interface.

(Casey Fredericks)[28]

On one level, contemporary technoscience seems to perpetuate the rationalist approach preached by the Enlightenment. On another level, the Gibsonian configuration of cyberspace as a *hallucinatory* experience alludes to science's involvement with the irrational. At the same time, while ongoing developments in scientific research emphasize the importance of specialization and expertise, an ever-growing body of data becomes daily available to an ever-growing body of Internet browsers. Cyberculture thrives on these ambiguities: rationality and irrationality coexist within its territory, as do specialist and amateur types of involvement. One of the major questions we need to address today is the following: are the non-specialists in a position to produce novel forms of knowledge or are they reduced to passive consumers of only haphazardly connected data? Arguably, modes of information chronologically antecedent to cyberspace, primarily broadcast, have already capitalized on the consumption by a passive audience of information emanating from a powerful centre. It may be fruitful, therefore, to focus not so much on the extent to which cyberspace's redefinition of knowledge is calling into question human agency as on the extent to which such a shift dethrones conventional ideas of reason and system to create scope for new constellations of human experience.

One of cyberpunk's main contributions to contemporary reassessments of issues of knowledge and agency lies in its fusion of mythological and technological motifs. John Shirley's 'Wolves of the plateau' offers a vivid description of the interplay of technology and mythology. The story's protagonist, Jerome, has a chip installed in his brain. As he tries to use it to achieve his practical plan – escape from confinement – he realizes that the chip is not just a technological artefact but also a mythological text:

> Jerome's chip communicating with his brain via an interface of rhodopsin protein; the ribosomes borrowing neurohumoral transmitters from the brain's blood supply, reordering the transmitters so that they carried a programmed pattern of ion releases for transmission across synaptic gaps to the brain's neuronal dendrites; the chip using magnetic resonance holography to collate with brain-stored memories and psychological trends. *Declaiming to itself the mythology of the brain; reenacting on its silicon stage the personal Legends of his subjective world history.*[29]

The picture painted by Shirley suggests that the technological *dream* of a brain systematically mapped out with the aid of genetics and cybernetics can easily turn into a *nightmare*, as the scientifically modified organ goes on being haunted by troubling reminders of the psyche's unspeakably complex fabric.

The nightmares of technoscientific reason are central to the thematic and structural organization of Gibson's *Trilogy* and consistently highlighted through the juxtaposition of technological and mythological tropes. Cyberpunk charts an ambivalent mythopoeia in which new forms of life are seen to emerge from technology and, at the same time, the digital universe is permeated by mysticism and occultism. Cyberspace seethes with vampires, mambos, shamans, mermaids, Faustian and Mephistophelean characters, ghosts, visionaries and soothsayers. AIs, console cowboys and the ruthless leaders of profit-driven multinational corporations are themselves redolent of the creation deities, heroes and villains of traditional lore. What these figures underscore is the intrinsic strangeness of the everyday, the ultimate uncanniness of anything we may deem familiar. *Neuromancer* abounds with references to mythology and lore, ranging from Rastafarian beliefs and practices to traditional icons such as the Hanging Garden of Babylon.[30] In *Count Zero*, the mythological dimension gains novel urgency through the invocation of voodoo figures. The would-be computer cowboy Bobby Newmark is about to be killed by the program he is testing when he perceives a female voice and hallucinatory images – 'Girlvoice, brownhair, darkeyes — . . . Darkeyes, desertstar, tanshirt, girlhair' – which alert him to the fact that 'it's a trick'.[31] The matrix-generated phantom rescues him, as it were, by making him recognize that the killer program cannot actually destroy him. This makes Bobby a 'chosen of Legba . . . master of roads and pathways, the loa of communication',[32] and hence a crucial pawn in the game played by Two-a-Day and his voodoo associates. The coalescence of technoscience and magic is further evoked through minor characters. The Korean biomedic who runs the portable neurosurgery module designed to scan Mitchell for lethal implants is a cutting-edge cyberscientist who also, however, 'knows black medicine from both ends'.[33] And Harry, the man who delivers the software supposed to enable Turner 'to pilot the jet that would carry Mitchell to Hosaka's Mexico City compound', wears around his neck an assortment of amulets: 'loops of fine steel chain, rawhide, bits of animal horn and fur, brass cartridge casings' and 'a crooked bit of bent gristle' which turns out to be 'a coon's pecker'.[34]

In *Count Zero*, voodoo is described as a '*structure*' that 'isn't concerned with notions of salvation and transcendence' but rather with 'getting things *done*' by recourse to *many* gods, spirits'.[35] Voodoo does not constitute a religion, mythology or mystical system so much as a business: it is an eminently 'professional priesthood'.[36] Such a business is very tricky indeed, for its leader, Two-a-Day, makes himself invaluable by supplying corporations with precious data but also finds himself in awkward situations which require a little bit more than strategic thinking and diplomacy. For example, corporations often download onto him, and require him to test, suspect programs which it would be too risky for the corporations themselves to probe. The most dangerous wares are the icebreakers, namely programs designed to penetrate the security systems built around top-secret corporational information. ICE is produced by artificial intelligences, for 'nothing else is fast enough to weave good ice and constantly alter and upgrade it'.[37] The AIs are not in themselves wholly autonomous, for the Turing police is always on the alert, lest they should become too smart. If the people (such as Lucas) downloading problematic goods onto Two-a-Day are not willing to carry out the necessary tests themselves, neither is Two-a-Day foolish enough to undertake the operation himself. This is where cheap hackers like Bobby enter the game as unwitting test-drivers. In the testing process, the unsuspecting cowboy may succeed in breaking the ice, encounter apparently meaningless data and abandon the programme as something of a waste of time. However, the ice may also fry the user 'dead'.[38] Bobby's experience is extraordinary because it falls in neither of these possible categories, and this is what makes him – in terms of voodoo – very special indeed.

As it happens, Bobby finds his role rather arduous to grasp. Lucas describes voodoo to him as a 'metaphor'[39] but to Bobby, who like most cowboys is practically illiterate, this word means little or nothing at all. He hazards the guess that 'metaphor' may refer to an electronic 'component', a 'capacitator', but that is about the size of his engagement with rhetorical parlance. What Lucas has in mind, however, is a system – such as voodoo and cyberspace themselves – wherein multiple meanings coexist and where 'the language of street tech' and the language of magic seamlessly interweave. In Lucas's discourse, technology is mythologized to the point that science and magic, the deck's microcosm and cyberspace's macrocosm, the mambo's microcosm and the spirits' macrocosm, become virtually indistinguishable:

> Think of Jackie as a deck . . . Think of Danbala as a program . . .
> 'Okay,' Bobby said . . . 'then what's the matrix? . . . what's cyberspace?'
> 'The world,' Lucas said.[40]

A similar worldview emerges from the subplot centred around the character of Wigan Ludgate. Having made a fortune, largely at the expense of politically unstable Third World governments, Ludgate experiences some 'major paradigm shifts' and becomes 'convinced that God lived in cyberspace, or perhaps that cyberspace *was* God'.[41] Occasional attempts are made to rationalize voodoo's infiltration of the matrix, yet these are confused, half-hearted and extremely hesitant, as evinced by Jammer's somewhat hysterical tirade:

> 'There's no way in hell there'd be anything out there that you had to talk to in fucking bush Haitian! . . . Beauvoir and Lucas and the rest, they're businessmen first. And those Goddamn things know how to make *deals*! . . . Could be they're virus programs that have got loose in the matrix and replicated, and got really smart . . . Or maybe the AIs have found a way to split parts of themselves off into the matrix.'[42]

Even the incredulous Finn ultimately acknowledges the animistic infrastructure of cyberspace, as indicated by a telling exchange with Molly in which he describes the belief-system of Lucas and his associates:

> 'Hoodoos. Thought the matrix was full of mambos 'n' shit. Wanna know something, Moll?'
> 'What?'
> 'They're right.'[43]

The character of Angie Mitchell in *Count Zero* and *Mona Lisa Overdrive* is central to the interweaving of technoscience and animism. As a consequence of a Faustian pact sealed by her father with unnamable forces willing to supply him with priceless data, Angie has had complex programs inscribed in her very brain, which enable her to access, in dreams, the voodoo world and cyberspace itself – the voodoo world *being* cyberspace or, at any rate, a very substantial component thereof: 'Her father was dead, seven years dead, and the record he'd kept of his life had told her little enough. That he'd served someone or something, that his reward had been knowledge, and that she had been his sacrifice.'[44] The technomythological nature of Angie's experiences is foregrounded through the juxtaposition of attempts at scientific explanation and an emphasis on their magical attributes. Having scanned her, Rudy fumbles for words capable of accurately describing the physiology of Angie's brain: 'What is it, some kind of cancer? . . . It's all over her head . . . Like long chains of it. . . . It's some kind of . . . Not an implant. Graft.'[45] But what is most prominent is the preternatural quality of Angie's dreams, her possession by myriad shapes and voices as, unconscious, she is repeatedly heard 'talking in the tongues'.[46] Angie herself refers to voodoo as a 'religious' structure and dismisses her friend Porphyre's sarcastic assessment of it as a mere matter of 'chickenbone and pennyroyal oil'.[47] In the closing sections of *Count Zero*, Angie and Turner are actually led by a voodoo voice speaking through the girl's body and urging them to 'find Danbala's horse'.[48] When they reach their destination, Angie is instantly welcomed by the mambo Jackie as 'the Virgin of Miracles' sent by Danbala.[49] As the voodoo epidemic rapidly spreads, Bobby himself is *possessed* by voodoo forces, and in the novel's climactic moments he confronts the villain Herr Virek in the form of 'Baron Samedi, Lord of Graveyards, the loa whose kingdom was death'.[50] The mythological infrastructure of scientific knowledge could hardly be conveyed more emphatically.

Mythological references centred on vampirism abound in *Mona Lisa Overdrive*. For instance, the voodoo goddess 'Mamman Brigitte', known as 'the eldest of the dead', visits Angie's dreams very much as an *undead* in the appropriate setting of 'whitewashed cemetery walls'.[51] The reference to Bobby as the 'Count' immediately conjures up in Little Bird's mind the image of the 'vampire', and later Slick, as he observes that the Count is being drained 'dry' by the electronic apparatus to which he is connected, remembers 'Bird's vampire talk'.[52] As Kumiko walks around the utterly impersonal, grey room to which Sally has taken her, she notices that 'there was something vampiric about the room . . . something it would have in common with millions of similar rooms, as though its bewilderingly seamless anonymity were sucking away her personality'.[53] Vampirism also features in the shape of a subcultural group, the Draculas, physically identifiable by their 'black raincoats', and their 'bone-thin, bone-white faces'.[54] Vampires, moreover, are surrounded by a plethora of spectres and hybrids: grotesquely distorted mutants, such as the 'palmetto bugs' produced through manipulations of the DNA of cockroaches,[55] and metamorphic figures, such as the 'centauri' of *Mona Lisa Overdrive*,[56] and the dinosaurs, talking mountains and bodies made up of 'writhing' television images of *Virtual Light*.[57]

The appeal to heterodox mythologies is, among other things, symptomatic of a desire to escape the squalor of everyday megalopolitan existence, to forge alternative forms of cohesion among increasingly alienated individuals. According to Darko Suvin, 'a solution logically latching onto cyberspace, and allowing surrogate reconnecting (*re-ligio*) between disparate people and their destinies ... is then religion'.[58] This reading is corroborated by Samuel Delany, who maintains that 'the hard edges of Gibson's dehumanized technologies hide a residing mysticism'.[59] The *dance of data* to which Gibson keeps referring is also a Gothic *dance of death*. As McCaffery emphasizes, Gibson, in depicting 'the world space of multinational capitalism', delineates an eminently contemporary technological situation. Yet his narratives concurrently reverberate with supernatural and mythological notes – in 'the mystical sense that our creation and re-creation of data and images produces systems capable of merging with one another into new intelligences' and that this, however, may not exorcise 'the uneasy recognition that our primordial urge to replicate our consciousness and physical beings ... is *not* leading us closer to the dream of immortality, but is creating merely a pathetic parody, a metaexistence'.[60]

If cyberpunk supplies legion alternative religions as a means of forging some sense of cohesion in an otherwise alienating environment, it is also the case that Gibson does not idealize those systems. In fact, he consistently underscores their dogmatic and ungenerous stance. This is vividly brought out by *Virtual Light*'s dubious neo-Christian communities – the most suspect consisting of a bunch of TV addicts who, besotted with 'Reverend Fallon' and his teachings, believe they will find Jesus by unceasingly watching movies, preferably old ones. The iconoclastic Skinner voices Gibson's scepticism about such spiritualistic opiates. Commenting on the cult that has grown around the figure of the AIDS martyr Shapely, the old man remarks: 'Same shit all over. Always some of 'em, anyway, makes you wonder how these damn religions last so long or what started it in the first place.'[61]

Heterodox belief systems such as voodoo may well be invoked in order to forge a sense of solidarity out of featureless societies in which multiculturalism often amounts to acute partitionings and unrelieved loneliness. Yet when Gibson voices certain suspicions about religions of all sorts, he points not so much to the west's willingness to learn from them as to its urge to idealize them as a corrective for its own emptiness. *Other* religions are not embraced by cyberpunk characters out of a desire to understand new lessons. Rather, they are valued in so far as they may counteract dominant value systems, supply evidence for the survival of faith and eventually just confirm the inability of cyberpunk's dystopian culture to embrace any creed for more than a fleeting moment. Geert Lovink's comments on 'contemporary nihilism' are especially relevant in this context. They suggest that when the west accepts or even values other traditions, this is because it is uneasy about *its own* loss of traditional beliefs and envies those who might still be capable of consistent devotion. When it goes as far as appropriating them, it is still fundamentally incapable of consistently participating in their rituals:

> Who would wish to visit upon another a dull life like our own, culminating as it does in likewise padded solitude? Tolerance means envy of the other's simplicity. . . . Gurus, healing stones, skyward apparitions, voodoo, and encounters all slip past, without one having ever a chance of sharing these experiences.[62]

Pat Cadigan's *Tea From an Empty Cup* explores the clash between western and non-western attitudes to the supernatural by drawing together technology and mythology in the context of virtuality. By taking a 'gel cap'[63] that facilitates access to alternative worlds full of erotically stimulating images, the user is supposed to discover not only the bliss of human orgasm but also the potent sexual energies that enliven a whole 'creation myth' – a myth based on cosmic conflict and on its resolution through ecstatic experiences that bring together erotic pleasure and laughter. Cadigan uses this idea to highlight racial and cultural differences in the approach to both technology and mythology. Thus the Japanese supplier of the cap believes in the interconnection of science, legend, sexuality and cosmic balance, and on the necessity of willingly yielding to the messages of myth. The white buyer, by contrast, is sceptical and governed by purely materialistic concerns that leave no room for myth and 'magic'.[64] Here we witness the conflict between a culture that views sex as the animating force of an inexhaustibly fertile universe and a culture in which sex is commodified and in which technology has become a means of divorcing the erotic from any mythological associations. Ironically, the 'white guy' is not totally impervious to the lessons of myth. When he is about to receive the object that may equally prove a blessing or a curse, he inadvertently turns to *Faust*: 'What doth it profit a man to gain the whole world and lose his soul?' Yet he has no idea where these words come from or indeed why they have occurred to him at this particular juncture. Hardened by his drably secular and positivistic background, he has no means of making sense of what he calls a 'premonition'. Disturbed and surprised, he remarks: 'it wasn't just a feeling. It was more like a vision. Or *almost* a vision. But it wasn't *my* vision.'[65]

The intermingling of mythologies and technologies suggests that as human civilization intermittently gasps for breath, things change and yet remain the same. Gibson explores this paradox in *Count Zero*, by recourse to two contrasting interpretations of the temporal configuration of cyberspace. The view that things change is embraced by the Finn: 'Didn't use to be this way. . . . I been in the trade forever. Way back. Before the war, before there was any matrix, or anyway before people *knew* there was one.' Lucas, on the other hand, advocates the idea that no real change has ever occurred; any modification of space simply amounts to an increasing sense of fragmentation and dispersal. In response to the Finn's depiction of a cyberspace that 'every year . . . gets a little more crowded' with mythical and spectral forms, Lucas states: 'the *world* has always worked that way'.[66] For Lucas, cyberspace is the world and the world is cyberspace – that is, anything we may haphazardly negotiate as *reality* is populated by wandering hosts of hybrid shapes and garbled polyphonies, both in the mythological conception of voodoo and in the technological exchange of electronically mediated messages and experiences.

In *Mona Lisa Overdrive*, the idea of change acquires fresh resonance. The assumption that 'It Changed' is accepted and the main reason adduced to explain the change is that 'when the matrix finally knew itself', when it 'attained sentience, it simultaneously became aware of *another* matrix, another sentience' – and of the fact that this was not necessarily *human*. Cyberspace is construed as 'the sum total of data in the human system' but the sum total ultimately neither sums up nor totalizes knowledge, for the moment it becomes aware of itself it also becomes aware of its limits and of the otherness that stretches beyond – and crosses over – its own boundaries.[67] Change consists of ruptures occasioned by self-awareness. Harking back to the plot of *Neuromancer*, the young Angie of *Count Zero* describes the process thus:

Once, there was nothing there, nothing moving on its own, just data and people shuffling it around. Then something happened and it . . . It knew itself. There's a whole other story, about that, a girl with mirrors over her eyes and a man who was scared to care about anything. Something the man did helped the whole thing know itself . . . And after that, it sort of split into different parts of itself . . .[68]

The *other* territory, thrown into relief by the splitting up of the matrix 'into all those hoodoos', includes non-human manifestations of being, and despite – or possibly because of – this attribute, it enhances the scope for *play*: 'it's all so much more amusing, this way'.[69]

Through myriad allusions to mythological motifs, fabulous creatures and heterodox rituals, Gibson also proposes underlying analogies between contemporary cyberculture and imaginary systems (particularly, as noted, voodoo). Voodoo is largely based on a concoction of magic, witchcraft, sorcery, superstition, African rites and Christian beliefs. Still active in Haiti, the West Indies and various parts of America, it combines – like the germane practice of obeah – abstract belief and material performance. Voodoo does not generally commit itself to intellectualizing agendas that aim at translating physical objects into disembodied concepts. In fact, it makes ideas inseparable from their concrete manifestations. Health and sickness, love and hate, wealth and poverty are concepts, no doubt, but they are consistently connected with material sources and material symbols, with the everyday objects that people both treasure and dread and with the earth to which everything returns. (The word obeah indeed refers to something buried into the ground to bring about change.) By analogy with voodoo, contemporary cyberculture stresses the importance of the material dimension. Although all sorts of experiences are continually translated into intangible data and information, our lives and identities are heavily defined by the tangible products that surround us and that symbolize cultural fantasies and anxieties. These objects often acquire a fetishistic status as markers of our being and destiny. Gibson emphasizes the hold of material objects laden with mythological connotations.

In *Count Zero*, in particular, cyberpunk's magical infrastructure manifests itself not only through voodoo but also through the enduring legacy and charisma of talismanic objects. The robotic

'Boxmaker' discovered by Marly in the orbital venue connected with the Tessier-Ashpool dynasty is a hypermechanical, if somewhat old-fashioned, aggregate of 'arms' equipped with 'pliers, hexdrivers, knives' and welded to a complex system of 'cables and optic lines'. Its function is to preserve the family's mythological reputation through the production of nostalgic artworks, by collecting into boxes disparate mementoes of the family's past: 'A yellowing kid glove, the faceted crystal stopper from some vial of vanished perfume, an armless doll with a face of French porcelain, a fat, gold-fitted fountain pen.' The emotional impact of this 'slow-motion hurricane of lost things'[70] is powerful. It demonstrates that technology and mythology are fundamentally interdependent and mutually sustaining. The 'Sandbenders' project described in *Idoru* proceeds from a similar assumption. Sandbenders are highly sophisticated computers that challenge the idea that hardware should be purely functional and utterly divorced from aesthetic principles. The conception of a jeweller dissatisfied with 'the way consumer electronics were made, a couple of little chips and boards inside these plastic shells', the Sandbenders have 'solid bronze' cases, 'ebony inlays', 'control surfaces' carved out of 'fossil ivory, turquoise, rock crystal'. These objects appeal to people for their sensuous properties, for their deployment of the aesthetic and tactile attributes of materials *qua* materials. The underlying technology remains unaltered from a practical viewpoint but in emotional and affective terms it is indeed transformed by its coupling with ancient substances in which legion untold myths, half-forgotten stories and hazy recollections are embedded: 'a lot of people liked that, like they had their music or their memory, whatever, in something that felt like it was *there*. . . . And people liked touching all that stuff: metal, a smooth stone.'[71] Technology does not erase myths and myths, in turn, rely on technology for their perpetuation.

A further aspect of voodoo that makes it somewhat akin to cyberculture is its intermingling of disparate historical and geographical motifs within a multilayered palimpsest of narratives: the kind of text that Internet browsers encounter in their exploration of available data. It is also worth noting that Gibson's creative activity has something in common with voodoo. As already mentioned, *Count Zero* describes voodoo as a *structure* for getting *things done*. It does not abide by universal principles but rather operates contingently, organizing whatever happens to be at hand into a system for working out specific problems and freely discarding it when it is no longer relevant. In this respect, voodoo could be regarded as a form of *bricolage*. Terence Hawkes describes this practice as 'a "science of the concrete" (as opposed to our "civilized" science of the "abstract") which ... classifies and arranges into structures the *minutiae* of the physical world in all their profusion'. These structures are '"improvised" or made up' and constitute contingent 'responses to an environment'.[72] Gibson is something of a *bricoleur* himself. He does not always plan his work according to abstract criteria or systematic research. Much of the time, he lets things take their course, allows himself to be grabbed by unexpected possibilities and builds narrative structures out of unforeseen coincidences. For example, it was by casually leafing through a copy of *National Geographic* that Gibson came across an article about Haitian voodoo and it is from this that he gleaned the basic ideas developed in *Count Zero*. Gibson does not appeal to any transcendental principles in describing his sources of inspiration. In fact, he candidly conveys a desire to write stories and a willingness to deploy whatever materials may fit into his general project. Ultimately, his aim is not 'to provide specific predictions or judgments' but rather 'to find a suitable fictional context in which to examine the very mixed blessings of technology'.[73]

The idea of cyberspace itself occurred to Gibson somewhat by chance. In an interview with McCaffery, the writer describes his source of inspiration thus:

> I was walking down Granville Street, Vancouver's version of 'The Strip', and I looked into one of the video arcades. I could see in the physical intensity of their postures how *rapt* the kids were. . . . These kids clearly *believed* in the space games projected. Everyone I know who works with computers seems to develop a belief that there's some kind of *actual space* behind the screen, someplace you can't see but you know is there.[74]

FICTION, THEORY AND THE LANGUAGE OF SCIENCE

The interweaving of mythological and scientific discourses creates an interdisciplinary field that challenges the reductionist tendencies of specialist knowledge. In this respect, it is comparable to the relatively recent phenomenon of 'Science Studies', a multi-discursive discipline that, according to Dorothy Nelkin, 'has attracted historians, philosophers, scientists, ethicists, sociologists, political scientists, and anthropologists' with 'no common conceptual framework' and 'no common methodology'.[75] The relative amorphousness of Science Studies has rendered it unpalatable to hard-core scientists, who view this discipline as a fad without clear aims or a genealogy, and its agenda as confused. This position is voiced by, among others, Paul Gross and Norman Levitt in *Higher Superstition*.[76] However, Science Studies has the undeniable advantage of relating science to other discourses, thus making it relevant to non-scientists. As Nelkin observes: 'As a distinct area of teaching and research, science study programs were first organized in the late 1960s in response to demands for "relevance" that grew out of the political currents of that time.' In the 1970s and 1980s, the emphasis shifts to the issue of determinism: scholars in the area of Science Studies become mainly concerned with the extent to which technology and science develop autonomously and with the extent to which they are socially and culturally determined. This concern has two principal spin-offs: *structural functionalism*, focusing on the ways in which the 'scientific community' operates in terms of 'norms, its system of rewards and sanctions, its organization into specialties, and its patterns of communication'; and *social constructivism*, exploring 'the process through which scientific knowledge is developed, how "facts" are created, incorporated, or resisted, and *how new knowledge becomes certified as scientific or excluded as myth*'.[77] Historical and anthropological approaches have further complicated these issues, by interrogating the concept of value-neutrality,[78] and by examining the impact of political and legal dispensations on technological systems.[79]

Today, Science Studies and related disciplines concerned with the relationship between technoscience and cyberculture are particularly keen on exploring various interconnections among technology, culture and society. According to Stanley Aronowitz and Michael Menser:

These relations involve a kind of complexity which prohibits us from claiming that any one of the three is distinctly prior, primary, or fundamental to one of the others. Various kinds of relations ensue (and are possible): technology shapes culture; science epistemologically grounds technology; science as an epistemology presupposes the technological; (techno)culture produces (techno)science; culture is always technological but not always scientific, and so on.[80]

By incorporating elements of mythology, fantasy and the supernatural into the fabric of technoscientific cultures, cyberpunk further complicates the picture painted by Aronowitz and Menser. It stresses that many contemporary disciplines are not insulated but rather interdependent. They supplement one another in much the same way as bodies and prostheses do. In the process, new discourses are engendered. As Haraway observes: 'Prosthesis is semiosis, the making of meanings and bodies.'[81]

The collusion of mythological and technological themes is one of the main strategies used by cyberpunk to produce alternative 'meanings' and 'bodies'. This interplay affords opportunities for linguistic experiment. It becomes possible to talk about fictional situations by recourse to scientific registers and, conversely, about science with reference to the figures of storytelling. Yet interdisciplinarity of this kind is a controversial issue and hackles sometimes rise when non-scientists are seen to make forays into the territory of science. The possibility of a rhetorical dialogue between science and other discourses is often anathema to professionals who, like the physicists Alan Sokal and Jean Bricmont, accuse thinkers such as Lacan, Kristeva, Deleuze, Guattari, Virilio, Lyotard and Baudrillard of *abusing* scientific ideas and terminologies in their writings. Sokal and Bricmont find the appropriation of words and concepts originally associated with the natural sciences, primarily physics, by intellectuals in the human sciences (psychology, sociology, cultural theory) contemptible on various levels. Their central argument is that those intellectuals distort scientific theories and vocabularies by 'either using scientific ideas totally out of context, without giving the slightest justification . . . or throwing around scientific jargon in front of their non-scientist readers without any regard for its relevance or even its meaning'.[82] Sokal and Bricmont believe that the abusers utilize concepts about which they have 'an exceedingly hazy idea . . . without bothering much about what the words actually *mean*', that they merely exhibit 'a superficial erudition', and that their approach to language displays 'a veritable intoxication with words, combined with a superb indifference to their meaning'.[83] This kind of argument obviously pivots on the notion that certain meanings are the incontestable property of certain words and that certain words, in turn, are unequivocally owned by certain contexts.

An important part is played, within the critique presented by Sokal and Bricmont in *Intellectual Impostures*, by the potential usefulness of scientific concepts as metaphors for non-scientific situations. While not totally denying this possibility, the authors none the less maintain that the intellectuals under attack are not capable of thinking or writing metaphorically in satisfactory ways:

> [A] metaphor is usually employed to clarify an unfamiliar concept by relating it to a more familiar one, not the reverse. . . . We fail to see the advantage of invoking, even metaphorically, scientific concepts that one oneself understands only shakily when addressing a readership composed almost entirely of non-scientists.[84]

Intellectual Impostures is questionable on three counts. Stylistically and rhetorically, it is *deconstructive* (that is, self-dismantling) because it lapses by its own criteria. The register it adopts to describe the putatively undisciplined, shallow and vague intellectuals who constitute its target is itself patently value-judgemental and opinionated. The *Preface* assures readers that an analytical treat is in store for them, yet, page after page, condemnatory reviews peppered with extensive quotations and scanty evidence of close reading feature a lot more prominently than analyses. The language is accordingly non-scientific. For example, we are told that Kristeva's 'sentences are more meaningful than those of Lacan but [that] she surpasses even him for the superficiality of her erudition';[85] that Deleuze and Guattari's references to quantum mechanics are 'totally devoid of meaning';[86] that Virilio's project is 'diarrhoea of the pen';[87] and that the general mood conveyed by such writers is a 'lackadaisical attitude toward scientific rigour' conducive to anti-empirical and apolitical positions.[88] Thematically, *Intellectual Impostures* makes a dubious distinction between writers whose appropriation of scientific images is acceptable (because they are merely peddling fantasies) and writers who abuse science (because they are applying their theories to so-called reality). What is not being taken into account, at this juncture, is the impact of fictional visions on projects carried out by practitioners in the technoscientific domain. For instance, the project launched by John Walker on behalf of the software company Autodesk was explicitly inspired by Gibson's writings, and indeed a demo called 'Cyberspace' after Gibson's *Neuromancer* was exhibited at the 1989 SIGGRAPH Conference.[89] (In response to Autodesk's appropriation of his neologism, Gibson 'threatened to sue' the company,[90] suspecting 'that technical people who like [his] work miss several layers of irony'.[91]) Chris Chesher notes that the architect Michael Benedikt was also influenced by Gibson in his design of 'a usable virtual space', consisting of 'a matrix of cells' which represent institutions and properties through which users can cruise, and through which power relations 'can be controlled, commodified and mapped'.[92]

The third count upon which Sokal and Bricmont provide a redoubtable critique is possibly the most crucial in philosophical terms. This concerns the role of figurative language. The two writers concede that they may be 'interpreting' their subjects 'too literally and that the passages [they] quote should be read as metaphors rather than as precise logical arguments'.[93] It could be argued, however, that what Sokal and Bricmont are interpreting too literally is not the philosophers themselves so much as the role of *metaphor* in both its linguistic and broadly cultural import. As indicated earlier, *Intellectual Impostures* defines metaphor as a basically *clarifying* mechanism. Indeed, its authors find it hard to accept that scientific images may be adopted by non-scientists not for the purpose of illumination but rather out of what they perceive as a perverse inclination to hide 'vacuity or banality ... behind deliberately obscure prose'.[94] The flaws of this position may be documented by reference to two main discourses. On the aesthetic level, the assumption that metaphor is unproblematically intended to operate as a simplifying device is inaccurate. The golden age of metaphor, the Renaissance, actually associated this trope with extreme complexity and intricacy. In his dedication to *The Faerie Queene*, Edmund Spenser famously described it as a 'dark conceit'.[95] If readers are to be enlightened by metaphor, they must first feel puzzled and defamiliarized. On a broader philosophical plane, Sokal and Bricmont's understanding of metaphor is conspicuously blind to arguments that it is difficult to see how they could possibly have missed in their extensive research into poststructuralism and postmodernism – namely the proposition that metaphor is not simply a figure of speech but an underlying mechanism of signification at large, whereby meaning is continually produced through metamorphoses, transpositions and displacements that render *all* concepts and terms tropological.

Metaphor is a structure of thought and signification that exposes the ambiguities of both theory and praxis by pursuing, or appearing to pursue, contradictory aims. On the one hand, it may seem to celebrate an ideal of unity by establishing powerful bonds between superficial images and the latent meanings that such images are supposed to stand for. On the other hand, in setting up correspondences between logically incongruous components, metaphor displaces the idea of any fixed values. There is no demonstrable reason, in other words, for which *an* image should incontrovertibly lead to *a* meaning. There are only contingent agreements as to what a pertinent reading might consist of, and these are always negotiable. The adoption of a scientific image, concept or term as a means of illustrating – or better, exploring – a philosophical or critical issue undoubtedly does produce a metaphorical formation of symbolic correspondences. But the function of such a formation is neither to clarify difficult ideas nor to unravel discursive intricacies. If anything, the opposite is the case: a metaphorical constellation based on a dialogue between different disciplines serves to *complicate* matters, to underscore the complexity of even the apparently most obvious phenomena, and to remind us that all vocabularies of both a specialist and an everyday kind come about as a result of ongoing processes of interdisciplinary borrowings, metaphorical exchanges, rhetorical migrations. If we were to refrain ourselves from using a word like *relativity* for fear of misappropriating Einstein's theories, we might as well erase the word *breakdown* from our vocabulary since this popular way of describing psychosomatic collapse is, after all, a metaphor gleaned from the field of mechanics. Were we to inspect the origins of the most common fragments of our languages, we would soon find that very many of them derive from areas that would once have been regarded as specialized.

On the one hand, cyberpunk may not come directly into Sokal and Bricmont's line of fire since it is classifiable as a fantasy genre, entitled to take certain liberties because in incorporating scientific concepts it does not muddy the waters too severely. Fact and fiction, in other words, could be said to remain discrete:

> If a poet uses words like 'black hole' or 'degree of freedom' out of context and without really understanding their scientific meaning, it doesn't bother us. Likewise, if a science-fiction writer uses secret passageways in space—time in order to send her characters back

to the era of the Crusades, it is purely a question of taste whether one likes or dislikes the technique.[96]

On the other hand, cyberpunk could be said to *abuse* scientific concepts because its images – both those based on legitimized scientific concepts and those invented for the purposes of its plots – are deployed to comment on *very real* cultural conditions and prospects. Moreover, cyberpunk underscores technoscience's involvement in a discourse of imaginary distortion and irrationality that interweaves scientific registers and ideas with scenarios based, as we have seen, on fantasy and myth. If Sokal and Bricmont were to believe that the writings of an author like Gibson were underpinned by thorough scientific research, they might just about condone his interweaving of science and fantasy. Yet Gibson himself claims no specialist expertise in any area of modern science and even candidly admits to knowing relatively little about computers. What he is truly interested in is 'collage'.[97]

Gibson openly admits that although the register he uses often *sounds* like 'technical and professional jargon', much of the time there are no real scientific vocabularies in which his language can be grounded. Words and phrases that suggest specialist scientific knowledge are, in fact, frequently drawn from subcultural imagery and inflections, from 'dope dealers' slang, or biker talk', for instance. 'Flatlining', one of Gibson's best-known terms, 'is ambulance driver slang for "death"'.[98] In terms of the arguments put forward in *Intellectual Impostures*, Gibson could be said to abuse not just contingent scientific vocabularies but also their very essence as reliable transmitters of knowledge. Indeed, if patently non-scientific registers such as slang can be handled so that they sound scientific, what chances do genuinely scientific registers have of protecting their boundaries against alien intrusions? Some practitioners in the natural sciences assume that their language describes true facts and feel uncomfortable when they discover that their terminologies may be appropriated by people outside their domain. Cyberpunk ironically problematizes their predicament by suggesting that phrases apparently derived from science may turn out to be no more scientific than a commercial caption or a snippet of subcultural lingo.

What is more, Gibson has stated that he is 'more interested in the *language* of, say, computers' than he is in the 'technicalities'. He also owns up to the fact that it was his relative ignorance of computers that enabled him to romanticize them.[99] In an interview with Salza, he further elaborates on his relationship with technology:

> I never was a technical guy and never will be. I'm a writer, and poetry and pop culture are the two things which fascinate me most. . . . However, I feel obliged to be ambivalent towards technology. I can't be a 'techie', but I can't hate it, either.[100]

Gibson's playful approach to technology should not be mistaken as either superficiality or arrogance. In fact, he concedes that 'some of the SF authors who are actually working scientists do know what they're talking about' and that for those who, like him, endeavour 'to present a world that doesn't exist and make it seem real', it is sometimes necessary to 'more or less pretend' they are 'polymaths'.[101]

Ultimately, the appropriation of scientific terminology by non-scientists and/or in non-scientific contexts should not be seen as a form of parasitical exploitation of serious experts by clownish bricoleurs. Indeed, it produces new and imaginative idioms that often combine, in a highly ironical vein, sense and nonsense, sophisticated articulation and formless babble. In Samuel Delany's 'Among the Blobs', for example, an entertaining register is created through the juxtaposition of technical language and infantile inarticulateness. The 'Blob' is described in specialist terms as:

> . . . a largely mucusoid emulsion contained in a selectively permeable membrane within which drifted a nucleus, various nucleoli, vacuoles, ribosomes, mitochondria, and chloroplasts, the whole a symbiotic intrusion of eucaryotic and procaryotic cells from a less vulgar moment in the pluroma when all was closer than it is today to organic soup, to inorganic matter.[102]

The reference to 'soup' is probably sufficiently bathetic in itself to deflate the scientific pretensions of the Blob's portrait. Furthermore, physiological complexity is not paralleled by developed linguistic competences, for the Blob's vocabulary amounts to 'Burble, burble . . . burble.'[103]

In conclusion, it could be argued that by bringing together diverse registers and discourses, mythological motifs and technological issues, cyberpunk is in a position to highlight the fact that scientific and narrative structures are analogous, for both continually move from one mythology to another. According to Fredericks, the trans-lation of *any* mythical structure into a belief system (scientific or otherwise) is circumstantial and provisional: 'speculative science and myth-making interact: the concepts, world-views, and images . . . are located at various points along a myth-science interface'.[104] Scientific thought, argues Italo Calvino, combines precision with a poetic element that is intrinsic to its 'posing of conjectures': it sets up, tests, validates and discards hypotheses in 'a possibly infinite series of approximations'.[105] Science is not oriented towards merely practical outcomes or the atomistic accumulation of data. In fact, it includes the possibility of novelty being experienced as a concomitant of a creative dialogue between the observer and the phenomena under investigation, from which data may be subsequently extrapolated. As John Willett points out, Galileo 'was amazed by the pendulum motion as if he had not expected it and could not understand its occurring, and this enabled him to come at the rule by which it was governed'.[106]

CHAPTER 3

CYBERPUNK AND THE BODY

> The body has not disappeared . . . it has become the infinitely penetrable body. . . . Life uses and violates borders, and life constructs media of its own to fill up the extra spaces. The amoeba and the fertilized egg are both sacs of juice and slime – one grows by splitting itself, the other by being split.
>
> (Peter Wilson)[1]

THE CYBERBODY

In cyberculture, the body is often conceived of as a fluid entity. Much recent scholarship concerned with the relationship between the biological organism and technology has stressed the body's lack of clear boundaries. Especially relevant to this context are the notions of 'biosociality' and 'technosociality'. The first term has been put forward by Paul Rabinow to describe a new way of producing bodies through biologically based technologies. Biosociality emphasizes the inadequacy of the principle of finitude, according to which humans are neatly bounded, by highlighting the instability of matter and form. This is borne out by research into the nature of the human genome which evinces a picture of virtually unlimited recombination. As François Jacob observes, 'nature operates to create diversity by endlessly combining bits and pieces'.[2] Technosociality, for its part, refers to the merging of nature and technology in a shared environment. According to Allucquere Rosanne Stone, this merging is based on a 'phantasmatic social interaction' wherein the 'boundaries between the living and the non-living' keep shifting, and identity is pluralized as a 'model of multiplicity outside a unitary physical body'.[3]

Rob Hardin's cyberpunk poetry offers graphic confirmation of the body's precarious boundaries by foregrounding the interpenetration of life and death. The poem 'Penetrabit: Slime-Temples' suggests that life cannot be unproblematically associated with the organism's healthy development. It is in ailing organisms that we often detect the most forceful signs of vitality and energy. The more rapid the organism's deterioration, the more intense its physiological activity. Life and death are inseparable in the 'Slime-Temples' of the body ravaged by illness. So are order and chaos: the apparently random, 'gibbering spirals' of protoplasm and 'scrolls' of neural reactions actually have a proclivity for creating patterns. Such patterns convey a sense of order but are also 'attended by failure and death', which suggests that death may be the only available state of stability. The poem 'nerve terminals' questions even this marginal hope of balance by stressing that death itself generates incessant movement and change. These phenomena, moreover, are metaphorically compared to forms of expression and communication, to language and music:

> Reanimated sentences
> crawl searchingly through palaces.
> . . . ellipses crumble, swapped for noise . . .
> *our symphonies*
> are insect seas.

The rotting corpse vibrates not just with life but also with sexual energies, as its uneven tissues are compared to 'love-bit scars'. Cyberpunk's frequent association of sexuality with unsavoury aspects of materiality is also vividly demonstrated by 'Fistic Herm-aphrodites', where human relationships are equated to insectile ones. The sexual life of centipedes does not come across as especially exciting:

> The newlyweds cough up larvae, smiling apologetically.
> Their desires read like a homework assignment
> and, at the base of the fifth pair of walking legs,
> their genital ducts have not yet evolved.

However, human sexuality itself is associated with a destiny of emotional frustration, as erotic yearnings are confined within 'the walls of the microwave' and 'bits of garden': a stifling world of petty domestic comforts. To what extent, Hardin implies, is human sexuality different from that of so-called inferior creatures? What Hardin repeatedly stresses is that life has no choice but to constantly rearrange its patterns in a frenetic attempt at self-propagation and that, in the process, its inextricability from death becomes obvious. Living cells inevitably wander in a 'necropolis of spirals' ('Penetrabit').[4] Moreover, the transformations dramatized by Hardin's cyberpunk poetry bear witness to the momentous impact of technoscience on current perceptions of embodiment.

Among the various technologies concerned with the relationship between the organic and the artificial, bio-engineering and bionics (biological electronics) have played a particularly prominent part. The first concentrates on the possibility of applying technological principles to the body by studying the structure of the living organism in terms of the mechanical properties of substances such as bone and muscle. The second is concerned with the application of biological processes to technology and works on the premise that certain design principles characteristic of the human body may be used as models for the production of new mechanical devices. Cyberpunk offers an imaginative articulation of these and other related developments in technoscience to show that the body is the ever-changing product of technologies that are always tied to specific cultural contexts. Thus it echoes contemporary critical perspectives on the relationship between the body and technology such as the ones advocated by Michael Feher and by Judy Wajcman. For Feher, the body is not 'a transhistorical set of needs and desires' but rather 'a reality constantly produced, an effect of techniques promoting specific gestures and postures, sensations and feelings'.[5] As a result, the body becomes a shifting territory, a battleground for competing structures of meaning, that cannot be explained away as a stable part of nature. Technology conceptualizes and systematizes the body in accordance with specific cultural requirements. Wajcman observes: 'technology is more than a set of physical objects or artefacts. It also fundamentally embodies a culture or set of social relations made up of certain sorts of knowledge, beliefs, desires, and practices.'[6]

A number of new technologies are increasingly deployed to map out and discipline the body down to its tiniest elements. As Anne Balsamo observes:

Consumption is monitored technologically through the use of

such devices as electronic scales, sugar-diabetes tests, blood pressure machines, fat calipers. A range of new visualization techniques contribute to the fragmentation of the body into organs, fluids, and gene codes . . . whereby the body becomes an object of intense vigilance and control.[7]

Medical technology is in a position to monitor and expose the most intimate internal processes: for example, portable units can check continually vital signs such as pulse rate and blood pressure.[8] Olfactory technology, for its part, provides security systems such as 'Scentinel'. This obtains an 'odour profile' of anyone seeking access to a high security area and compares it with the profiles in its memory.[9] In *Idoru*, Gibson supplies a comparable illustration of technological mechanisms of surveillance. Airline passengers are subjected to DNA testing, as a means of proving their identities, by having hair samples taken and matched against the DNA displayed in their passports in the form of bar codes.[10]

Cyberculture pivots on a contradiction: a growing fascination with the body, testified by all sorts of media, coexists with an increasing infiltration of the body by technologies that seem to take its materiality away. According to Christine Boyer, the desire underlying the systematic management of the body's minutest functions appears to be 'to annihilate the materiality of the body' and thus produce an organism 'released from its physical restrictions, a body evacuated, devastated, disintegrated, disappearing'.[11] Yet the purging, honing and sculpting of the physiological apparatus also point to an ongoing fascination with the most intractably material aspects of embodiment. In this respect, they do not signal the demise of the flesh but actually constitute forms of resistance to what Rosi Braidotti has called 'the old myth of transcendence as flight from the body', the idea of 'transcendence as disembodiment'.[12]

Cyberpunk offers an ironical line of resistance to the concept of 'transcendence as disembodiment'. Indeed, according to Nick Land, it 'does not subscribe to transcendence, but to circulation; exploring the immanence of subjectivity to telecommercial data fluxes: personality engineering, mind recordings, catatonic cyberspace trances, stim-swaps, and sex-comas'.[13] In Gibson's work, the body is undoubtedly altered by technology but not transcended. The material dimension plays a crucial role: flesh can be vat-grown; organs can be lifted out of the body and replaced with brand new ones; exoskeletons enable the terminally sick to retain motility and a modicum of metabolic functions; mirror-shade implants allow people to see in the dark and retractable blades may be inserted under one's fingernails. At the same time, the physical dimension is emphasized by Gibson's setting: a planet filled with *gomi* (waste, garbage, detritus) and with various forms of 'Thomasson', i.e. 'useless and inexplicable monuments'.[14] As Veronica Hollinger points out, 'the "average" cyberpunk landscape tends to be choked with the debris of both language and objects'.[15] Gibson's fascination with the bodily qualities of gomi and Thomassons mirrors his own stylistic proclivities. In an interview with McCaffery, he describes his way of writing thus: 'stitching together all the junk that's floating around in my head. One of my private pleasures is to go to the corner Salvation Army thrift shop and look at all the junk.'[16] Moreover, as Bruce Sterling observes in his preface to the collection of short stories *Burning Chrome*, the material traits of cyberculture are of vital importance to Gibson because he is concerned with presenting 'the future from the belly up, as it is lived, not merely as dry speculation. . . . In Gibson's work we find ourselves in the streets and alleys, in a realm of sweaty, white-knuckled survival.'[17] Gregory Benford further points out that Gibson 'concentrates on surfaces as a way of getting to the aesthetic of an age'.[18] As the elements that classic humanism would have regarded as the core of the self are projected onto the superficial spectacle of a technologically mediated existence – that is, as the human *inside* becomes interchangeable with an eminently artificial *outside* – technology, in turn, penetrates the body and its frail dermal casing: as Darko Suvin points out, 'for cyberpunks technology is inside, not outside, the personal body and mind itself'.[19]

Cadigan's *Tea from an Empty Cup* emphasizes the body's penetrability by technology. In a world saturated with media-processed narratives, one may never be in a position to ascertain a body's origins or its destiny. The powerful 'Celebrity Aristocrat' Joy Flower (something of a cyberpunk adaptation of the Evil Queen of fairy tale and Gothic fiction) thrives on a network of 'Boyz', whose bodies are considered extremely valuable as long as they enjoy her favours but fall into total oblivion the moment this is no longer the case. Speculations about the Boyz' fate give rise to a byzantine web of narratives that invariably draw attention to the body's vulnerability. Joy's own body may be the unfortunate result of faulty biotechnology. The hypothetical nature of the stories built around Joy and her coterie vividly underlines the insecure status of the body in cyberculture:

> There were rumours of the usual kinky sex things, as well as the unusual. Joy Flower was sexually insatiable owing to an experimental brain implant gone wrong. No, gone *right*. No, she was really a celibate procurer for a cabal of rich and powerful perverts. . . . Other things were hinted at in almost inaudible whispers, about the Boyz who had vanished. Dead in hideous ways. No, *worse* than dead, shut away in secret clinics and hospitals, braindead but maintained on life support as their bodies were parted out to rich and powerful invalids who needed their hearts, livers, lungs. No, they were installed in the world's fanciest barn, pumped full of nutrients, massaged daily for a month, then butchered and roasted for the palates of a cabal of rich and powerful flesh-eaters.[20]

Cadigan's cyberbodies are definitely not immaterial entities. Take the case of the 'kid' who, having chosen to visit a 'post-Apocalyptic Noo Yawk Sitty'[21] in Artificial Reality (computer-based simulation aided by a 'hotsuit' lined with 'wires and sensors') ends up dead while online as a result of a 'classic ear-to-ear'.[22] And what of the 'guy who didn't open his parachute in a skydiving scenario and was found dead with every bone in his body shattered'?[23]

Gibson's and Cadigan's narratives make it quite clear that the body's technological editing is not something that can be unproblematically cherished. Many cyberpunk characters pursue the dream of self-reinvention driven by consumer desires that almost invariably entail exploitation and abuse. Organ banks and support vats offer promises of immortality but their beneficiaries are most likely to be the hyper-rich. The donors often provide body materials without having given their consent and indeed prior to dying. 'Now, some night, you get maybe too artistic,' Case is told early on in *Neuromancer*, 'you wind up in the clinic tanks, spare parts.'[24] Marge Piercy's *Body of Glass* likewise presents the body as an assemblage of commodified parts, circulating endlessly in a world ruled by oppression and violence. The cyborg Yod, created by the male scientist Avram with the assistance of Malkah, a woman, is humanized by his sexual urges (he has an affair with Shira, Malkah's granddaughter) and by his aggressive disposition (he kills Avram when he is sent by his maker onto a mission that would certainly cause his own destruction). As an artificial body, Yod is disturbingly akin to natural human bodies that similarly oscillate between loving and destructive impulses. When he wonders about his synthetic nature, he is reminded that human beings are no less artificial than he. If Yod closely resembles humans, the human cast of *Body of Glass* turns out to resemble cyborgs. Shira tells him:

> 'Yod, we're all unnatural now. I have retinal implants. I have a plug set into my skull to interface with a computer. I read time by a corneal implant. Malkah has a subcutaneous unit that monitors and corrects blood pressure, and half her teeth are regrown. Her eyes have been rebuilt twice. Avram has an artificial heart . . . we're all cyborgs, Yod.'[25]

Cyberpunk and cyberculture invite us to address fundamental questions about embodiment and about the body's relation to both space and time. They prompt us to examine where and when our experiences take place and the part played by our bodies in the context of such experiences. As many cyberpunk writers show, we only ever perceive and come to know things as bodies – that is, membranes of flesh and blood – rather than as incorporeal consciousnesses, even in the most thoroughly virtualized situations. The ways in which we negotiate ideological, ethical and aesthetic issues are not abstract, for they pivot on the construction of cultural bodies of perception and knowledge. Such bodies are not static configurations any more than the individual organism is unchanging. They actually permutate at all times; they are always, in other words, *in the process of becoming embodied.* Knowledge is embodied, ultimately, because experiences are inscribed (both as memories and as expectations) in our very cells. Human identity, in turn, is not an assemblage of immaterial data; it is in fact, as Roland Barthes observes, 'a *tissue* of quotations'.[26] The practices through which this 'tissue' is woven constitute a complex ritual structure through which the body is ceremonially textualized. According to John Monk, 'There are name-giving ceremonies, password-issuing ceremonies, the elaborate ceremonies of academic awards, job interviews, medical consultations, legal proceedings and commonplace rituals, like buying food, gossiping or going to work – all contributing to the fabrication of individuals.'[27] Immersion in the virtual environments produced by technoscience does not automatically amount to an experience of disembodiment, for it is grounded in ritual/ceremonial experiences of an eminently material nature. The body is extended by technology, as its sensory faculties are stretched beyond familiar territories, and at the same time it is humbled into a recognition of its limitations. Either way, the human—technical interface requires a continual reassessment of the body's meanings.

IDORU: THE BODY AS PERSONALITY CONSTRUCT

The 'idoru' is 'a personality-construct, a congeries of software agents, the creation of information-designers': a 'synthespian'.[28] Thus, it exemplifies the idea that bodies are technological products and that technology, in turn, embodies specific cultural forms of production and consumption. What is most intriguing and para-doxical about the idoru is that it is an immaterial construct, on the one hand, and an object of erotic desire, on the other. One of the novel's leading threads is the arrangement of an *alchemical* marriage between the synthetic star and a meat-and-bones rock star. Another is the notion that the idoru, though artificial, carries traces of a personal history. Indeed, it is inscribed in a web of memories, vest-iges of submerged life stories and fleeting glimmers of lost objects, scenes, colours and sounds. Commenting on his first face-to-face experience of the idoru, Laney is overwhelmed by a cascade of images that have no obvious connection with its cyberworld and, in fact, hark back to an ancient landscape that resonates with legendary echoes:

In the very structure of her face, in geometries of underlying bone, lay coded histories of dynastic flight, privation, terrible migrations. He saw stone tombs in steep alpine meadows, their lintels traced with snow. A line of shaggy pack ponies, their breath white with cold, followed a trail above a canyon. The curves of the river below were strokes of distant silver. Iron harness bells clanked in the blue dusk.[29]

At the same time, the idoru is inconceivable apart from the operations of nanotechnology, that branch of contemporary tech-noscientific research that most drastically unsettles the material boundaries of both animate and inanimate objects, thereby making

the very distinction between the animate and the inanimate somewhat obsolete:

> Imagine. Containers that automatically change shape or depth
> as you add more content. Furniture that automatically adjusts
> itself to fit your body. Microscopic robots that repair people from
> within, selectively eliminating damage from viruses, aging, or
> injury, among other things.[30]

(*Virtual Light* also makes reference to nanotechnology by describing
its products as 'these things that kind of *grew*, but only because they
were made up of all these little tiny machines'.[31])

Gibson's inscription of the idoru's cyberbody in a world of temporal and spatial dislocation turns it into a concurrently technological and mythological palimpsest. The idoru superimposes upon
one another diverse textual layers, with each layer covering yet never
erasing the previous ones, in a virtually endless process of increasing
complexity: 'Rei's [the idoru's] only reality is the realm of ongoing
serial creation . . . . Entirely *process*; infinitely more than the combined sum of her various selves. The platforms sink beneath her, one
after another, as she grows denser and more complex.'[32] Furthermore, the idoru is described as 'the result of an array of elaborate
constructs that we refer to as "desiring machines"', '*aggregates of
subjective desire*', 'an architecture of articulated longing'.[33] It is
probably irrelevant to speculate about the likelihood of Gibson having borrowed the phrase *desiring machines* from Gilles Deleuze and
Felix Guattari. What is interesting, however, is the pattern of analogies that soon surfaces if we compare Gibson's treatment of the
cyberbody with the version of corporeality portrayed by the two
philosophers. The picture presented by Gibson finds a close correlative in Deleuze and Guattari's assertion that:

> There is no such thing as either man or nature now, only a process
> that produces the one within the other and couples the machines
> together. Producing-machines, desiring-machines everywhere . . .
> the self and the non-self, outside and inside, no longer have any
> meaning whatsoever.[34]

At the same time, Gibson's speculations about the viability of *mar-
riages* between humans and synthetic constructs points to the fact

that their interpenetration is inevitable because neither of them is ever whole or self-sufficient. Deleuze and Guattari concur: 'Desiring-machines are binary machines . . . one machine is always coupled with another. . . . Desire constantly couples continuous flows and partial objects that are by nature fragmentary and fragmented.'[35]

If the coupling of biological and artificial entities serves to organize bodies and desires, it must be emphasized that no organization is ever conclusive. Any structure of meaning and desire entails as a corollary the possibility of unpredictable change. The idoru, specifically, is a thoroughly assembled construct but the construct only *works* – as an organization of data – in so far as it undergoes ongoing transmutations and in so far as it is allowed to have *its own* dreams.[36] In other words, any organization, albeit necessary for meaning and communication to occur, is never final. It is inherent in the nature of any organism that it may become *dis*organized. Desiring-machines organize our functions and feelings according to what is culturally expected of us. An idoru or idol star, for example, serves to channel the media-generated yearnings of fans and consumers into an intricate structure of mutating images. However, desiring-machines like the idoru also make us aware of a tantalizing alternative – what it might be like to enter a zone of anarchic flow:

> Desiring-machines work only when they break down, and by continually breaking down. . . . Desiring-machines make us an organism; but at the very heart of this production, the body suffers from being organized in this way, from not having some other sort of organization, or no organization at all. . . . Every coupling of machines . . . becomes unbearable to the body without organs. Beneath its organs it senses there are larvae and loathsome worms, and a God at work messing it all up or strangling it by organizing it. . . . [T]he desiring machines attempt to break into the body without organs, and the body without organs repels them, since it experiences them as an over-all persecution apparatus.[37]

The idoru is an organized body-construct produced by technological means. It is also a means of organizing the bodies of its fans by technologically harnessing their subjective desires. At the same time, however, it is a fluctuating body whose technological permutations are capable of evoking mythological images. In regimenting other beings' desires, the idoru simultaneously shatters their sense of wholeness by exposing them to a chaotic universe of decomposition. Neither Gibson nor Deleuze and Guattari propose either a celebration of a totally fluid existence (the body without organs) or an acceptance of regimentation; rather they propose a dialectical relationship between flux and order. Desiring-machines are not, ultimately, categorizable as either policing agencies designed to discipline the body or subversive agencies inciting the body to rebellion. Endowed with ambivalent powers, desiring-machines simultaneously generate, as Cathryn Vasseleu notes, spaces for the 'mechanization of passions' and spaces for 'characterizing the technology in corporeal terms'.[38]

This ambivalence is dramatized in *Idoru* through the combination of high technology and psychic powers, virtuality, mysticism and the harsh realities of profit-driven corporations wherein 'lives' are routinely 'destroyed, and sometimes re-created, careers crushed or made anew in guises surreal and unexpected' in a 'ritual letting of blood' involving media leviathans and naïve fad-hunters.[39] Laney exemplifies the text's overall ambiguity by uniting the mystical traits of the traditional soothsayer and those of the cyberspace expert defined by his relationship with computer networks. These elements coalesce to produce highly uncommon skills:

> [Laney] had a peculiar knack with data-collection architectures . . . he was an intuitive fisher of patterns of information: of the sort of signature a particular individual inadvertently created in the net as he or she went about the mundane yet endlessly multiplex business of life in a digital society. . . . He'd spent his time skimming vast floes of undifferentiated data, looking for 'nodal points'.[40]

This peculiar talent is fundamentally the product of chemical experiments, 'drug trials' to which Laney was subjected as an inmate of a 'Federal Orphanage' in his teens. The tests were designed to research the physical and psychological effects of super-illegal substances potentially able to turn their users into monomaniacal automata.[41] Laney underlines the hybrid status of his powers by describing them both in scientific terms, as an ability to process 'broad-spectrum input' through 'pattern recognition', and in imaginary terms, as analogous to 'seeing things in clouds . . . .'

Except the things you see are really there.' In this context, the human body is rendered ephemeral by its intercourse with technology, codified on the basis of its symbiotic relationship with machines and indeed *produced* by machines. Yet the body still plays a pivotal role as the marker of individual agency, what makes one particular 'signature' recognizable as belonging to a specific person. Thus Laney has difficulties tracing the rock 'n' roll hero Rez's personality because Rez has been constructed in purely corporational terms and cannot therefore 'generate patterns'. Trying to identify Rez's signature within hordes of data, all Laney keeps finding is an utterly disindividualized image: 'it's like trying to have a drink with a bank'. Even in a thoroughly digitalized culture where all experience, both personal and collective, may ostensibly be divorced from its material agents, the individual body stubbornly goes on asserting itself as the bearer of traces which, were the body to be elided, would become totally inaccessible. You cannot construct a pattern of any kind about someone who is 'not a person', who 'doesn't drink' and for whom 'there's no place . . . to sit'.[42]

THE GHOST

In blurring the dividing line between the natural and the artificial, cyberpunk also calls into question the body's reality. As we have seen, technology does not erase the body's materiality. Rather, it problematizes it by underscoring its involvement with virtual phenomena: simulated bodies, synthetic organisms and personality constructs. The physical body is not removed from the picture. It is actually required to reassess the meaning of its concreteness by negotiating with its immaterial counterparts. This state of affairs is by no means exclusively peculiar to cyberculture. In fact, it harks back to the age-old phenomenon of *haunting*, as an experience that hinges on the (more or less troubling) encounter between material and immaterial bodies, the flesh and the phantom.

There is a potently physical dimension to the phenomenon of spectrality, for the state of being or feeling haunted, as Avery Gordon has stressed, 'is not simply one of cognitive doubt, or of the unknown'.[43] The sense of uncertainty elicited by haunting is not a purely intellectual phenomenon, since it impacts directly on the body and on the senses. It is as material entities that we perceive the presence of immaterial beings, that we become aware of *other* bodies and

on their influence on our lives. Haunting reminds us that our knowledge of the world is always lacunary, for what we know is constantly
punctured by inexplicable mysteries. Simultaneously, it makes us
aware of both the powers and the limitations of our senses: of our
occasional ability to perceive what *is not there* and of our frequent
failure to perceive what *is*. The rhetoric of haunting points to a
breakdown of representation and signification whereby the spectre
stands simultaneously for a *site* we wish to avoid and a *sight* we are
not allowed to avoid. As Maurice Blanchot observes, 'What haunts
us is something inaccessible from which we cannot extricate ourselves. It is that which cannot be found and therefore cannot be
avoided.'[44] That which haunts us is both inaccessible and inevitable;
we cannot avoid it for the very reason that we cannot access it. We go
on seeking it *because* we cannot find it. The ghost goes on inhabiting
our space because it has no place of its own; it marks a placeless
place, an absent presence. At the same time, we always share what we
call *our* space with ghosts and virtual bodies.

Gibson dramatizes three main types of haunting: the haunting of
space; of people by other people; of people by their own obsessions.
The Malibu villas among which Angie wanders in her directionless
search for meaning are haunted by the absence of their 'restless resi-
dents'. They are 'entropic' spaces peopled by ghosts bred by their
slow decomposition: 'She imagined the rooms empty, flecks of cor-
rosion blossoming silently on chrome, pale molds taking hold in
obscure corners.' The haunting of these spaces mirrors Angie's own
haunting by an omnipresent gaze:

> She was accompanied, on these walks, by an armed remote, a tiny
> Dornier helicopter that rose from its unseen rooftop nest when
> she stepped down from the deck. It could hover almost silently,
> and was programmed to avoid her line of sight. There was some-
> thing wistful about the way it followed her, as though it were an
> expensive but unappreciated Christmas gift. . . . [H]er solitude . . .
> was under constant surveillance.[45]

There are, of course, more subtle ways of haunting people by technological means, as suggested by Sally's sinister warning that Kumiko
may be 'kinked':

> 'Maybe your dad, the Yak warlord, he's got a little bug planted in

you so he can keep track of his daughter. You got those pretty little teeth, maybe daddy's dentist tucked a little hardware in there one time when you were into a stim.'[46]

When they are not physically persecuted by other people and their technological weapons, Gibson's characters are, more often than not, hounded down by their own afflictions and paranoid ambitions. Angie feels persecuted by her environment because she is first and foremost plagued by her own nightmares: the result of biotechnological manipulation and drug addiction. Gentry, for his part, is haunted by his monomaniacal quest for the 'Shape', the 'overall form' of cyberspace: 'The apprehension of the Shape was Gentry's grail.'[47] Indifferent to any interest or activity outside this fixation, he would spend 'days on end with his decks and FX-organs and holo-projectors', to come out only 'when he got hungry'.[48] The female character in Marc Laidlaw's 'Office of the Future' is likewise simultaneously haunted by her surroundings and by her own inner space. She keeps all the lights in the house off 'in order to keep the headaches away'. Yet the headaches, far from being thus tamed, acquire an independent life of their own. In the unbroken silence of the dusty house, she feels them 'circling around her like wolves, closing in' and darkness only provides an illusion of protection. Indeed, it is incapable of exorcizing the ghosts spawned by a densely material space, cluttered with 'steel desks, cork partitions, rows of filing cabinets': a mounting stack of objects and data that threaten to stifle her 'from the walls on all sides'.[49]

Through these images, cyberpunk implicitly reminds us that even 'a culture seemingly ruled by technologies of hypervisibility' and intent on having us believe that 'everything can be seen'[50] , as Gordon expresses it, inevitably contains simmering absences, vacuous presences, gaps and secrets, and that this mainly invisible or hidden world is not a fantasy world but a crucial portion of social reality. Indeed, social reality only ever holds itself together through the denial, disavowal or repression of an unnamable *something*. According to Gordon, 'Haunting is a constituent element of modern social life. It is neither pre-modern superstition nor individual psychosis; it is a generalizable social phenomenon of great importance. To study social life one must confront the ghostly aspects of it.'[51] There is always a gap between what we see and what we know. Visibility and invisibility are, in this respect, inextricably interconnected. As Rainer

Maria Rilke observes, 'We are bees of the invisible. We madly gather the honey of the visible to store it in the great golden hive of the invisible.'[52]

Gibson exposes the paradoxes of a culture of hypervisibility through settings that combine presence and absence. These settings would not, at first sight, seem to leave much scope for invisibility. Indeed, with their proliferation of gomi and Thomassons, they appear to epitomize a world of overwhelming presences, a glut of visibilities. Yet the origins of the objects that cram those spaces are more often than not obscure and inexplicable. Hence they are traversed by intimations of a nothingness that undermines all illusions of wholeness, presence and ultimately visibility itself. Junk, waste, trinkets and machines whose original functions remain utterly unfathomable also unsettle the idea of ontological necessity: if these objects *had to* exist by virtue of some metaphysical mandate, they might justifiably be expected to be rather better defined than they are in terms of origin, form and function. As it happens, they constitute a synthetic jungle of haphazardly juxtaposed bits and pieces. As random portions of being, these objects bring to mind Heidegger's *Dasein*, the contingent manifestation of a superior Being tarnished and degraded by being sunk in a social environment of anonymity and idle prattle.[53] Cyberpunk seems to have little time for metaphysical concepts such as that of a foundational Being. Its narratives, even when they utilize supernatural motifs, are scarcely concerned with transcendental forces beyond contingent and material relations of power and practices of consumption. Heidegger's reflections on technology are also pertinent to this argument. For Heidegger, technology has a lamentable knack of *concealing* Being, of obfuscating its purity and depredating its intrinsic truth. However, in so far as all forms of cultural existence emanate from Being – however fallen and depraved they may be – technology itself is part of Being's inscrutable unfolding. Cyberpunk's anti-idealistic universe concurrently underscores and parodies this message: it highlights the inevitability of technology and, at the same time, our inability to demonstrate the existence of a pure Being behind its operations.

In cyberpunk fiction, the relationship between the visible and the invisible plays an important part. We are repeatedly reminded that what we see is inseparable from what we do not and cannot see: a footprint is only visible in the absence of the footwear that has produced it; a digital configuration of data is only visible in the absence of the physical structures that the data signify. Sight is a site of tension between presence and absence and much of what we see cites – but does not represent – what we might be seeing instead. Cyberpunk emphasizes the pockets of invisibility that fold and unfold within the visible. Indeed, the matrix itself is not only a site-less site – 'There is no there, there'[54] – but also a sightless sight: a fog of visions endlessly receding towards the black infinity of spaces between mirrors.

Nothing is ever *fully* visible. The discourse of spectrality, as intimated earlier, attests to this idea. It demonstrates that there are always gaps in our systems of vision – and hence of knowledge – and that we are haunted by these lacunae because we do not know how or where to situate them. We only ever see contingent and transient manifestations of things, not the things themselves in their entirety. Moreover, the objects we see are not autonomous, for they depend on the context formed by other visible objects and, more importantly, by countless invisible ones. What does exist is inevitably crossed by the nothingness that it may easily have been instead. As Terry Eagleton comments:

> [W]hat we see when we contemplate something is merely a kind of snapshot or frozen moment of the temporal process which goes to make up its true nature. . . . No object ever swims into view other than against the background of some 'world'. . . . We can see something because it is present to us; but what we cannot usually see is what enables this presentness in the first place. . . . Finally, what we do not see in an object is that it might just as well never have been.[55]

Of considerable interest, in the context of contemporary articulations of the dialectics of visibility and invisibility, are images of *hidden* aspects of biology that advances in science and photography have recently disclosed. While enhancing our grasp of the real, these images simultaneously open up *fantastic* realms, landscapes and forms. These worlds, moreover, are *inside* us: in their uncanny complexity of structure, colour, composition and texture, those images remind us that *otherness* is an internal dimension of our being. As Baudrillard points out in *The Transparency of Evil*, this eerie recognition amounts to: 'Not being oneself – but never being alienated either: coming from without to inscribe oneself on the figure of the Other, within that strange form from elsewhere.'[56]

THE STRANGER

Fictional constructions of the *alien* have consistently been utilized as metaphors for various threats of invasion and disruption of the familiar, the visible, the known. These threats are identifiable as long as the alien *looks* alien. When an element of invisibility creeps in, and the alien becomes unnervingly indistinguishable from humans, the threats gain fresh urgency. There is a vital difference, for example, between H.G. Wells's *The War of the Worlds* (1898) and Jack Finney's *The Body Snatchers* (1955). In the former, the Martians who disrupt the suburban world in which they land are overtly, even rudely, other: they retain something of a head, but their bodies are atrophied and furnished with tentacles. In the latter, a somatic blurring of the boundary between alien and human, producing considerable difficulties in differentiating between the two, turns into a serious cause for panic. Cyberculture complicates this trend and underscores the alien's potentially unrecognizable omnipresence. Monsters are never far away, or, as Freddy Krueger warns in *Freddy's Dead: The Final Nightmare*, 'Every town has an Elm Street.'

The work of the Swiss painter H.R. Giger visualizes the *stranger within* in the shape of surreal creatures that are made particularly weird by the scientific precision of their depiction. These could be read as visual interpretations of a deep sense of self-alienation. According to Timothy Leary:

Giger mercilessly shows us the anabolism and catabolism of our realities. In these paintings we see ourselves as crawling embryos, as fetal, larval creatures protected by the membrane of our egos, waiting for the moment of our metamorphosis and new-birth. We see our cities, our civilizations, as insect hives, ant colonies peopled by larval crawling creatures. Us.[57]

Giger is succinctly described in *Virtual Light* as: 'Real classical. Bio-mech.'[58] This definition of an artist still deemed, nowadays, quite innovative and controversial is an ironical commentary on the dynamics through which cultures construct their canons. *Idoru* refers explicitly to the Swiss artist in comparing Tokyo's 'nanotech buildings' to 'Giger's paintings of New York'[59] and, less overtly but more graphically, in its depiction of 'a Franz Kafka theme bar' which displays 'chairs molded from some brown and chitinous resin', 'insectoid mandibles', walls that imitate 'wing cases and bulbous abdomens' and 'a curving stairway molded to resemble glossy brown carapaces'.[60] The club's decor instantly evokes Giger's bio-mechanoid creations, their insectile shapes, their soft and vulnerable flesh precariously bounded by chitinous armours, their tantalizing metamorphoses, and their baffling juxtapositions of the organic and the constructed.

Otherness and haunting take various forms in Giger's work but the main emphasis is consistently placed on the Gothic character of cyberculture, as futuristic technologies coalesce with mystical and supernatural motifs. Human bodies are violently penetrated, dis-membered, randomly reassembled, or forced into unholy com-munions with prosthetic implants that, far from enhancing the body, actually violate it with a gusto worthy of the Marquis de Sade. While the human organism is engulfed by monstrous, macabre and gro-tesque shapes that almost invariably translate into instruments of torture, inanimate objects (even as *lowly* an object as a toilet seat) acquire organic attributes. From the now familiar monsters designed by Giger for *Alien* and *Alien 3* to his motor landscapes, ghost trains, alien furniture, *Erotomechanics* (1980) and *Necronomicons* (1990), the artist's leading thread is an elaborate interpretation of the intim-ate relationship between mythology and technology. This is conveyed through a style that unites ancient traditions of the occult and their re-workings within contemporary culture. The *Baphomet Tarot* (1993) is a classic example of Giger's (cyber)Gothic style in its com-bination of technological imagery and satanic motifs revolving around the intriguing shapes of the pentangle and of the horned deity of the abyss.

As Marina Warner comments, the images produced by modern science exhibit telling points of contact with older iconologies, in that the sense of reality becoming more and more visible (and intelli-gible) is intertwined with the sense that the visible does not disclose rational structures but rather fantastical and puzzling forms:

The flow of images these days, swollen by new technologies, brings us a flood of messages about material phenomena, from the structure of a strand of DNA to the beautiful, blowing plumes of uncreated stars caught by the Hubble telescope. . . . But the ways such images are structured, in form, colour and composition, as well as the ways they are received and understood . . . reveal deep connections to iconologies that precede the disclosures and revelations of these scientific breakthroughs.[61]

What often makes such images unsettling is that they tend to capture processes that go on *inside* the body. Donna Haraway concurs:

The blasted scenes, sumptuous textures, evocative colors, and ET monsters of the immune landscape are simply there, inside us . . . the hillocks of chromosomes lie flattened on a blue-hued moonscape of some other planet . . . the auto-immune disease-ravaged head of a femur glows against a sunset on a dead world.[62]

William W.A. Ewing's *Inside Information* supplies a fascinating and mesmerizing gallery of images of this kind. While documenting in great detail the scientific matrix of the photographs included in his collection, Ewing remarks that 'it is difficult to believe that these fascinating pictures are not out-takes from some popular science-fiction film'.[63] He credits twentieth-century advances in the imaging of the body's innermost recesses (such as micrography and various scanning techniques) with the unprecedented ability to depict 'physiological processes as well as morphological and anatomical structures'.[64] At the same time, however, he reminds us that the images thereby created are indeed *images* that, though not attempting to distort reality, are inevitably the result of *techniques*. For example, colour is often used creatively in endoscopic and micrographic photography: it may be added to monochromatic images, or altered to produce starker contrasts between different zones than would otherwise be the case. From a medical point of view, this creative manipulation of *nature* could be described as simply 'user friendly', as a way of enabling the viewer 'to differentiate detail'.[65] However, Ewing is also aware of the aesthetic implications of these techniques. The point is that no image is a neutral rendering of reality, however scientifically advanced the tools and media at the maker's disposal may be, for the maker is always operating decisions. As Martin Kemp and Ken Arnold observe:

Whether we are dealing with an artist making a detailed rendering, a photographer who judges lighting, exposures and printing, or a technician adjusting the emission and parameters of the receiver in an ultrasound scan, complex series of choices are made, which involve what we may call artistry, in the sense of using skill to give a selective, effective and even appealing depiction.[66]

The micrographic photographer Manfred Kage corroborates this argument by emphasizing the aesthetic dimension of all images, even the most *documentary*. Indeed, he likens his search for, and selection of, appropriate images derived from scientific materials to Duchamp's approach to *found objects* and to the Surrealists generally. These were the very artists who, according to Ewing, 'seized upon an invisible reality which would only be confirmed, and charted, in the last quarter of our century, by scientists'.[67] At the same time as science delivers previously invisible images as seemingly imaginary shapes, followers of spiritualistic movements endeavour, paradoxically, to rationalize their own icons in quasi-scientific terms. Warner cites an intriguing example of this trend:

In America, where the cult of angels has become a new popular frenzy, one writer seriously calculated that the dimensions commonly represented were inaccurate, and that in order to fly, a grown angel, even a slender one, would need at least a fourteen-foot wing-span.[68]

Jeanette Winterson ironically implies that the present-day angelomaniac's rationalizing efforts echo ancient attempts to name and quantify the unfathomable regions of mysticism and faith:

The old sceptics used to say that if Hell existed, where is it? What part of the Universe does it occupy? What are its coordinates? It had to be a latitudinal Hell, a longitudinal Hell. A Hell subject to tape measure and set square.[69]

Humans are strangers to themselves and reason alone is unlikely to help them deal with the dilemmas engendered by this condition. The discipline of linguistics emphasizes the notion of self-alienation by showing that those elements of discourse that should most accurately define individuals, namely personal pronouns, are in fact the most vacuous indices of identity: personal pronouns are *shifters* that only carry meaning in a specific context. Anybody can be 'I', so how can there be anything special about *my* 'I'? Anybody's I is inevitably criss-crossed by the traces of countless and faceless Is and destined to err endlessly through their crowd. The phantasmatic nature of the linguistic shifter has digital correlatives in two manifestations of the I other than the personal pronoun with which all computer users will be familiar. Sean Cubitt describes them as 'the blinking cursor/insertion point that stands just ahead of every last letter' and the 'nomadic I-bar/arrow and its various metamorphoses – the pointer-tool'.[70] According to Cubitt, both of these digital functions metaphorically underline the rootless status of the subject I, its strangeness to itself: 'The cursor as perpetual tourist meanders through a landscape which is always foreign', and the pointer, in turn, 'circulates . . . a zone deprived of semantic content' seeking 'a home from which its very freedom has exiled it'. Furthermore, just as there is no evidence for any metaphysical necessity behind the arbitrary actions of the human I, so the movements of its digital siblings are guided by a piece of machinery that is also very much a mindless toy: 'the mouse in the hand is blind' and 'runs its errands tail-first'.[71]

Analogies between the human I and the digital I intimate that understanding the precarious anchorage of *any* subject position is the precondition of our ability to come to terms with the stranger within.

BURNING CHROME AND *MONA LISA OVERDRIVE*: THE BODY AS COMMODITY

Implants and transplants, genetic restructuring, and the consumption of an unthinkably complex galaxy of data do not make the body impregnable. In fact, they throw into relief the commodification of corporeality by world-wide power games, largely based on the illicit trade of body parts. Biotechnology does not make the body stronger and more durable. If anything, it shapes it on the model of the commodity doomed to planned obsolescence, in a post-millennial society run amok. Technological transformations of the body are dictated by ideological and economic imperatives. *Neuromancer*'s Case, for instance, is subjected to enhancing surgery so that he may become an able-bodied pawn in the service of corporational sleaze. Molly seems to have deliberately chosen to have her body prosthetically improved. Yet the concept of free choice is over-shadowed by intimations that without her artificial adjuncts she would have no power whatsoever within a social structure that will only accommodate her as a ruthless mercenary. Things appear to be quite different for the cyber-aristocracy able to postpone death by having their cells preserved in support vats. After all, they own the economies by which people like Case and Molly are manipulated. However, Gibson does not offer one single instance of successful return to the realm of the flesh by any of the characters fortunate enough to be kept marginally alive. *Count Zero*'s Virek, for example, retains the power to project virtual semblances of his body in a wide variety of simulated contexts. Nevertheless, there remains a gap between these apparitions and the unsavoury reality of a physical body reduced to seething hordes of cancerous cells. Moreover, the apparitions themselves are ultimately killed off.

These examples suggest that *all* of Gibson's bodies – those of the powerful and of the disenfranchised alike – are engaged in an ambivalent partnership with medical technologies that prove simul-taneously enabling and oppressive. Of course, Gibson is depicting a future world, an essentially hypothetical fantasy world. Yet there is already evidence in the present for medical technologies that empower and disempower at the same time, thus intimating that Gibson's vision is more of an amplification than a distortion of current conditions. An interesting and in many ways harrowing example of present-day technology's ability to both strengthen and disable our bodies comes from the field of research into Alzheimer's disease. 'Critical Art Ensemble' have documented this issue with ref-erence to 'a new radical map, acquired through the use of positron-emission tomography'. Such a map:

> . . . reveals the part of the brain affected by Alzheimer's disease, and the degree to which the brain has been eroded by the disease. This map can help physicians diagnose Alzheimer's up to ten years before symptom onset. The comedy begins with the admis-sion that there is no way to predict when symptoms will begin to appear, and there is still no known treatment for the disease.[72]

The essay goes on to point out the paradoxical character of the enterprise, as a tantalizing illustration of science's potential knack of restoring the body to health and, concurrently, as a depressing recognition of the unknown. A person diagnosed with Alzheimer's and unable to know when the symptoms will start manifesting themselves or indeed *if* they will is unlikely to feel particularly elated by the findings of the medical gaze. Moreover, the project discussed by 'Critical Art Ensemble' bears points of contact with Gibson's speculations on the future of medical technology because it exposes the interdependence of scientific and economic issues. Just as surgery and biotechnology in cyberpunk are by an large predicated on economic imperatives, so the Alzheimer's case underlines the possible financial repercussions of developments in the diagnosing of the disease:

> Since the process of visualization . . . is of little use for the patient already diagnosed with the disease, it must be asked: who could benefit from this information? . . . Those who would benefit most from this information are insurance companies and the employer of the person likely to be afflicted with the ailment.[73]

Several of Gibson's stories collected under the title of *Burning Chrome* highlight the ambiguous character of the relationship between the body and technology. In 'Johnny Mnemonic', thousands of data are stashed in the protagonist's head as so many megabytes. His brain has been modelled through microsurgery to resemble a computer and he cannot know or remember any of the information filed in the cabinet of his head. Eventually, Johnny ends up 'making good money' as a result of a Squid being able to 'read the traces of anything that anyone ever stored' inside him by detecting the passwords buried in the chips of his computerized brain.[74] Squids, incidentally, are superconducting quantum interference detectors, formerly used for military purposes, and Johnny's partner, specifically, is a cyborg dolphin – 'surplus from the last war' – combining very perceptive sensor units and a 'clumsy and prehistoric' structure.[75] Despite Johnny's eventual success, however, there are hints throughout the story that the character's condition is comparable to some unnameable disease over which he has no control or to a demonic possession by forces that cannot be exorcized: 'The program. I had no idea what it contained. I still don't. I only sing the song, with zero comprehension.'[76] Right at the end, Johnny fantasizes about the healing moment that will remove this *cancer* (as it were) from his body: 'one day I'll have a surgeon dig all the silicon out of my amygdalae, and I'll live with my own memories and nobody else's'.[77]

'Johnny Mnemonic' was made into a film (directed by Robert Longo and starring Keanu Reeves as the protagonist) in 1995. Gibson wrote the screenplay of his original story and was pleased with both the product and its reception. Prior to *Johnny Mnemonic*, Gibson's experiences in film had consisted of the co-writing with Tom Maddox of an *X-Files* episode entitled 'Killer Switch' and of a few misadventures. His screen adaptations of 'Burning Chrome' and 'Neuro-Hotel' never made it to the production stage. More importantly, his script for *Alien 3* was almost entirely scrapped, the only trace of his labour retained by the movie being the image of the prisoners with bar codes tattooed on their necks. Shortly before the release of *Johnny Mnemonic*, Gibson stated: 'It is only fair that the first script of mine that goes into production should come from . . . my early career', further confirming the importance of the piece (originally written in 1980) as 'the root source of *Neuromancer* and *Count Zero*'.[78]

'The Belonging Kind' vividly dramatizes the body's precarious boundaries. *What* exactly are the woman pursued by Coretti and her drinking companions, as their bodies alter drastically from one bar to the next in all their physiognomic and vestimentary signifiers of age, status and class? Are they replicants, mutants, ghosts? On the one hand, these bodies epitomize the fluidity of the technological body, famously conveyed by the T-1000 of *Terminator 2: Judgment Day*; on the other, they hark back to Proteus, the shape-shifting deity of ancient mythology. Both the technological and the mythological connotations of startling metamorphoses are conjured up by Gibson's narrative, through descriptive details that are simultaneously reminiscent of Ovid, R.L. Stevenson and Franz Kafka, in a pot pourri of dreamlike images. For example:

. . . it was there, in the light of a streetlamp, like a stage light, that she began to change. The street was deserted.

She was crossing the street. She stepped off the curb and it began. It began with tints in her hair – at first he thought they were reflections. But there was no neon there to cast the blobs of color that appeared, color sliding and merging like oil sticks. Then the colors bled away and in three seconds she was white-blond. He was sure it was a trick of light until her dress began to writhe, twisting across her body like a shrink-wrap plastic. Part of it fell away entirely and lay in curling shreds on the pavement shed like the skin of some fabulous animal.[79]

In 'The Belonging Kind', the body is encoded as a function of *interior design*. The protean bodies that the protagonist obsessively follows from one boozing hole to the next are, ultimately, postmodern items of furniture and decor. They are 'human fixtures'[80] defined entirely by their sartorial attributes, be these 'shapeless Salvation Army overcoats' or 'bright suburban leisurewear', elegant evening gowns or soiled factory clothes.[81]

In 'The Gernsback Continuum', the ephemerality of a human body uncertain of its own reality is paralleled by the transitoriness of the body of built space. The unfulfilled visions of 'the first generation of American industrial designers' of the 1930s have survived primarily in the form of sketches, such as that of a conclusively non-airworthy, 'grandiose prop-driven airliner, all wing, like a fat symmetrical boomerang with windows in unlikely places', a 'grand ballroom and two squash courts'. This sketch appeals especially to the imagination of the narrator, an architectural photographer. Although he is already well aware that 'it is possible to photograph what isn't there',[82] his psychosomatic equilibrium receives a severe blow when, preparing for a shot of a tangible building, he finds himself penetrating the 'fine membrane' of probability:

> Ever so gently, I went over the Edge – And looked up to see a twelve-engined thing like a bloated boomerang, all wing, thrumming its way east with an elephantine grace, so low that I could count the rivets in its dull silver skin, and hear – maybe – the echo of jazz.[83]

The shock is formidable and is experienced in eminently physical ways, as though the airliner's improbable body had somehow managed to breach the very boundaries of the narrator's own body. The vision produces an unbearable sense of anxiety which no amphetamine is capable of relieving. This demonic weight may only be lightened through the protagonist's self-submission to popular technologies of the tritest order. Indeed, he is advised to 'watch lots of television, particularly game shows and soaps', for it is only 'really bad media' that 'can exorcise your semiotic ghosts'.[84]

The narrator's vulnerability stems primarily from his exposure to a culture that makes the body redundant (for example, by translating architectural three-dimensionality into the flat surfaces of imaginary drawings) and simultaneously emplaces it as the supreme ideological icon. The body is marginalized by the fantastic character of an environment that is only available in the guise of visionary sketches and, occasionally, in that of the 'relentlessly tacky', spectral buildings that tend 'mostly to survive along depressing strips lined with dusty motels, mattress wholesalers, and small used-car lots'.[85] The 'streamlined buildings' of 'Thirties design' are the aborted children of 'an alternate America . . . that never happened' – a submerged body worthy of attention solely for 'some lost sect that had worshipped blue mirrors and geometry . . . white marble and slipstream chrome'.[86] At the same time, both architectural and physiological bodies become pivotal to the most ominous ideological projects: 'When I isolated a few of the factory buildings,' the narrator observes, 'they came across with a kind of sinister totalitarian dignity, like the stadium Albert Speer built for Hitler.'[87] Concurrently, his hallucinations are peopled by racially harrowing stereotypes: white, blond and blue-eyed Americans, 'smug, happy, and utterly content with themselves and their world', redolent of 'the sinister fruitiness of Hitler Youth propaganda'.[88]

'The Winter Market' marginalizes the body's materiality by turning it into a vehicle for simstim (simulated stimulation) dreams commercially edited into popular chillers and thrillers. At the same time, it foregrounds the physical dimension in its least savoury manifestations. The character of Lise incarnates this paradox. On the one hand, she is intensely physical: her identity is defined by a fatal, devastating illness which induces extreme pain and may only be kept at bay by the donning of an exoskeleton. A contraption that Lise never divests herself of, being incapable of tolerating the sensation of total passivity to which nakedness condemns her, the exoskeleton accentuates the character's bodiliness by mapping the body's inside on the outside, thereby *doubling* her materiality. On the other hand, Lise's interfacing with technology attenuates her corporeality, for her ultimate aim is a total escape from the 'hated flesh' and a fusion with the 'hardwired godhead' of a Hollywood dream of 'stardom and cybernetic immortality'.[89] Lise does achieve her objective, for by the end of her ordeal we find that she has 'merged with the net'.[90] Her fame is based on a rare ability to 'dive down deep, down and out, out into Jung's sea, and bring back ... dreams'. These archetypal dreams can be accessed by 'neuroelectronics' and hence transformed into commodities, digital packages for consumption by an avid 'market' of computer users longing to see their deepest fantasies embodied in visible shapes.[91] Throughout the story, Lise's broken, crumbling body is always on the scene (though ostensibly marginalized by cybernetics) and screaming to be released from 'the bonds of polycarbon', yet longing for the departure to be marked by bodily contact, by a 'hand she couldn't even feel'.[92]

In 'Rock On', Pat Cadigan deals with themes analogous to those explored by Gibson in 'The Winter Market'. While Lise's faculties are harnessed to the electronic production of visual images, the mind of Cadigan's Gina is used as an organic synthesizer for the production of rock 'n' roll hits. Her employer, Man-O-War, has considerable musical ambitions but the tapes he produces never turn out to be 'as good as the stuff in the head, rock 'n' roll visions straight from the brain'. Gina, the human synthesizer (ominously dubbed 'synner' and hence 'sinner'), has the power to access Man-O-War's visions, 'to get everyone in the group dreaming the same way' and 'to rock them and roll them the way they couldn't do themselves'. A miraculous catalyst, Gina is instrumental to the construction of a collective dream or, perhaps, a *consensual hallucination*: 'anyone could be a rock 'n' roll hero then. Anyone! In the end, they didn't have to play instruments unless they really wanted to, and why bother? Let the synthesizer take their imaginings and boost them up to Mount Olympus.'[93]

One of the stories collected in *Burning Chrome* that draws attention most explicitly to the body's penetration by technology is 'Hinterlands'. Here the natural body is posited as less real than machines. For example, the protagonist Toby is so used to hearing the voice of his boss, Hiro, through a mechanical 'bonephone implant'[94] that when he perceives the real tone and timbre of Hiro's voice he is somewhat unsettled: 'It was strange to hear him acoustically, not as bone vibration from the implant.'[95] Ironically, reality proves more unfamiliar and defamiliarizing than its simulation. While the body is technologized, technology is endowed with a pulsating body of its own. Toby is especially sensitive to the physical and almost sexual connotations of the information that flows relentlessly through his orbital workplace:

A constant stream of raw data goes pulsing home to Earth, a flood of rumours, whispers, hints of transgalactic traffic. I used to lie rigid in my hammock and feel the pressure of all those data, feel them snaking through the lines . . . lines like sinews, strapped and bulging, ready to spasm, ready to crush me.[96]

'Burning Chrome' encapsulates some of Gibson's recurring concerns in his exploration of the relationship between the body and technology. First, it emphasizes the ambivalent nature of cyberspace as a map of incorporeal geometrical abstractions, on the one hand, and a physical world in which ICE can literally *kill* illegitimate hackers, on the other. Second, 'Burning Chrome' highlights certain structural analogies between the physical organism and computer technology. Its main male characters are portrayed thus:

Bobby Quine and Automatic Jack. Bobby's the thin, pale dude with the dark glasses, and Jack's the mean-looking guy with the myoelectric arm. Bobby's software and Jack's hard; Bobby punches console and Jack runs down all the little things that can give you an edge.[97]

Moreover, Gibson's encoding of his characters' identities on the basis of technological metaphors is inseparable from their association with esoteric discourses. The story utilizes the symbolism of the tarot, for example, to describe the characters' yearning for omens, signs and premonitions that may enable them to catch prophetic glimpses of what the future has in store for them.[98] Finally, 'Burning Chrome' typifies cyberpunk's paradoxical configuration of the body by simultaneously presenting the natural body as an *incomplete* entity, wholly dependent on the possibility of prosthetic enhancement, and highlighting the central role played by that body in the acquisition of the valuable prosthesis. Rikki, for example, is driven by the desire to purchase the 'Zeiss Ikon Eyes' which, in her fantasies, will enable her to become a simstim star.[99] It is her ambition to edit her natural form in such a way that the body itself may be transcended in the pursuit of virtual fame. But in order to purchase the coveted prosthetic adjunct, Rikki (like Molly in *Neuromancer*) has no choice but sell her body for the dubious delight of 'closet necrophiliacs'.[100]

Moving from *Burning Chrome* to *Mona Lisa Overdrive*, it could be argued that one of the novel's main achievements lies in its ability to throw into relief the body's puzzling complexity, a feature of our being that is vividly captured by Bryan Turner's words: the body is 'at once the most solid, the most elusive, illusory, concrete, meta-phorical, ever-present and ever-distant thing (a site, an instrument, an environment, a singularity and a multiplicity)'.[101]

Above all, *Mona Lisa Overdrive* examines the extent to which the already fraught relationship between the body and science has been recently problematized further by the confluence of sexuality and technology. On one level, the novel highlights the enduring hold of pre-cybernetic sexual modalities even in the midst of a thoroughly technologized environment. For example, Eddie, Mona's pimp, expects the girl's erotic tales to be rhetorically *edited* so as to suit his personal fantasies. Although he could give vent to those fantasies by using a deck and appropriately selected software, he prefers Mona to supply him with salacious detail in her physical presence: 'What Eddie wanted to hear was that it hurt a lot and made her feel bad, but she liked it anyway.'[102] The body's intract-able materiality is here central to the sexual experience. By con-trast, the interfacing of the physical act with high technology has deflating effects: when Mona gets into bed with Michael, after he has arranged for his cutting-edge digital gear to record every moment of what is to come, she finds that 'the fun was gone, and she might as well have been with a trick'.[103] Regular involvement with cybertech on a professional basis desexualizes even those whose fame rests on libidinal glamour. Sense/Net stars Angie Mitchell and Robin Lanier, for instance, are professional sex icons but are unable to translate simulated erotic harmony into fleshly contact:

> She [Angie] remembered the one night they'd spent together, in a windblown house in southern Madagascar, his passivity and his patience. They'd never tried again, and she'd suspected that he feared that intimacy would undermine the illusion their stims projected so perfectly.[104]

Mona Lisa Overdrive, like *Burning Chrome*, stresses that physicality is only apparently suppressed by technology. This is borne out by the fact that while Gibson's console cowboys and cyberspace addicts pursue a fantasy of dematerialization, others cling on to a mechanical model that emphasizes the corporeal dimension. Slick, in particular, articulates a technological dream of an intensely physical character by constructing imposing anthropomorphic automata. Slick's quest for bodiliness is testified by his commitment to the principle that his constructs *must be physical*. In creating the Judge, in particular, he aims for maximum physicality by rejecting media and materials of an overly ethereal kind. In building the Judge's hand, a lethal 'buzzsaw', Slick finds that: 'Electricity, somehow, just wasn't satisfying; it wasn't *physical* enough. Air was the way to go, big tanks of compressed air, or internal combustion if you could find the parts.'[105] The Judge is 'nearly four meters tall, half as broad at the shoulders, headless' and made largely of 'scavenged parts'.[106] The bodiliness of Slick's enterprise is underscored by the Frankenstein-ian flavour of his task. Moreover, his creatures are composite constructs that metonymically encapsulate the patchwork character of Gibson's dystopian cyberculture as a whole.

The physical dimension is also underscored, incidentally, by the Tessier-Ashpools' reliance on the *material* replication of the family via genetic manipulation as a means of perpetuating its mythical power. Although the family's economic and cultural prestige could easily be asserted through purely cybernetic channels, what they deem vital to the maintenance of their legend is 'the labyrinth of blood'[107] running through virtually endless 'pairs of cloned embryos'. The somatic features of various Tessier-Ashpools are accordingly stressed to convey their pathetic folly and savage lyricism. Just consider the portrait of Marie-France's countenance, 'the planes of her face' diffracted 'in a tortured, extended fugue'.[108] In their addiction to the physical dimension, testified by their obsessive recourse to cloning and cryogenics under the relatively lenient aegis of 'orbital law', the Tessier-Ashpools have engineered a situation in which it is 'hard to keep track of which generation, or combination of generations, is running the show at a given time'.[109] Paradoxically, the body's enduring significance may only be asserted by randomly disseminating it across both space and time.

Returning to Slick's project, it is noteworthy that the aesthetic of bulk is supposed to serve therapeutic purposes. Deprived of his memory by harsh penal experiments, Slick builds his robots in an effort to salvage, however marginally and haphazardly, the right to recollect: 'He could remember every step of the Judge's construction, if he wanted to, and sometimes he did, just for the comfort of being able to.'[110] Furthermore, Slick's project – with its emphasis on immanence and materiality – could be read as an attack against metaphysical pretensions. These are embodied by his house-mate Gentry's obsessive conviction that cyberspace has a 'Shape' and that its 'apprehension' is the ultimate and uniquely valid quest.[111] For Slick, by contrast, it is utterly irrelevant whether or not cyberspace has a form of any kind, for the guises in which the matrix may manifest itself are only ever the product of arbitrary decisions on the part of powerful corporations. Some of those guises may prove more pleasing to the senses than others but ultimately it is merely a contingent question of taste.

What both Slick and Gentry draw attention to is the question of whether cyberspace can be regarded as a *body* in its own right. Indubitably, the commercial dimension of the Internet, the World Wide Web and virtual reality suggests that cyberspace is a *commodified* body akin to the bodies of the fictional characters discussed in the previous pages. However, a number of critics have proposed that cyberspace is indeed a body, despite its apparent immateriality, not only because of its commodified status but also because of its sensuous qualities. Indeed, the appeal of virtual domains is not reducible to their technological functions. It is, in fact, an eminently aesthetic phenomenon whereby pleasure is derived from the digital network's ability to represent graphically a bewildering array of data. These electronic representations are aesthetically enticing in that they combine the cool edge of geometrical and algebraic precision with the warm edge of chromatic play. Vilem Flusser is one of the critics who have emphasized that the digital *apparitions* produced by computers are aesthetically enticing, and that their polychromatic worlds are akin to art and indeed beautiful. Flusser draws on the shared German etymology of '*Schein* (apparition)' and '*schon* (beautiful)'[112] to corroborate his argument. He also comments on the tendency to 'distrust these synthetic images' and suggests that the main reason for this wariness is not, as it has commonly been assumed, that 'they are hazy figments hovering into nothingness' but actually that 'they are worlds that we ourselves have designed, rather than something that has been given to us, like the surrounding world'.[113] Flusser thus draws attention to the difficulty, arguably exacerbated by cyberculture, of coming to terms with the absence of transcendental principles able to determine what we are and how we should live. It is up to human beings themselves to ideate, describe and compute reality, in an understanding of the part played not merely by their minds but also by their senses.

In his own evaluation of the aesthetic import of the body of cyberspace, Michael Heim emphasizes that there is something deeply *erotic* about the appeal of digital images:

> Our fascination with computers is more erotic than sensuous . . . our affair with information machines announces a symbiotic relationship and ultimately a mental marriage to technology. . . . The world rendered as pure information not only fascinates our eyes and minds, but also captures our hearts. We feel augmented and empowered. . . . This is Eros.

Heim's argument relies on a classical conception of the erotic as the product of a feeling of personal inadequacy conducive to a quest for self-fulfilment. Accordingly, it posits the erotic as 'deeper than the play of the senses' owing to its engagement with metaphysical objectives. When this understanding of the erotic, as opposed to the sensuous, is projected onto the digital realm, computers are construed as a means of pursuing self-realization rather than as providers of merely pleasing images. This is an intriguing and in many ways persuasive argument. Yet in recognizing its strengths we should also be aware of its potentially detrimental commitment to binary thought. For example, Heim theorizes an adversarial relationship between 'the aesthete', as someone who 'feels drawn to casual play and dalliance', and 'the erotic lover', as someone who 'reaches out to a fulfilment far beyond aesthetic detachment'. The 'ontology of cyberspace' is associated with the erotic rather than the aesthetic because computers are envisaged as vehicles for the transcendence of our flawed material selves.[114] However, while it may be the case that many people interact with machines – more or less lovingly – to strengthen their sense of personal power and to stretch the boundaries of their knowledge, many others seek and find pleasure in digital technology without harbouring any metaphysical fantasies. The limitations of Heim's argument are due to the fact that his definition of the erotic relies substantially on the equation between the erotic and the metaphysical search for the infinite advocated by Plato in *The Symposium*. In this text, the Greek philosopher constructs a hierarchical structure that posits heterosexual attachments as base and overly corporeal, their only redeeming trait being their usefulness in propagating the human species. Next comes homosexual love involving adult males and boys as a more refined form of yearning for harmony and beauty. More refined still is the love binding kindred souls in pursuit of philosophical truth and just laws. At the culminating point of the pyramid stands the most authentic image of the erotic, namely a longing to contemplate the Pure Form of Beauty unfettered by carnal longings.[115]

However, the erotic also epitomizes everything that destabilizes the unity of identity, knowledge, narrative and history, as documented by Roland Barthes in *A Lover's Discourse*. Here the erotic is associated with emotions and images that stubbornly resist categorization – with the *atopic* (placeless, unlocatable) realm in which all signs, from the most trivial to the most sublime, are overwhelmingly meaningful and utterly meaningless. Barthes's erotic discourse is a series of fragments that may only cohere through a totally arbitrary act of narrative ordering.[116] If Barthes's version of the erotic is brought into play alongside Plato's, then Heim's opposition between the aesthetic/sensuous and the erotic becomes problematic. Plato's desensualizing ideal is only *one* version of the erotic and its authority can hardly remain unchallenged under the pressure of anti- or post-metaphysical approaches. If cyberspace, in turn, is *erotic*, this is not simply because it affords opportunities for transcendence of the limitations of the flesh. It is also erotic in the Barthesian sense, as a kaleidoscopic universe of fragments that we may string together into coherent stories, only to realize that such stories do not reflect a metaphysical necessity and could, in fact, have been something quite different.

The body's tenacious presence in the apparently decorporealized domain of the matrix is borne out by the endurance of sensory and sensuous experiences as an integral part of cybernavigation. For example, Angie, returning to *reality* from the virtual realm, finds that sense impressions gleaned in the latter survive, albeit spectrally, after pulling off the trodes. Specifically, she notices that the taste of a drink consumed in simstim still lingers on her tongue: 'She sat up and took a swallow of beer, which mingled weirdly with the ghost-flavor of Tally's recorded wine.'[117] If gustatory impressions from cyberspace are capable of infiltrating ordinary life, it is also the case that virtuality is portrayed by Gibson as a situation that engages intensely the entire sensorium. At one point, Angie is instructed (in the course of an electronic test of her sensory responses) to stroke her bedspread and 'the raw silk and unbleached linen' become increasingly alive under her touch: 'Angie felt the weave thicken beneath her fingertips. . . . She could distinguish the individual fibers now, know silk from linen. . . . Her nerves screamed as her flayed fingertips grated against steel wool, ground glass . . .'[118] The dreams experienced by Angie as, by virtue of her brain implants, she is capable of accessing the matrix without even the need for trodes, are themselves acutely physical: 'there really was something *there*, another person – at least three of them – speaking through Angie. And it *hurt* Angie when they spoke, made her muscles knot and her nose bleed.'[119] As for Bobby, much as he is translated into a cybernetic construct, his physical being repeatedly displaced and increasingly attenuated, the body obstinately asserts itself in its least palatable configuration, as a 'wasted thing . . . strapped down in alloy and nylon, its chin filmed with dried vomit'. Even in his most explicitly digital incarnation, Bobby remains incontrovertibly material, the data he represents forming a 'solid rectangular mass of memory bolted above the stretcher'.[120]

THE DOLL

Gibson also addresses issues of materiality and corporeality by examining the relationship between the human body and inanimate imitations of it: dolls, for example. Dolls are anthropomorphic projections: images of our humanity imprinted on a non-human world. Yet dolls are, fundamentally, artificial *things* (be they stuffed or hollow) which, in sporting their resemblance to humans, simultaneously allude to the artificial status of human beings themselves. Gibson utilizes the image of the doll precisely to evoke the artificiality of human appearance, as evinced by the description of Kumiko's father, 'his eyes flat and bright, like the eyes of a painted doll'.[121] Dolls are both attractive toys, incarnations of the body perfect and disturbing reminders of the synthetic nature of all identities. As images of the ideal body become more and more industrial and streamlined, identity is increasingly conceived as an effect of mass-production.

Dolls emanate particularly unsettling vibrations in the context of voodoo, a crucial point of reference in both *Count Zero* and *Mona Lisa Overdrive*. Roaming the contaminated wasteland of Dog

Solitude, Slick comes across 'the wingless hulk of an airliner', which turns out to host some rather unexpected guests:

> Stuck his head inside and saw hundreds of tiny heads suspended from the concave ceiling. He froze there, blinking in the sudden shade, until what he was seeing made some kind of sense. The pink plastic heads of dolls, their nylon hair tied up into topknots and the knots stuck into thick black tar, dangling like fruit. . . . [A]nd he knew he didn't want to stick around to find out whose place it was.[122]

The dismal spectacle of dolls laced with voodoo accoutrements is here rendered particularly disturbing through defamiliarization, as the meaning of the plastic heads in such an environment is quite unfathomable. The doll, this classic incarnation of timeless beauty, flawlessness and candour, is a metamorphic icon capable of crossing over into the realm of the monstrous and the infinitely menacing. As the character of Mouse in Walter Mosley's *Gone Fishin'* knows well, few things are as effective in delaying a pursuing foe as the hanging of a voodoo doll along his path. Mosley offers a chilling image of the kind of uncanny transmutation to which the supreme icon of manufactured charm is liable:

> Dom handed Mouse a doll that had been burned and mutilated. It had once been a white baby doll but the hard-rubber skin was now burnt black . . . . The brown hair was clipped short and the arms were straight out as if it were being crucified on an invisible cross. The eyes were painted over as the white wide eyes you see on a man when he's frightened and trying to see everything coming his way.[123]

There is a further factor that makes dolls disturbing: their *scale*. Perfection is built into a miniaturized structure. In cultures where power is conventionally associated with imposing size (giants, Titans, the Sublime), it is at least disorienting to find perfection coupled with diminutive dimensions. (Technophobic attitudes to electronic culture may be partly explained in the light of this tradition, the very dimensions of microcircuitry calling into question conventional associations between volume and power.) There is something almost unbearable about the marriage of smallness and perfection. Perhaps this is due to the fear that the small-and-perfect may become more and more so, *ad infinitum*, until its attributes are no longer perceivable. Gaby Wood examines these issues in her case study of Caroline Crachami – one of the most tantalizing nineteenth-century exhibits beside the Elephant Man – as a *curiosity* whose uncanny reputation rests on the mythology of size and on the collusion of organic and doll-like attributes. Commenting on the sight of Crachami's skeleton (on display in the Hunterian Museum, London), Wood points out that the 'smallness and the proportion of the thing (an adult shape the size of a newborn) are breathtaking'.[124] Crachami's eeriness is heightened by her association with *dolls*: she is human, indeed a suffering and heavily abused human, yet the relics through which her career is documented – tiny silk socks, ballerina slippers, a thimble and a ruby ring – might well have belonged to a doll.[125] As Wood argues:

> The general sense of wonder surrounding the Sicilian Fairy was to do with her being an adult in miniature, or with her resemblance to a doll. . . . Crachami's main strength as an exhibit was certainly her ability to befuddle her viewers' sense of scale.[126]

Some of the most unsettling connotations of the image of the doll are conveyed by Gibson in *Neuromancer*, where the show staged and enacted by Peter Riviera, and indeed entitled 'The Doll', epitomizes the darkest and most intrusive facets of virtuality. In the show, the 'doll' is the product of Riviera's own projections and, specifically, of his sexual attraction to Molly. Standing in a 'ghostly cube' emanating from the actor's 'holographic aura', Riviera virtualizes the image of a room, therein that of a bare mattress and gradually, upon the mattress, that of the spectral woman – the *doll* – about whom he fantasizes. The female figure takes shape slowly, in a crescendo of distressingly vivid metonymic fragments: a hand whose nails are 'coated with a burgundy lacquer', its skin 'unbroken and unscarred', opens the sequence and then:

> The act progressed with a surreal internal logic of its own. The arms were next. Feet. Legs. The legs were very beautiful. . . . Then the torso formed, as Riviera caressed it into being, white, headless, and perfect, sheened with the faintest gloss of sweat. Molly's

body. Case stared, his mouth open. But it wasn't Molly; it was Molly as Riviera imagined her.[127]

In this passage, the image of the doll is used to expose some unappetizing truths about the ways in which human beings give synthetic form to their fantasies out of the fragmentary sense impressions evoked by real people, who are thereby reduced to infinitely malleable psychic debris. No wonder Case and Molly find Riviera's show intolerable. The doll, this ancient symbol of untainted beauty, turns out to be a monstrous assemblage of scraps of memories and desires.

As Boyer has observed, dolls, like puppets and mannequins, also 'represent the mass-production of identity, whether woman as commodity (that is as prostitute or doll) or man as automaton'.[129] As indicated in the preceding paragraph, the image of woman as doll is emphasized by Gibson to comment on the exploitation of the female body. The image of man as automaton, conversely, is questioned. This image embodies the Futurist fantasy of a hard, sealed and machine-like male physique, capable of opposing the sense of boundlessness conventionally associated with the female body. In Gibson, the powerful men who, like *Count Zero*'s Virek, rely on complex machinery for their endurance are scarcely describable as bounded. The body's reduction to a mob of ravaged cells swarming incessantly in the artificial womb of a support vat could hardly be farther from Marinetti's vision, that of a machine-body based, as Andrew Hewitt puts it, on:

> . . . order, discipline, force, precision, and continuity. . . . With the machine I mean to leave behind all that is languorous, shadowy, nebulous, indecisive, imprecise, unsuccessful, sad, and melancholy in order to return to order, precision, will, strict necessity, the essential, the synthesis.[129]

Gibson's rejection of the image of the mechanical superman underlines his view of corporeality as a phenomenon that, in both its natural and its simulated manifestations, eludes synthesis and order.

CHAPTER 4

CYBERPUNK, GENDER AND SEXUALITY

> Gender, like the body, is a boundary concept. It is at once related to physiological sexual characteristics of the human body (the natural order of the body) and to the cultural context within which that body 'makes sense'. The widespread technological refashioning of the 'natural' human body suggests that gender too would be ripe for reconstruction.
>
> (Anne Balsamo)[1]

TECHNOLOGIES OF THE GENDERED SUBJECT

Those who maintain that the body has disappeared tend to support their argument by emphasizing the replacement of the physical organism by technological extensions of the body's senses and organs. Commenting on McLuhan's anticipation of this view in the mid-1960s, Benjamin Woolley asserts: 'Television has become our eyes, the telephone our mouth and ears; our brains are the interchange for a nervous system that stretches across the whole world – we have breached the terminating barrier of the skin.'[2] Arthur and Marielouise Kroker adduce as further evidence for the demise of the physical body the mounting panic surrounding bodily issues such as AIDS, addictions of various sorts and eating disorders which underscore the basic flimsiness of the organism.[3] Anne Balsamo, by contrast, argues that:

> The body may disappear representationally in virtual worlds . . . but it does not disappear materially, either in the interface with the VR apparatus or in systems of technological production. . . . [M]yths about identity, nature, and the body are rearticulated with new technologies.[4]

Balsamo supports her position by focusing on the relationship between technoscience and issues of gender and sexuality. Technologies of the reproductive body seem to promote the dissociation of procreation from intercourse: is this an a-gendered agenda? Maybe, yet biotechnology still associates reproduction with the female body, encapsulated by the icon of the *artificial womb*. Moreover, aesthetic ideals that make muscularity central to certain versions of feminine sex appeal bear witness to the gendered status of practices such as body-building. At the same time, cosmetic surgery, which still uses the female body as its primary raw material, encourages technologies that objectify the gendered subject according to the principle of metonymy: 'the physical female body is surgically dissected, stretched, carved, and reconstructed',[5] with a closer and closer focus on isolated details, made available by the development of technologies of inner visualization. These technologies are gendered mechanisms of surveillance, which open up the female body to a piercing medical gaze, for example in the use of laparoscopy as a means of aiding the process of *in vitro* fertilization. The configuration of the female body as a cyborg uterus, its manipulation by the fitness and beauty industries and its subjection to penetrating technologies bear witness to the fact that the meat-and-bones body has *not* melted into thin air as a result of cybernetic interventions. In fact, it is central to the perpetuation and reformulation of legion technologies of subjectivity.

In Gibson, cosmetic surgery is used (like biotechnology) as a leitmotif designed to emphasize the body's constant construction by the social and economic structures of cyberculture. Digital technologies play a central role in contemporary approaches to cosmetic surgery. In the first place, these consist of imaging techniques based on a computer's graphic applications. Once the part of the body to be subjected to surgery has been displayed on the screen, any or all of its features can be manipulated – reduced, enhanced, erased, smoothed out – through various tools. The body becomes a canvas upon which the surgeon's artistic and designing skills are tested. The problem with the analogy between art and surgical construction is that while artists – though inevitably influenced by trends – by and large strive for variety, cosmetic surgeons follow, as Balsamo puts it, 'the logic of assembly-line beauty'[6] and aesthetic criteria that idealize certain traits and exclude others. The prostitutes that people the Kafka bar in Gibson's *Idoru* have been produced according to these very tenets:

'Routine plastic surgery lent them a hard assembly-line beauty. Slavic Barbies.'[7] Gibson also draws attention to the racial dimension of surgical editing. For example, the Japanese women described in *Neuromancer* undergo surgery in order to remove the epicanthic eyelid fold and thus achieve a Western look. The reverse procedure is adopted by the Panther Moderns (an underground political organization that harks back to the 1960s Black Panther movement in advocating violent resistance to racist behaviour). Case, at one point, encounters a Panther boy whose countenance has been modified so as to achieve not a westernized image of aesthetic excellence but rather a challenging, subtly animalistic appearance: 'Dark eyes, epicanthic folds obviously the result of surgery, an angry dusting of acne across pale narrow cheeks. . . . [T]he boy moved with the sinister grace of a mime pretending to be a jungle predator.'[8]

A further problem is raised, in the discourse of cosmetic surgery, by considerable levels of confusion about the relationship between aesthetic and medical considerations. Is the beauty myth perpetuated by technological procedures merely the embodiment of aesthetic ideals? Or is the production of putatively flawless bodies a means of promoting health? Some surgeons are adamant about the clinical necessity of cosmetic surgery. For example, R.T. Farrior and R.C. Jarchow state that cosmetic surgery is about 'medicine and not the beauty parlor' and that 'in our society many cosmetic surgical procedures are not a luxury but are considered necessary'.[9] It would seem pertinent to wonder, however, *who* exactly is in a position to establish what is *necessary*. Susan Irvine takes up the necessity issue in her account of the increasing popularity of cosmetic surgery in the UK. She persuasively argues that it is difficult to draw the line 'between the things we all consider acceptable and the things that some of us don't', and that condemning certain forms of surgical intervention upon the body may be hypocritical in a world that takes the dyeing of grey hair and the removal of leg hairs somewhat for granted. Yet Irvine is also eager to point out that once one has entered the self-ameliorating circuit, there is a risk of not knowing where to stop – 'and the effects themselves can become addictive'. Weighing up various arguments both in favour and against cosmetic surgery, Irvine also documents the case of a patient who, having undergone a surgical facelift, ends up in a somewhat schizophrenic position: 'my face does not belong to me. . . . I used to feel young and look old. Now I look young and feel old.'[10]

The dubious delights of cosmetic surgery are sharply brought into relief by Sterling's fiction. In *Schismatrix*, Kitsune undergoes radical transformations that seem almost miraculously advantageous: 'They gave me to the surgeons,' Kitsune recalls. 'They took my womb out, and they put in brain tissue. Grafts from the pleasure centre, darling. I'm wired to the ass and the spine and the throat, and it's better than being God. When I'm hot, I sweat perfume. I'm cleaner than a fresh needle, and nothing leaves my body that you can't drink like wine or eat like candy.' However, on closer inspection it turns out that the technological manipulation of Kitsune's body has been a means of disciplining her no less than a means of enhancing her: 'they left me bright,' she observes, 'so that I would know what submission was'.[11] The gift of awareness, a potential blessing, may well amount to a curse.

Gibson often emphasizes the least appetizing aspects of cosmetic surgery by underscoring its role in the economic and sexual reification of women. He depicts a horrifying reality in which women either are subjected to surgery so as to be turned into lucrative whores or else subject themselves to prostitution so as to be able to afford expensive surgery that may enable them to pursue their dreams of success and independence. *Idoru*'s Slavic Barbies fall into the former category. Molly in *Neuromancer* and Rikki in 'Burning Chrome' typify the latter. Both Molly and Rikki raise the money that will enable them to obtain their precious implants by submitting themselves to neural cut-outs that disconnect the conscious mind from the body and thus enable them to participate in their clients' sadistic fantasies as mere *meat puppets* best suited to the unsavoury requirements of closet necrophiliacs.

It is in *Mona Lisa Overdrive* that cosmetic surgery becomes a central theme and plot device. Indeed, it operates as a potent metaphor for the blatantly iniquitous power relations that govern Gibson's universe. The novel shows that the reconstruction of the body through surgery is not merely a medical process but also, perhaps more importantly, a political and ideological phenomenon. It is by no means coincidental that the main technologically restructured body presented in *Mona Lisa Overdrive* is that of an economically powerless, politically disenfranchised and SINless (that is, lacking the single identification number that provides citizens with legal rights) young woman. Indeed, this demonstrates that it is the vulnerable body of the poor and the exploited that supplies the raw material out of which the powerful and the affluent fashion their destinies. Mona's surgical transformation serves to protect Angie, a famous and wealthy simstim star. And the need to protect Angie stems, in turn, from the greed, jealousy and insanity of a more powerful woman still, namely Lady 3Jane Tessier-Ashpool. It is ominous that behind the gruesome exploitation of a defenceless female should lie the interests of other, more influential, women. This is not to say, however, that the world portrayed in *Mona Lisa Overdrive* is a matriarchy, for Angie and 3Jane are themselves cogs in a profit-driven and deeply patriarchal corporational machine. Rather, the fact that Mona's victimization can be traced back to the agendas of two other female characters can be read as a metaphor for one of the least delectable truths about technological metamorphoses of the body – that is, the fact that the body ideals that cosmetic surgery is supposed to help us achieve are, despite their origins in predominantly male fantasies, often internalized, publicized and promoted by women themselves.

The political dimension of Mona's ordeal is conveyed in various ways. At the most basic level, she is handled like a disposable commodity by Eddie, the pimp who sells her to Gerald, the New York plastic surgeon charged with the task of turning her into a replica of Angie. Significantly, Eddie ends up dead, for, powerful as he may be in relation to Mona, he is none the less an economically insignificant pawn in the broader power game of which he has no inkling. At a further level, Mona is fed the familiar political rhetoric of freedom of choice and individual autonomy so central to the logic of capitalism and so consistently abused by its practices: 'You're having some work done. All of it reversible later, if you want, but we think you'll be pleased with the results. Very pleased.'[12] Clearly Mona has no choice, no freedom, no autonomy. As for the 'results', pleasing as they may be, they consist above all of a profound sense of dislocation and identity splitting: 'the face with bruised eyes looking at her from the other bed, nose braced with clear plastic and micropore tape, some kind of brown jelly stuff smeared back across the cheekbones ... Angie. It was Angie's face.' Unable, as yet, to connect Angie's image – her own reflection in a mirror, of course – and her body, Mona observes: 'She's so beautiful,' whereupon Gerald remarks: 'You, Mona. That's you.' At this point, the pathetic role-playing awaiting many a subject of cosmetic surgery begins: 'She looked at the face in the mirror and tried on that famous smile.'[13]

The fact that Mona gradually gains a grasp of her new identity by inspecting her features and expressions in a mirror echoes Lacan's hypotheses on the mirror phase as the stage of human development in which the child first acquires a sense of itself as a separate entity by beholding its specular reflection while simultaneously experiencing a split between the I that sees and the I that is seen. At the same time, Mona's experience highlights our dependence on the sense of sight and submission to a scrutinizing gaze: although the eyes that Mona meets in the mirror are, from a literal viewpoint, her own, they also embody, figuratively, the controlling gaze of the system that owns her body, requires it to look in a certain way, and forces it to survey itself constantly for evidence of its ability or its failure to conform to the expected image. Mona has always been an Angie Mitchell fan and many have commented on her physical resemblance to the popular simstim star. But fantasizing about being somewhat like a media icon and actually becoming her are not one and the same thing. Ultimately, like the woman cited by Irvine, Mona is left with the feeling that she is both herself and somebody else – the two selves uncomfortably locked in the same body. Her sense of displacement is heightened by the realization that, even if she decided to return to her former image, there would probably be no visible evidence for the pre-surgery Mona. Uncertain, hungry, longing for a dose of wiz and, above all, desperately lonely, Mona just does not know any more what she really wants or what she truly wishes to look like:

> She looked in the mirror. Gerald said he could put it back the way it was, someday, if she wanted him to, but then she wondered how he'd remember what she'd looked like. . . . Now she thought about it, maybe there wasn't anybody who'd remember how she'd looked before. . . . It gave her a funny feeling, like who she'd been had wandered away down the street for a minute and never come back. . . . The teeth were nice; the teeth you'd wanna keep anyway. She wasn't sure about the rest, not yet.[14]

No less crucial than cosmetic surgery are the technologies deployed by cyberculture to construct the body (especially the female one) with a focus on the issue of reproduction. The tendency to technologize the female body in the context of reproduction is borne out by consistent analogies between the biological organism and mechanical structures. In her essay on 'Anthropological Knowledge', Emily Martin supplies some classic examples of this technosomatic imagery drawn from mainstream anatomy textbooks such as Arthur Guyton's (1981) and Eliot G. Mason's (1983). Here the female body is equated to a system of control and some of its physiological processes are accordingly defined. Menopause is seen as a breakdown of central control and menstruation as a failure to reproduce on the part of an idle or disused machine.[15] At the same time as bodies are described in technological terms, machines are often invested with bodily and specifically sexual attributes. Claudia Springer has pointed out that the 'forceful energy' of the machines of the early Industrial Age has often been associated with 'virile masculinity'. On the other hand, 'ships and boats' have been linked to femininity, very possibly because of their Freudian connotations as womb-like vessels.[16] The contemporary computer is ambiguous. Indeed, electronic technology is connected with a feminine stereotype because it is silent, inconspicuous and miniaturized, with a masculine stereotype because of its amazing powers and with an asexual identity due to its bland physical appearance. Concurrently, an opposition can be observed between industrial technology as energetic, 'noisy', 'thrusting and pumping'[17] (and hence akin to conventional notions of masculinity) and electronic technology as quiet and subdued (and hence comparable to patriarchal conceptions of femininity). Springer observes that this opposition is embodied, within cyberculture, by the contrast between the phallic and hypermasculine cyborgs of popular cinema and the '"feminized" computer with its concealed, passive, and internal workings'.[18] Taking into consideration a further stereotype, the one based on the association of the female body with a troubling sense of *mystery*, it could also be argued that digital technology is metaphorically feminine to the extent that even experts find it somewhat impenetrable. As Sterling notes: 'Computers are fearsome creations, redolent of mystery and power. Even to software engineers and hardware designers, computers are, in some deep and basic sense, hopelessly baffling.'[19]

Scientific devlopments have affected deeply dominant representations of sexuality and reproduction. In the nineteenth century, people had ambivalent attitudes towards machines: they cherished the new opportunities that machines afforded but simultaneously dreaded the possibility that technology may take over their lives. The fear of the machine was often displaced onto the female body as a reproductive system. Like the machine, woman was often construed as concurrently seductive and menacing, as an uncanny being capable of generating life and yet unable to produce any meanings or values. This spawned many negative images of the female body as an overwhelming and unruly force of nature that it was incumbent upon science to restrain by systematically controlling its reproductive capacities. The stereotype of the *hysteric* was a product of these disciplinary practices. The tendency to displace the dread of technology onto the female body is clearly exemplified by Fritz Lang's classic film *Metropolis* (1926). The fear that machines may get out of hand is interwoven with the fear that female sexuality may become uncontrollable. Law and order in the city of Metropolis depend on the destruction of the lascivious robot Maria. Moreover, several science-fictional plots articulate deep-seated anxieties about women's reproductive functions by toying with the idea that male-dominated forms of *technological* reproduction may supplant *biological* reproduction. None the less, even as the female body is thus marginalized, its influence persists through many displaced references to procreation, in the disturbing forms of aliens and mutants. Horror films such as *Leviathan*, *The Fly*, *Alien* and *The Invasion of the Body Snatchers* articulate the fear of reproduction in relation to the theme of bodily invasion. They stress that bodies can be violated and contaminated at all times, and that conception and birth are always (at least potentially) synonymous with the breeding of monsters.

As Adele Clarke has commented, contemporary reproductive processes centred on techniques such as 'artificial insemination (AI) available on a limited basis since the 1930s, in vitro fertilization (IVF), embryo transfer (ET), gamete intra-fallopian transfer (GIFT), and an array of hormonal and other infertility treatments' impact directly on women's bodies and are not only instrumental to the redefinition of natural reproduction but also to a potential reconceptualization of the *raw materials* supplied by the female body.[20] Hence a series of interrelated questions must be addressed:

When will there be transplantable wombs and fallopian tubes? Which women's bodies would seem most likely as donors of wombs, tubes, life? Will families be approached to donate whole brain-dead women's 'living cadavers' to serve as free-standing wombs to be implanted via IVF? . . . Will free-standing technoscientific wombs be cyborgs?[21]

Like Clarke, Monica Casper underscores the transformations undergone by the female body as a result of technoscientific interventions. She argues that 'to talk about fetal cyborgs and technofetuses' – i.e. embryos made possible by technological practices – 'is necessarily to talk about maternal cyborgs, or what I call technomoms'.[22] The processes through which fetuses are technologically produced do not leave the so-called *natural* maternal body intact. This body may well go through all the motions *naturally* associated with pregnancy, regardless of how the baby-to-be has ended up there. Yet it is culturally pigeon-holed as a technological construct and it is accordingly monitored through sophisticated technologies of vision.

Such technologies, moreover, are also routinely brought to bear on the bodies of pregnant women who are not pregnant as a result of technoscientific interventions. Any pregnant woman's body subjected to scanning is technologized, for this practice turns her body into a technological *spectacle*: it allows 'a fetus *in utero* to be seen by those outside of a woman's uterus; these technologies transform embodied fetuses into symbolic film images'.[23] Ultrasound plays a particularly prominent role and indeed embodies a typically western addiction to fantasies of revelation and conquest. As Michael Harrison points out, ultrasound enables scientists to 'render the once opaque womb transparent, letting the light of scientific observation fall on the shy and secretive fetus'.[24] Discovery myths, Casper suggests, are sometimes allied to a related fantasy of territorial penetration. This is borne out by cases in which 'a phallic condom-covered wand is inserted into a woman's vagina' in order to produce a clearer image of what is going on inside the womb.[25] In the light of these observations, it would be preposterous to claim that the technologization of reproduction makes the body redundant. The procedures described above actually point to the centrality of the body in both its born and unborn configurations. For one thing, the fetus is increasingly ideated as a body in its own right from the earliest stages of *in utero* development. According to Alan Findlay:

The fetus is thought of nowadays not as an inert passenger in pregnancy but, rather, as in command of it. The fetus, in collaboration with the placenta, (a) ensures the endocrine success of pregnancy, (b) induces changes in maternal physiology which make her a suitable host, (c) is responsible for solving the immunological problems raised by its intimate contact with its mother, and (d) determines the duration of pregnancy.[26]

Moving from the specific discourses of cosmetic surgery and repoduction to a more panoramic examination of the impact of cyberculture on the gendered body, it is noteworthy that contrasting approaches to the relationship between technology and gender are central to some of the liveliest debates in contemporary feminist theory. Particularly important are the diverse responses to the conventional association of femininity with nature that animate such debates. Some critics contest that association by arguing that it has traditionally provided the basis for the domination of female nature by a male technocracy supported by the alliance of patriarchy and science. Others embrace the femininity—nature connection as a means of asserting an oppositional female identity, capable of counteracting the potentially tyrannical hold of male technoscience. This line has gained momentum as a result of theoretical and political trends that capitalize on the cross-pollination of gender issues and ecological issues. Carolyn Merchant, for example, argues that women's self-association with nature – in opposition to technology – may pave the way to their emancipation from 'cultural and economic constraints that have kept them subordinate to men'. In tandem, feminism and ecology may be in a position to produce a subversive critique of capitalism and of its aggressive, competitive and ultimately destructive modalities of development and progress. 'Juxtaposing the goals' of feminism and ecology 'can suggest new values and social structures, based not on the domination of women and nature as resources but on the full expression of both male and female talent and on the maintenance of environmental integrity'.[27]

The tendency to link environmental and patriarchal forms of oppression and violence is pivotal to the ethos and to the activities promoted by ecofeminism. As Maria Mies and Vandana Shiva observe, 'Wherever women acted against ecological destruction or/ and the threat of atomic annihilation, they immediately became aware of the connection between patriarchal violence against women, other people and nature.'[28] Ynestra King, one of the most

influential voices in the field, states: 'ecofeminism is about con-
nectedness and wholeness of theory and practice. It asserts the special strength and integrity of every living thing.' King lends a
spiritual/mystical flavour to the project by asserting that women are
in a privileged position to understand the violence perpetrated by
patriarchal dispensations on the natural environment: 'We have a
deep and particular understanding of this both through our natures
and our experience as women.'[29] Central to spiritual ecofeminism is
James Lovelock's *Gaia* principle, according to which the Earth is a
physical, living being. Ecofeminist critics such as Paula Gunn Allen
and Carol Christ develop this idea in eminently mythological terms
by invoking ancient and traditional images of Mother Earth as an
all-embracing Goddess.[30] By embracing these ideas, many ecofemi-
nists hope to transform the power structures of patriarchy and its
dogmatic attachment to rationalist philosophies. As Victor Margolin
points out:

> For ecofeminists, the narrative of Goddess spirituality has been a
> powerful impetus to political action. They have led and partici-
> pated in demonstrations against acid rain, the destruction of the
> rain forests, the depletion of the ozone layer, and the proliferation
> of nuclear weapons and have, as well, been involved in numerous
> other causes related to a healthy environment.[31]

Thus ecofeminism is both a form of protest against the damage done
in many camps to the earth's ecology and a means of mobilizing
women as a community. Such a community may forge a distinctive
identity for itself by cooperating with the earth's living energies.

The idealization of the earth and of women's relation to it is also a
trait of the kind of feminist science fiction that, as Joan Gordon
states, 'dreams of a pastoral world, fuelled by organic structures
rather than mechanical ones, inspired by versions of the archetypal
Great Mother'.[32] A good example of the anti-mechanical proclivities
of much feminist science fiction is Joan Slonczewski's *A Door Into
Ocean*, where the 'Shorans' use genetic engineering to shape their
world, yet refuse mechanical forms of engineering disassociated
from the organism.[33] Another example is Joanna Russ's *The Female
Man*, where people who could benefit from teleportation would
rather walk. Their world, 'Whileaway', is in many ways the product
of arcadian nostalgia. However, Russ's novel also presents a picture

of femininity that departs from the stereotype of the nurturing woman longing to strengthen her connections with an idealized matriarchal past. In the opening section, in particular, we are presented with a 'female man' named Janet who is loving and caring but also familiar with violence: 'I love my daughter . . . I love my family . . . I love my wife . . . I've fought four duels. I've killed four times.'[34]

Many feminist critics acknowledge technology's inevitability. Others go even further and encourage women to side with technology, in the belief that, as long as women either passively regard technology as oppressive or actively rebel against it by embracing nature, they merely perpetuate the faulty logic of essentialism: namely, the approach that links the *essence* of femininity to nature, and that of masculinity to science. For these critics, there is nothing to be gained from the claim that women have a *special* connection with nature. In fact, such a claim may only serve the interests of a metaphysical system that positions women as objects trapped in a *natural condition*. Rosi Braidotti argues that technology should neither be inscribed as women's enemy nor be idealized as their ally. Both technophobia and technophilia are blinkered attitudes. Technophobia is likely to amount to the 'fatal attraction of nostalgia', to a 'flight' that 'has the immediate effect of neglecting by sheer denial the transition from a humanistic to a posthuman world'. Technophilia may turn out to be equally limited if it merely amounts to a 'phantasy of multiple re-embodiments', the idea that cybertech opens up a Cockaigne of endless self-reinvention at no cost. One bemoans the loss of a golden age that has plausibly never obtained; the other celebrates the advent of a golden age that will plausibly never obtain. What Braidotti proposes, as an alternative, is a confrontation of the 're-locations for cultural practice' fostered by postmodernity that neither 'mourn the loss of humanistic certainties' nor relish the kaleidoscopic promises of 'polymorphous re-embodiments'. Feminist philosophy informed by postmodernist approaches to the phenomenon of embodiment has much to contribute to the understanding of those *re-locations*. According to Braidotti, the key contribution consists of simultaneously asserting and debunking certain validated signifying practices:

> [T]he new is created by revisiting and burning up the old. Like the totemic meal recommended by Freud, you have to assimilate the dead before you can move on to a new order. We need rituals of

burial and mourning for the dead, including and especially the ritual of burial of the Woman that was. . . . The answer to metaphysics is metabolism, that is to say a new embodied becoming.[35]

Ultimately, addressing women's relation to technology does not amount to severing the tie between the female body and nature but is rather a means of *denaturalizing* certain dogmatic conceptions of nature and the natural. This process has led to a radical interrogation of three interrelated notions: (1) the naturalness of reproductive processes; (2) the naturalness of biological life; (3) the naturalness of the boundary between the natural and the technological. According to Marilyn Strathern, new reproductive technologies do not 'interfere with nature' but actually with 'the very idea of a natural fact': that is, they force us to reassess the distinction between supposedly natural and cultural phenomena.[36] Michelle Stanworth subscribes to this problematization of the concept of the natural:

> [T]he attempt to reclaim motherhood as a female accomplishment should not mean giving the natural priority over the technological – that pregnancy is natural and good, technology unnatural and bad. It is not at all clear what a 'natural' relationship to our fertility, our reproductive capacity, would look like.[37]

Sarah Franklin draws attention to the interplay of the biological and the technological in the development of human life by focusing on the image of the fetus as an autonomous *sitter* of *portraits* taken by endoscopic means, its autonomy underlined by the mother's absence from such images and by the invisibility of the invasive tools for visualization.[38] How could biological growth be described as wholly *natural* when even the tiniest form can be the object of cultural constructions and digital imaging?

GENDER ROLES IN CYBERPUNK

Cyberpunk's approach to gender roles is highly ambiguous, for it appears both to perpetuate and to subvert stereotypical representations of masculinity and femininity. This ambiguity is borne out by conflicting interpretations of the gender and sexual attributes of some of cyberpunk's best-known characters. Nicola Nixon, for example, describes Gibson's females as 'depoliticized and sapped of any revolutionary energy'.[39] Timothy Leary totally disagrees with Nixon's reading and celebrates those characters as 'strong, independent' and 'heroic'.[40] Joan Gordon, less euphorically and perhaps more persuasively than Leary, also argues that cyberpunk's representations of femininity are often positive:

> At first glance it [cyberpunk] seems to be overtly masculinist science fiction – men are men, waving guns and knives, competing like all getout and plugged up to the gills with pollutant technology. But look at the women in mirrorshades – Molly in Gibson's *Neuromancer*, Deadpan Allie in Cadigan's *Mindplayers*, for instance – aren't they tougher than the rest? I would suggest that cyberpunk is covert feminist science fiction. On that night foray into the underworld which is the central experience of ... cyberpunk, men and women travel as equals.[41]

Gibson's *Virtual Light* amusingly comments on the stereotyping tendencies of certain gender polarizations fostered by technology. Describing Rydell's enthusiastic response to computer imaging as 'a kid in high school', faced with the challenge of sculpting 'things out of nothing, out of that cloud of pixels or polygons or whatever they were', the narrator observes: 'the girls were always doing these unicorns and rainbows and things, and Rydell liked to do cars, kind of dream-cars, like he was some designer in Japan somewhere and he could build anything he wanted'.[42] The irony, here, lies with the fact that the girls' overtly fantastic constructs are not, after all, that different from Rydell's ideations, given the latter's own fantastic character. The courier responsible for the delivery of the virtual glasses containing plans for the urbanistic metamorphosis of San Francisco is himself hooked to a digital dream – that of the woman he encounters through another pair of virtual glasses in a white house, among candles and wine, night after night over many long and lonesome years.[43] When he steps out of this fantasy world to have a go at real sex, he makes fatal blunders: for one thing, as the heroine Chevette is quick to realize, he has got 'asshole' written all over him – and violent death is his reward.[44]

In *Neuromancer*, Case is – potentially – a reincarnation of the macho crook of classic crime fiction, yet he never conveys an image of triumphant masculinity. He is symbolically emasculated by mycotoxin, a fungal poison developed by the Russians as a warfare weapon that blocks his ability to access the matrix, and later injected with endorphin inhibitors meant by his tormentors to make him experience as much pain as possible. Case's mental atrophy, emotional dislocation and physical frailty do precious little to evoke impressions of virility. At one point, his scrambled consciousness is aptly mirrored by his surroundings, a waiting room decorated with genuinely surrealist gusto: 'A pair of bulbous Disney-styled table lamps perched awkwardly on a low Kandinsky-look coffee table in scarlet-lacquered steel. A Dali clock hung on the wall ... its distorted face sagging to the bare concrete floor.'[45]

Molly's gender connotations are also ambivalent. Reminiscent of the *tough dame* of that mean-street genre traceable back to Chandler's crime fiction, she may alternatively be read as an image of the liberated woman or as a stereotype. It is up to the individual reader, ultimately, to decide what to make of the kind of *toughness* displayed in a passage like the following:

'Because you try to fuck around with me, you'll be taking one of the stupidest chances of your whole life.'
She held out her hands, palms up, the white fingers slightly spread, and with a barely audible click, ten double-edged scalpel blades slid from their housing beneath the burgundy nails.
She smiled. The blades slowly withdrew.[46]

Molly is described as a *working girl*, which in this context could mean a *street samurai* or even a ninja, namely a tenacious fighter (in Japanese history, a samurai was a defender of feudal lords and a ninja a member of a related group of less honorable repute). But Molly's title also reflects the fact that she has been a prostitute and indeed one of rather a special kind. As hinted at earlier, her task was to cater to the desires of sadists who enjoyed doing things to her while she was switched to a software programme and neurally cut out. Molly has pursued this unpalatable career so as to be able to pay for enhancing surgery leading, most famously, to mirrorshade implants and the insertion of those retractable and lethal fingernails. Molly's vulnerability is emphasized by the fact that she has suffered more acutely than other women in the same trade due to an incompatibility between the 'cut-out chip' implanted in her body to ensure she cannot be aware of or remember what is done to her by her clients and the 'circuitry' implanted by the 'Chiba clinics' where she undergoes regular surgery.[47] She starts remembering, eventually wakes up in the course of a particularly gory routine, is sacked and threatened with death. Molly's boss, it turns out, was planning to have her killed by a client as part of a state-of-the-art 'snuff' performance, faithful to a sadistic tradition that associates sexual pleasure with the killing of women and with necrophilic urges generally.

The theme of necrophilia can be related to a widespread tendency in western literature and art (especially noticeable since the nineteenth century) to interweave sexuality and death. According to Rudolph Binion, death is 'a piquant aphrodisiac', fuelled by necrophilic fantasies in both explicit and covert ways, which in the latter part of the twentieth century has pervaded not only high art but also various forms of mass culture.[48] The coupling of eroticism and death with an overt emphasis on necrophilic impulses has also been a means of constructing compelling gender stereotypes. This idea is exhaustively documented by Elizabeth Bronfen in *Over Her Dead Body*, by reference to the recurring topos of the lifeless female as an object of intense sexual yearnings. 'The aesthetic representation of death,' Bronfen maintains, 'lets us repress our knowledge of the reality of death.' When death is staged on the female body, its representation allows the viewer to repress not only the reality of death but also the sense of threat associated with femininity as 'the superlative site of alterity'.[49]

Molly's sexual exploitation and her encoding as an aesthetic representation of death may seem to endow her with a stereotypically passive identity. However, though physically and psychologically objectified according to the direst of patriarchal expectations, Molly is also sexually dominant and, in intercourse with Case, described as more competent and active than her partner.[50] Of course, it could be argued that even the image of an assertive and both sexually and professionally independent woman may contribute to the perpetuation of patriarchal stereotypes. Arguably, the reason for this type of woman being popular among male consumers of action fiction is that she incarnates the ideal of a hard, sealed and thoroughly technologized female body and is thus able to counteract the sense of threat traditionally associated with the soft, leaky and unbounded natural body of woman. Yet Molly's power should not be underestimated. Evidence for its scope is supplied by the fact that, in physically possessing Case, she is also instrumental to the surfacing of potent mental impressions in his confounded self: sex with Molly resuscitates in Case pictures of a lost cyberspace – 'his orgasm flaring blue in a timeless space, a vastness like the matrix'.[51] Molly's competence is also subtly conveyed throughout the novel by various descriptive details (not always overtly sexual but none the less erotic) which could alternatively be interpreted as a means of consolidating the negative stereotype of the castrating heroine or as assertions of her cold-blooded flair: just consider the image of Molly 'dissecting her crab with alarming ease', shortly followed by an even more menacing display of table manners: 'Molly . . . extruded the blade from her index finger, and speared a grayish slab of herring.'[52] Note also that Molly does not *cry*: her tearducts have been routed back into her mouth, so that if she feels like crying she *spits* instead.[53]

Molly has influenced subsequent fictional heroines, particularly Elektra in the comic book series *Elektra Assassin*, by Frank Miller and Bill Sienkiewicz,[54] and Abhor in Kathy Acker's *Empire of the Senseless*. The latter novel uses cyberpunk themes and imagery to speculate about the possibility of dismantling patriarchal ideology – the 'father' in all his material and metaphorical incarnations – through a sustained violation of all conceivable taboos. *Empire of the Senseless* is eerily utopian in its conception of an alternative world, attainable by stealing data from 'The Man'. The likelihood of achieving this objective is sustained by Abhor's cyborg determination: 'All I know is we're looking for a certain construct. Somewhere. Nothing else matters.' Yet the world presented by Acker is also a harrowing dystopia in which 'desire and pain're the same', where people are routinely subjected to 'neurological and hormonal damage' leading to syndromes more lethal than AIDS, where cities resemble gaping wounds in which 'poverty was writhing in pink', and where 'imagination was both a dead business and the only business left to the dead': 'In such a world which was non-reality terrorism made a lot of sense.'[55] As Andrew Ross points out, both Abhor and Elektra are 'steely, orphanesque survivors of a history of victimage that includes paternal rape, followed by repeated sexual predation on the part of violent males'.[56] The character of Swish in John Shirley's 'Wolves of the Plateau' is another striking example of an abused female, virtually destroyed by paternal repudiation. She is rather disturbingly portrayed as 'a woman with an unsightly growth, errant glands that were like tumours to her'. Her condition is the effect of the consumption of inordinate amounts of an artificial drug and her addiction, in turn, is the result of the longing 'to dampen the pain of an infinite self-derision that mimicked her father's utter rejection of her'.[57] Sarah in W.J. Williams's *Hardwired* is likewise portrayed as a victim of paternal abuse who, like Gibson's Molly, develops into a fatal killer by means of surgical enhancement. Ironically, for a character harshly oppressed by patriarchy, Sarah's main weapon is a 'cybersnake': an overtly phallic device that springs out of her mouth to assault her prey.[58]

VIRTUAL SEX

Issues at stake in debates about the impact of cyberculture on the body – especially the gendered one – are further problematized by the eroto-electronics of virtual sex. Virtual sex is supposed to be contact-free and therefore totally safe. This is no doubt good news from a medical perspective. However, this pre-emptive definition also makes virtual sex disappointingly anticlimactic. If it is prescriptively commendable on the basis of its aseptic virtues, what else may be expected of it in terms of physical gratification? Yet virtual sex is not ultimately reducible to a decarnalized experience. It does not point to the body's obsolescence but rather to the necessity of rethinking the body as an erotic entity. Like virtual sex, Gibson's cyberpunk explores alternative forms of sexual intercourse. Consider, as illustrative examples, the following passages:

After the third margarita their hips were touching, and something was spreading through him in slow orgasmic waves. It was sticky where they were touching; an area the size of the heel of his thumb where the cloth had parted. He was two men: the one inside fusing with her in total cellular communion, and the shell who sat casually on a stool at the bar, elbows on either side of his drink, fingers toying with a swizzle stick. Smiling benignly into space. Calm in the cool dimness. And once, but only once, some distant worrisome part of him made Coretti glance down to where soft-ruby tubes pulsed, tendrils tipped with sharp lips worked in the shadows between them. Like the joining tentacles of two strange anemones.[59]

Her nails were lacquered black ... the lacquer only a shade darker than the carbon-fiber laminate that sheathes my arm. And her hand went down the arm, black nails tracing a weld in the laminate, down to the black anodized elbow joint, out to the wrist, her hand soft-knuckled as a child's, fingers spreading to lock over mine, her palm against the perforated Duralumin.[60]

These extracts from Gibson's short stories 'The Belonging Kind' and 'Burning Chrome' draw attention to alternative forms of sexuality which bring into play organs other than the genitals: hybrid organs reminiscent of mythical shapes, on the one hand, and prosthetic adjuncts, on the other. In both cases, we are presented with an eroticism in which pleasure and horror are inextricably intertwined, as the abject, the tabooed and the sublime meet and merge in mutual suffusion. These alternative versions of sexual intercourse point not to the demise of the body but rather to the necessity of extending conventional notions of desire and pleasure into hitherto forbidden territories. This necessity has been highlighted by J.G. Ballard:

> I believe that organic sex, body against body, skin area against skin area, is becoming no longer possible. . . . What we're getting is a whole new order of sexual fantasies, involving a different order of experiences, like car crashes, like traveling in jet aircraft, the whole overlay of new technologies, architecture, interior design, communications, transport, merchandizing. These things are beginning to reach into our lives and change the interior design of our sexual fantasies.[61]

In other words, the collusion of technology and sexuality does not automatically amount to the demise of erotic and bodily experiences. Rather, it demands a reassessment of conventional notions of both desire and fulfilment. As Claudia Springer argues, such a reassessment may only be undertaken in the light of an ironical grasp of technology, as 'a contradictory discursive position, representing both escape from the body and fulfilment of erotic desire'.[62] Gibson, moreover, blurs the distinction between erotic objects and financial objects by enlisting the same forms of advanced technology to the pursuit of sexual pleasure and economic gain. In *Virtual Light*, for instance, Gibson plays with two pairs of cyberglasses: one pair offers scope for virtual sex, the other yields a plan to remap San Francisco to huge financial advantage. What's the difference?

Ostensibly incorporeal, clean and safe, cybereroticism actually requires a merging of biological bodies and machines that is intensely physical, for it forces its users to confront the uncertainty of their boundaries and the ambiguity of all sexual and gender roles. Virtual sex may seem to make the body obsolete by replacing physical contact with digitally simulated intercourse. Nevertheless, it does not take place in a vacuum. Its users are required to adopt certain bodies, or forms of embodiment, in order to interact with their simulated partners. Thus, virtual sex does not take the body away but actually multiplies its users' experiences of embodiment, to the point that, as stated in *Susie Bright's Sexual Reality*, 'you could look like anything and be any gender or combination of genders you want. There's no particular reason for you even to be a person.'[63] The whole sensorium is brought into play by the digital tools designed to aid virtual sex, and their sexual connotations are consistently underscored. Consider, for example, the image of the virtual 'bodysuit' presented by Howard Rheingold: 'something like a body stocking, but with the kind of intimate smugness of a condom' and with 'an array of intelligent sensor-effectors' embedded in its inner surface.[64] Karlin Lillington confirms the importance of tactile perception in the dynamics of cybersex:

> Aficionados of VR erotica are waiting for 'teledildonics', the ability to interact not just visually but through touch with a 3D computerized playmate. Already, the technology exists to create a 3D replica of a live model, who could be explicitly animated. . . . Add skin and texture to the model and you could have a virtual clone. . . . A research team in Germany has produced a prototype full-body sensory suit for virtual sex. The technology is clumsy now, but that's predicted to change.[65]

Pat Cadigan ironically underscores the physical character of virtual sex in *Tea from an Empty Cup*, where some users – very unromantically dubbed 'sexers' – are said to get so 'heated up' that they end up hurting themselves in the course of simulated stimulation. An especially amusing case is that of 'this one blowfish' who 'cut himself on the straps, broke some ribs'. The '*cute* part' of the accident turns out to be that his partner 'broke the *exact, same ribs*' at precisely 'the *exact, same time*'. Cadigan is here taking to farcical extremes the idea that the body is not suppressed by cybersex, for simulated stimulation can lead to prominently physical responses.[66]

The complexity of cybereroticism is further attested by the

existence of computer services that, while not being overtly sexual, still rely on an ethos of seduction and penetration. A case in point is the provision for businessmen of 'cyberhostesses' designed to help them make their public images more seductive and to penetrate the market in incisive ways. Intimacy and flirtatiousness are primary ingredients in the electronic dialogue between the businessman and his cyberhostess. Rachel Baker describes the cyberhostess as a 'digital "personal assistant"' that 'will cater for a person's information requirements' and make the user's 'needs and desires . . . public by logging them onto a sophisticated, commercially available database'. The cyberhostess is expected to help her guest project his personal identity onto the outside world in such a way that his most intimate characteristics 'become coordinated and accessible to devices and services'.[67] It is by no means coincidental that the digital assistant should be encoded as female. Indeed, it is pretty obvious that the businessman keen on fashioning an alluring and penetrating self-image is supposed to have greater chances of success if his efforts are supported by the conventions of a flirtatious boss—secretary relationship. Baker illustrates the growing cult of the cyberhostess with close reference to the services provided by 'Personal Data Fairy' (PDF), an Internet and data-marketing initiative that invites users to construct concurrently technological and mythological roles for themselves; the refrains used by the PDF's 'Cyberhostess Marketing Proposal' are indeed: 'be your own propagandist' and 'perpetuate your own myth'. The PDF demonstrates the importance of gender roles in the deployment of digital ventures and, at the same time, emphasizes an enduring fascination with the erotic body in both economic and psychological terms. The female character created as a means of guiding the ambitious man through the Internet is first expected to 'engage the client in intimate, personal conversations via e-mail'. As a corollary of this preliminary strategy, the hostess will develop her own 'character traits' and these will 'gradually become unique and personal to each client'. Ultimately, a truly professional hostess will be not only 'reliable' and 'thoughtful' but also 'entertaining', 'unpredictable' and above all 'seductive – will play with you and reveal herself over time' as a 'sexy, intimate female guide'.[68] Self-promoting and marketing tactics of an electronic kind could hardly exhibit erotic connotations in a more explicit fashion. Although the cyberhostess clearly does not exist as a meat-and-bones body, her virtual physicality is pivotal to her and her guest's professional success. Technological through and through, the digital assistant cannot, however, be interpreted as a purely artificial figure; nor can the eroticism she conveys be read as exclusively robotic.

Gibson, likewise, stresses that sex based on the interplay of the human and the technological is not *totally* mechanical, for powerful bodily energies are incessantly at work/at play. According to Sadie Plant, cybersex heralds 'a merging which throws the one-time individual into a pulsing network of switches which is neither climactic, clean, nor secure'.[69] Cyberpunk makes this patent by underscoring the sexual act's inevitable implication with the *meat* that its heroes are supposed to long to escape, and the association of intercourse with a sense of mystery:

> It was a place he'd known before; not everyone could take him there, and somehow he always managed to forget it. Something he'd found and lost so many times. It belonged, he knew – he remembered – as she pulled him down, to the meat, the flesh the cowboys mocked. It was a vast thing, beyond knowing, a sea of information coded in spiral and pheromone, infinite intricacy that only the body, in its strong blind way, could ever read.[70]

The fact that 'only the body' is capable of *reading* the 'sea of information' discharged by sexual intercourse underscores the enduring powers of the flesh. Moreover, a key word in the extract quoted above is 'remembered'. Remembering does not simply signify *recalling* data. It also means *introjecting* codes that are meant to give us a coherent identity. We retain a cultural and social self as long as we are able to remember how we are expected to act, think and feel. To this extent, *remembering* is also *re-membering*: producing a *whole* body out of the scattered limbs of western history. Its most inveterate antagonist is *dis-membering*, the processes through which the self is fragmented and dispersed. Gibson embraces the ethos of dismemberment: like Frankenstein's creature, Gibson's bodies stand out as the *disjecta membra* of a culture in which the light of scientific reason is insistently shadowed by dark and forbidding forces. The portmanteau title of Gibson's best-known novel is replete with these connotations. 'Neuromancer' hints at a romance plot and simultaneously invests the idea of romance with ambiguous undertones, the 'neu[ro]' prefix suggesting in one breath ideas of novelty (*new* romancer), psychological disturbance (*neurotic* romancer), magic (neuromancer/*necromancer*) and taboo (neuromancer/necromancer/ *necrophiliac*).

Furthermore, *Neuromancer* challenges the cultural codes that define individuals in sexual terms, as *either* active *or* passive. In the virtual interactions between Molly and Case, Case experiences things through Molly's body and thus catches a glimpse of what it might be like to be a woman. He realizes 'just how tight those jeans really are' and finds the 'passivity of the situation irritating'. At the same time, passivity is displaced from the female to the male body, as Molly is in a position to produce powerful tactile impressions without Case being able to reciprocate: 'she slid a hand into her jacket, a fingertip circling a nipple under warm silk. The sensation made him catch his breath. She laughed. But the link was one-way. He had no way to reply.'[71] Moreover, cyberpunk shows that, in accessing cyberspace, console cowboys both protract a myth of patriarchal dominance and are rendered impotent by their absorption in a disorienting array of data. As Deborah Lupton observes, 'For their male users . . . computers are to be possessed, to be penetrated and overpowered. . . . This masculinist urge to penetrate the system . . . represents an attempt to split oneself from the controlling mother.' Yet once the user has jacked into the matrix (which, by the way, means *womb*), the dominant feeling is not a sense of absolute control but rather one of 'engulfment', induced by the architectural complexity of the matrix as a whole and by the local geography of 'the inside of the computer body' as 'dark, enigmatic, potentially leaky, harbouring danger and contamination, vulnerable to invasion'.[72]

Neither cyberpunk nor cyberculture generally is unproblematically dominated by patriarchal imperatives. If there is a danger of cyberspace services perpetuating male myths of spatial conquest (as evinced by computer games based on a veritable obsession with mapmaking), it is also the case that women have both actively contributed to the construction of Net structures that address specifically feminine issues and developed their own distinctive versions of virtual reality. A particularly interesting case is *Osmose*, a virtual space developed by Char Davies (Director of Visual Research at Softimage, Montreal) and her team in the mid- to late 1990s. *Osmose* is based on a multilayered architecture comprising twelve interrelated levels: the Grid; the Clearing; the Forest; the Leaf; the Subterranean World; the Code World; the Pond; the Abyss; the Life-World; the Cloud; the Text World; the Ending. Natural forms and ideas characterized by a sense of non-linearity and flux play an important part in the system's overall structure. This emphasis on fluidity could itself be regarded as one of *Osmose*'s distinctively feminine traits. However, Davies and her team are no more interested in themes than they are in the physical functioning of their virtual construct. The phallic joysticks often used as means of navigational control in virtual reality are replaced, in *Osmose*, by overtly corporeal strategies. Variations in the immersant's experiences depend on her/his breathing patterns and rhythms: inhaling enables one to float upward and exhaling to descend. Body balance is also crucial, as modifications in one's centre of balance allow changes of direction. Davies's aim is to produce the feel of a smooth and supple environment unfettered by rigid maps, in which the body is accorded primary importance:

I believe that it is only through the body, through body-centred interfaces (rather than devices manipulated at arm's length) that we can truly access this space and explore its potential. Such emphasis on the body's essential role in immersive virtual space may be inherently female. The whole notion of space enveloping a body at its centre is probably feminine.[73]

CHAPTER 5

CYBERPUNK AND THE CITY

> The ceaseless transformation of the city into the post-
> human. Piles of ruin are continually tunnelled and
> reformed into an equation of billboards . . . as the body
> becomes a sum total of cosmetic surgery and replace-
> ment parts as the outfit to fulfil any desire.
>
> (Thom Jurek)[1]

Like the biological, erotic body, the body of the cybercity combines
materiality and immateriality. Digital technology tends to ideate the
city in immaterial terms as an abstract map or network of computer-
processed data. At the same time, however, contemporary cities are
very material indeed: crammed with ever-expanding and ever-
changing architectural structures, teeming with bodies and vehicles,
packed with commodities of all sorts. In cyberpunk, space is often
conceived of in immaterial terms as a product of the electronic mapping of abstract data. Yet its cities are emphatically material. The
mounting waste of desolate urban sites, the pervasiveness of crime
and disease, and the enduring fascination held by relics from bygone
ages underscore the cybercity's corporeal dimension.

Thus, while 'the young male protagonists of Gibson's tales live
for the exhilaration of the Net,' observes Nigel Clark, the main
'attraction of their fictional universe lies in the sensory richness and
complexity of the landscape *outside* the cybernetic realm . . . ter-
rains in which vibrant new signifying surfaces are layered over the
detritus of obsolescent forms'.[2] John Christie likewise points to the
material attributes of Gibson's settings – 'the meticulous superficiality', 'the texture of multi-media reference', the 'interest in
degenerative and pathological forms of capital' – as their most
appealing characteristics.[3] Fredric Jameson elaborates on the

economic significance of the sprawling and decidedly postmodern nature of Gibson's cities as the monstrous body of multinational corporations: all-encompassing systems that relentlessly engulf a feeble multitude of individual bodies. Gibson's 'technological bazaar' is 'sealed into an inside without an outside' which transforms 'the formerly urban' into 'the unmappable system of late capitalism itself'.[4]

SCIENCE AND SPACE

What does cyberpunk share with postmodern visualizations of space? What contemporary scientific perspectives are most relevant to its geographies? These questions may at least partially be answered by assessing the ideological and psychological significance of *maps*. Geographical maps are the product of complex practices aiming at rationalizing the world in systematic ways. No map is ever fully faithful, for maps fix into stable images worlds that are actually constantly changing. However, maps are often *presented* as accurate and reliable in order to lend a sense of permanence to human experiences of both space and time. Maps are metaphors, figures or tropes and should not, therefore, be confused with literal reality. Yet they claim to embody natural aspects of the world and it is on the basis of this claim that they repeatedly become *fetishes*, idealized objects of attraction. As Donna Haraway comments:

> Geographical maps can, but need not, be fetishes in the sense of appearing nontropic, metaphor-free representations, more or less accurate, of previously existing, 'real' properties of a world that are waiting patiently to be plotted. Instead, maps are models of worlds crafted through and for specific practices of intervening and particular ways of life. . . . The maps are fetishes in so far as they enable a specific kind of mistake that turns process into nontropic, real, literal things inside containers.[5]

Maps may be fetishized as rational grids exempt from the disruptive operations of rhetoric. Yet, as Gustav Metzger observes, they are products of specific ideological programmes, regardless of the degree of scientific accuracy to which may lay claim. For instance:

> The 'T-in-O' maps were more statements of faith rather than a

description of the world – they anchored faith. They described faith, they produced a feeling of security within the believers. The Hubble photographs support similar functions. Out there in the indescribable galaxies is a world so inhospitable to humanity that the imagination freezes. The Hubble photographs bring that immensity within our grasp, and so give a measure of comfort; ease a transition towards the new. . . . Maps and globes have always been more than merely descriptive. They are articles of faith, advancing the nation and culture producing them. They are weapons in a geopolitical endeavour.[6]

Maps are deconstructive (namely, self-dismantling) texts. They are abstract constructs based on the selection of details that pertain to a contingent geographical situation. Yet, as D.R. Fraser Taylor points out, they ask to be taken as 'holistic' representations of 'geographical reality' and hence as objective pictures.[7] Maps are concurrently supposed to provide relevant and referentially accurate descriptions of the here-and-now and to transcend their contingent contexts by pointing to a universal reality or nature. As argued in the previous chapter, developments in contemporary science have questioned conventional notions of objectivity and universality by displacing the very concept of *nature*. For example, research into the human genome has transformed traditional views on the body as a natural whole and thus produced an alternative *map*. In Haraway's words:

> 'Life', materalized as information and signified by the gene, displaces 'Nature', preeminently embodied in and signified by old-fashioned organisms. . . . [T]he genome, the totality of genes in an organism, is not a whole in the traditional, 'natural' sense but a congeries of entities that are themselves autotelic and self-referential.[8]

As the fantasy of the body as a coherent and unified organism is exploded, we are reminded that no map, no spatial organization of either people or objects, ever constitutes a unity. Nick Land brings this point home by exposing the metaphysical principle of spatial unity as fallacious: ' "Space is essentially one" (Kant). Kant lies.'[9]

In all its aspects, the spatial body portrayed by cyberpunk is a hybrid compound of often puzzling details, assembled in a surreal fashion. As already argued, it consistently combines technological, biological and fantastic elements. Charlie Blake confirms:

> [H]uman neuro-systems can be downloaded long after their corporeal vessels have ceased to function – only to be retrieved, like unwilling ghosts . . . . [C]yberspace is haunted not only by the voodoo gods and virtual zombies of a pre-millennial age . . . but by vampires, shape-shifters and chimeras of every conceivable kind.[10]

This breach of conventional boundaries also characterizes contemporary technoscience. Indeed, many of its projects do not appear to conform to the constraints of the natural world. Rather, they simulate realities of their own conception by extracting increasingly minute elements from the natural world – such as neurons and quarks – and by processing their data by reference to increasingly minute temporal scales – nanoseconds, picoseconds, femtoseconds. These minimalized elements are then reassembled into structures that are not perceivable *as such* in the visible world. These structures are always narrative and precarious for, as Jeanette Winterson points out: 'What we know does not satisfy us. What we know constantly reveals itself as partial. What we know, generation by generation, is discarded into new knowings which in turn slowly cease to interest us.'[11]

Technoscience works with partial epistemologies and tentative hypotheses. Its main task, as Jean-François Lyotard suggests, may well consist of a 'search for instabilities', for possibilities that inevitably stretch beyond the bounds of determinism and predictability. These often amount to 'a multiplicity of absolutely incompatible statements', which may 'only be made compatible if they are relativized in relation to a scale chosen by the speaker'.[12] In its relative indeterminacy, technoscience also interrogates the relationship between parts and wholes by making the *isolated detail* and the *holistic assemblage* alternately predominant. Indeed, while focusing on the tiniest components of a system, it simultaneously stresses that what is ultimately most tantalizing is not the individual detail itself so much as the unimaginably complex assemblages to which the detail alludes. This position is paradigmatically advocated by Edward de Bono, who argues that in the scientific analysis of systems:

... a detailed examination of the components will not, by itself, be very helpful any more than a detailed examination of a building stone will give a picture of the architecture of Venice. The organization of the system is as important, or more important, than the actual components.[13]

Felix Guattari likewise emphasizes the importance of the assemblage by maintaining that 'today's information and communication machines do not merely convey representational contents, but also contribute to the fabrication of new *assemblages* of enunciation, individual and collective'.[14]

The idea of the assemblage as a way of describing and representing space has also been invoked by recent developments in the visual arts. SCI-ART, for instance, focuses on the relationship between science and space, specifically the space of the human body as a map that, like the city, combines natural and artificial elements. SCI-ART capitalizes on the interplay of medical imaging, pharmaceutical science, artificial intelligence and genetics, and codes derived from photography, film, multimedia installations and fashion design, to explore the relationship between the physical body, the technologies that relentlessly impact upon it, and its artistic representation. Intriguing examples of SCI-ART cited by Tim Johnson in a review of one of its exhibitions include Susie Freeman's *Recoil*, where a 'contraceptive coil is shown against a ball gown' on which '6,550 contraceptive pills' have been sewn, in order 'to show the sheer substance of drugs needed to provide equivalent protection'; *One For The Road*, where 'the simplicity of an artificial hip joint is displayed next to a fabric of pockets containing a total of 10,000 pills – an estimation of the quantity of drugs a patient would require without such a replacement'; Richard Brown and Igor Aleksander's *Biotica*, a project that 'uses the technology of neural networks and virtual reality to create computer forms that explore Aleksander's ideas on how life controls itself and how we define it'; and *The Painter's Eye Movements*, a science/art collaboration initiated by the cognitive psychologist John Tchalenko, where the detailed examination of eye movement and brain activity in the painter Humphrey Ocean at work seeks to establish in what ways a skilled artist's brain workings differ from those of 'unskilled control subjects'.[15] SCI-ART thus foregrounds the processes through which we are constituted as interdisciplinary 'assemblages of enunciation' (to return to Guattari's words), while creating its own provocative assemblages.

Cyberpunk writers are equally attracted to the detail and to the assemblage in their representations of urban space. The aesthetic and psychological impact of their sprawling megalopolises derives from both a keen eye for the minutiae of setting and architecture and a concern with the multifarious ways in which these fragments coalesce into various compounds: the all-engulfing structures of multinational economies, the corporate identities of subcultural groups and, of course, the system of the matrix itself. Cyberpunk's cities come across simultaneously as boundless territories in which both human beings and objects endlessly circulate as so many fragmentary commodities and sealed conglomerates whose boundaries serve to protect the interests of privileged ranks. Cyberpunk thus suggests that space is not necessarily *either* sealed *or* boundless but rather *both* sealed *and* boundless at one and the same time. Research into the relationship between different ways of theorizing and representing space and different ways of constructing scientific knowledge yields a comparable message.

According to Emily Martin, western culture exhibits three main ways of charting space: the *citadel*, the *rhizome* and the *string figure*. The citadel is predicated on walls, on principles of impregnability and self-contained professionalism; it is the domain of specialists 'encased in a culture of their own ... one that has little to do with anything outside it. The walls of the citadel (seen from this perspective) are left intact.' However, the citadel is also rendered permeable by science's need to communicate with non-specialist audiences: 'We see how the making of facts, and the resources necessary to make them, depend on gathering allies in many places. Scientists must travel about into government agencies, manufacturing concerns, press offices, and publishing houses.'[16] The rhizome, a virtually boundless map charting the interplay of culture and science, is the model that follows from the recognition of the citadel's precariously delimited geography/architecture. The awareness that the 'walls of the citadel are porous and leaky' – for 'inside is not pure knowledge, outside is not pure ignorance' – is precisely what ushers in the rhizome as an alternative configuration. The rhizome has the obvious advantages of fluidity and openness: its space resembles a Borgesian world of multiforking paths which disqualifies the very concept of mapping. Yet this model, despite its emphasis on the endless ramifications of the culture—science relationship, has its limitations: it is 'too solid, monolithic ... slow-moving'.[17] The third type of map, the string figure, further complicates the scenario inaugurated by the rhizome, by generating, according to Jennifer Rich and Michael Menser, 'a conceptual telescoping of the shifting cartographies of science and culture'.[18] The string figure suggests that ramifications and bifurcations of the kind proposed by the rhizome *do* form maps and that such maps keep mutating at a staggering rate. Patterns are created so as to highlight their ephemerality and this condition of impermanence, in turn, may only be adequately documented through the creation of patterns. The citadel toys with maps based on the possibility of clear demarcations. The rhizome dispenses with maps in the service of sprawling undifferentiation. The string figure, for its part, acknowledges the role of maps as omnipresent yet transient constructs. In other words, the string figure proposes that, instead of negating the existence of maps, it would be more fruitful to take their pervasiveness on board as entities that are incessantly made and unmade.

On the scientific plane, the string figure alludes to a model for the possible relationship between energy and matter. Strings are 'linear distributions of mass-energy' which, according to John Barrow:

> ... could arise during a particular type of change in the material state of the universe during the first moments of the universe's expansion from the Big Bang. . . . They would exist as a network of tubes of energy which gradually become stretched and straightened by the expansion of the universe. . . . [Strings] arise because underlying symmetries of nature break in disconnected ways in different parts of space and these linear or sheet-like structures form at the boundaries between regions of different symmetry.[19]

These hypotheses have been developed by the Superstring theory put forward by Michael Green.[20] Such theories are based on the assumption that the basic elements of matter are not zero-dimensional points but rather linear strings, and that such strings unite, separate, loop and twist in a space that contains more than just four dimensions: a somewhat Gothic '*shadow world*', as Barrow puts it.[21] Winterson describes the Superstring as a scientific model that adopts 'no stable first principle'.[22] 'According to the theory,' she states, 'any particle, sufficiently magnified, will be seen not as a fixed solid point but as a tiny vibrating string. Matter will be composed of these vibrations. The universe itself would be symphonic.'[23]

DIGITAL MAPS: ON/OFF

At first sight, the cybercity appears to frame reality in terms of a digital apparatus with basic binary ON/OFF options, combinations and disjunctions which may seem to rationalize space. What is all too easy to forget about binaries is that there is always a *gap* between ON and OFF, that there is inevitably an *interval* between 0 and 1. As Sadie Plant observes, this discontinuity can be regarded as a metaphor for the technological dislocations of subjectivity and time documented by cyberpunk: 'The cores of identity become the ones and zeros of a digital printout'; simultaneously, electronic technology 'marks a fundamental shift in conceptions of history: a move away from linear development, and a return to the cyclical, now transformed into circuitry'.[24] In 'Max Headroom', Harold Jaffe likewise maintains that 'the human brain . . . fundamentally is no more than a binary system of off-on switches'.[25]

Computer language, moreover, provides metaphors for different ideations of space. It seems worth recalling, in this context, that the Boolean algebra on which the disarmingly *simple* logic of computers is based embodies a distinctively western, logocentric worldview; indeed, as Joanna Buick and Zoran Jevtic point out, it 'depends on electrical signals being "present" (1) or "not present" (0). . . . Computing decisions . . . involve comparing two pieces of data and using the logic operators AND, OR and NOT to determine what to do next.'[26] This system metaphorically perpetuates a metaphysical tradition that valorizes unity and presence and marginalizes disunity and absence. The One is idealized as a guarantee of order and stability: in Land's words, as the only 'positive pulse'.[27] Conversely, Zero is associated with absence, negativity, the void. However, non-presence turns out to play as vital a role in computing decisions as presence. This is borne out by alternative readings of the operations involved in the various *gates*. Let us first consider the basic principles according to which the gates function. The AND gate is based on the principle that if the two pieces of data involved are both 1, the output will also be 1 and that if one of the pieces is 1 and the other is 0, the output will be 0. In the OR gate, as long as one of the two pieces is 1, the output will be 1; for the output to be 0, both pieces of data must be 0. The NOT gate inverts the signal by transforming 1 into 0. In the NAND gate, if the two pieces are different the output will be 1, and if they are the same the output will be 0. In the NOR gate, if either piece is 1 the output will be 0, and if both are 0 the output will be 1.

If we now turn to figurative interpretations of these operations, we find that the principle of unity is not automatically glorified by digital language. The table presented below proposes contrasting readings of the five gates already described. Each reading alludes to different ideations of space based on either presence or absence, fullness or emptiness. The conventional readings reinforce the hold of the One; the alternative readings highlight the Zero's flair for *unlimiting* space.

AND   1 & 1 = 1

1 & 0 = 0

agreement yields unity;	unity is shattered
disagreement yields the void;	by nothingness:
presence is married to harmony	presence is vulnerable

OR   1 & 0 = 1

0 & 1 = 1

0 & 0 = 0

unity is the legitimizing factor:	the only balance
where 1 does not feature	available is produced
there is only the void	by the dominance of 0

NOT   1 = 0

| unity colonizes the void | 0 renders unity void |

NAND   1 & 1 = 0

0 & 0 = 0

1 & 0 = 1

0 & 1 = 1

unity is forced to address	unity is deconstructed:
its dependence on the void:	agreement yields 0;
1 needs 0 to be itself	disagreement yields 1

NOR $1 \& 0 = 0$
$0 \& 1 = 0$
$0 \& 0 = 1$

unity's dependence on the   only 0 provides unity
void is confirmed

To date, one of the most significant contributions to the debate on the relationship between digital technology and urbanology is William Mitchell's *City of Bits*, a study of the impact of cybertechnology on both architectural structures and life in the built environment. Mitchell argues that 'architecture and urbanism' are inevitably and deeply affected by 'the digital telecommunications revolution, the ongoing miniaturization of electronics, the commodification of bits, and the growing domination of software over materialized form'.[28] Mitchell also introduces the concept of *electronic agoras* to describe the peculiar realms created by digital technology as spaces that are concurrently antispatial and urban bodies that are simultaneously incorporeal. These territories are inhabited by *cyborg citizens* – the term cyborg alluding not so much to a literal production of biological/mechanical compounds as to the ordinary person daily involved in digital exchanges through online communication, attendance of wired lectures and participation in VR rides. These exchanges also impact on the architecture of civic institutions, as testified by online shopping malls and virtual museums, to generate what Mitchell terms a *recombinant architecture*.

Closely related to these developments are the virtual communities and community networks established by bulletin boards, MOOs and MUDs and electronic forums – what Mitchell terms 'soft cities'. This denomination, incidentally, harks back to one of the most influential theorizations of the postmodern city, namely Jonathan Raban's *Soft City*. Here, urban *softness* refers to a space in which 'nothing is fixed' and 'the possibilities of personal change and renewal are endless'.[29] It would be misleading to view Raban's account as an unproblematic celebration of the openness and fluidity of urban living, for the critic is actually aware of the perils inherent in this eminently unstable space. What *Soft City* does emphasize, however, is that there is always a gap between the urban body and its cartographic and bureaucratic representations:

The city as we might imagine it, the soft city of illusion, myth,

142

aspiration, nightmare, is as real, maybe more real, than the hard city one can locate in maps and statistics, in monographs on urban sociology and demography and architecture.[30]

This point is corroborated by Sean Cubitt, who is also concerned with the relationship between abstract and concrete aspects of the urban experience. The fact that in the 'manipulation of binary data' disparate sources coalesce, thus producing hybrid admixtures of 'physical data' and 'census statistics and tax returns', for example, problematizes the status of materiality in both spatial and temporal terms. Yet it is vital to remember that digital images 'encode information about an actually existing materiality' even though this is presented as a 'shifting pattern of energies from which the existence of objects can only be inferred'.[31]

The crumbling and overpopulated geographies and histories portrayed by cyberpunk bear witness to the overwhelming physicality of objects even as these are translated into the aseptic geometry of pixels. Thus cyberpunk stresses that digital ideations of reality as a cybernetic or computational box do not create an incontrovertibly *clean* grid. They also produce interstices and lacunae, and it is precisely in these unmapped, often neglected areas that disorder bursts out. The picture painted by Christine Boyer vividly documents this state of affairs:

> Reality is increasingly immaterial, and our modes of travel become static terminal transmissions. Meanwhile, the contemporary city stands with all its gaping wounds as crime escalates, megacities erupt, blood continues to spill, disease accelerates, and unemployment and undereducation continue.[32]

Rosi Braidotti corroborates this reading: 'urban space . . . has been cleaned up and refigured through postindustrial metal and plexiglass buildings, but [this] is only a veneer that covers up the putrefaction of the industrial space, marking the death of the modernist dream of urban civil society'.[33] Florian Rotzer further underscores the city's ambivalent status by showing that urban spaces have, historically, been constructed concurrently as privileged locations and as paradoxically dislocated or unlocalized spaces. Cities are 'the focus of power, capital, the movement of goods, labour, knowledge and culture' but they are also, increasingly, abstract constructs where 'information which travels through the networks' replaces material relations and physical movement.[34]

Pat Cadigan's *Tea from an Empty Cup* dramatizes the idea that digital technology has the power of severing the city from any conventional sense of location. In the novel, cities are indeed portrayed as disembodied entities. First, they are fundamentally video-simulated constructs for consumption by Artificial Reality (AR) users, who only ever know them as electronic representations with phonetically distorted names: 'post-Apocalyptic Noo Yawk Sitty' and 'post-Apocalyptic Ellay', for example.[35] Second, they are sea-buried ruins resulting from a series of earthquakes that are supposed to have annihilated Japan. However, Cadigan's cities' immateriality is only apparent. A number of AR junkies are killed online while *visiting* their favourite locations. If the cities themselves are ostensibly rendered incorporeal by digital technology, the fate of their AR tourists shows that the physical dimension still plays a very prominent role, as they are absorbed into a whirlpool of nightmarish chaos and violence. The situation here presented by Cadigan echoes Keith Piper's assertion that interactive media may constitute a kind of dystopian city, a 'riot zone with the user not as orderly citizen but as digital looter'.[36]Moreover, the demise of the physical Japan of old does not signal the total disappearance of the country's body. In fact, it triggers the desire to construct a New Japan: a new city-body woven from technology and ritual.

Gibson radically questions the association of cyberspace with a clean and rationalized geography. In stating that the computer matrix resembles an image of Los Angeles captured from 5,000 feet up in the air, he actually equates it to an urbanscape of bodily and cultural corruption.[37] Neither Gibson's cyberspace nor the material buildings and streets presented in his fiction abide by the rules of modernity, where the machine is often idolized as a means of fabricating mathematically pure, inorganic environments. Modernity appealed to the machine's purging powers in quasi-religious ways; in Calvin Coolidge's words: 'The man who builds a factory builds a temple. The man who works there worships there.'[38] With Gibson, we move from the modern utopia of the machine to the postmodern dystopia of the electronic matrix. The sprawling megalopolis eludes mapping, for the unknown, the uncanny and the alien insistently grow within its uncertain boundaries, in much the same way as disease proliferates within the flimsy casings of cyberpunk's bodies. In a drastic departure from the humanist model which, by recourse to Vitruvian parameters, required urban structures to reflect the harmony of the perfect body, Gibson draws attention to the dense and swarming territories that relentlessly mutate regardless of classical criteria.

With its emphasis on discontinuities and gaps and on the provisional character of all compartments and demarcations, cyberpunk's handling of space also mirrors some of the dilemmas faced by astrophysics. Research into the structure and functioning of galaxies since Edwin Hubble (1926) has shown that galaxies are not single and unified objects but rather agglomerates, complex structures with unstable boundaries and no homogeneous distribution of matter over space and time. The sum total of individual galaxies, moreover, does not match the mass of an aggregate. There is always a certain amount of *missing* mass. A well-known phrase often used to designate certain particularly elusive manifestations of matter is, arguably, *black holes*. A black hole is the product of a gravitational collapse of great intensity and momentum: the smaller the black hole, the greater its gravitational attraction; the greater its mass, the weaker its density. A black hole is analogous to a tunnel capable of sucking in both matter and light – the narrower the tunnel, the higher its suction powers. It is at black holes, pursuing the comparison between cyberpunk and astrophysics, that cyberpunk's sense of space consistently hints. Gibson's fiction, in particular, alludes to the dynamics of black holes on two levels. Orbital journeys of the kind described in the *Trilogy* suggest precisely the traveller's suction into a powerful conduct able to attract anything and anybody into its field. At the same time, the console cowboy's cybernavigation is based on the idea of physical and mental absorption into channels (those of the matrix) too strong to be resisted. The cybernaut is squeezed like toothpaste through the *black holes* of cyberspace.

Scientists intent on mapping the unchartable – the ultimate night sky of *Star Trek*, as it were – struggle to contain an ineffable remoteness. What their projects inexorably meet, argues Cubitt, is the intimation that on the edge of a galaxy, our own, which we still barely comprehend 'twinkle the beacons of galaxies that existed long ago' and are even less comprehensible: 'Cosmological observation can then only recall and refine a class of objects marked by their absence.'[39]

VENICE

In *Mona Lisa Overdrive*, Gibson makes the baffling inaccessibility of outer space a prominent feature of terrestrial and seemingly familiar cities. London, for instance, is portrayed as an almost impenetrable palimpsest, resulting from an incremental stratification of historical occurrences which, somewhat paradoxically, renders history itself unintelligible:

> T]he past . . . seemed the very fabric of things, as if the city were a single growth of stone and brick, uncounted strata of message and meaning, age upon age, generated over the centuries to the dictates of some now all but unreadable DNA of commerce and empire.[40]

However, the city that is arguably closest to the fluidity of cyberspace is Venice. Venice is prominent in Gibson's *Idoru*, in the guise of a virtual package that presents the city as an unknown, ancient space beyond the grasp of its user and, at the same time, as a paradigmatic incarnation of cyberspace. As Chia virtually roams her simulated Venice, as the 'stones of the Piazza [flow] beneath her like silk', and as she speeds into 'the maze of bridges, water, arches, walls', she has 'no idea what this place was meant to mean, the how or why of it'. What is quite clear, however, is that Venice, with her 'water and stone slotting faultlessly into the mysterious whole' in a 'default hour of gray and perpetual dawn', epitomizes the intrinsic character of cyberspace as a realm in which disparate elements blend in often unforeseeable ways and where the passing of time is hard to register.[41] Chia's rapport with her digital Venice parallels the perceptions of the matrix experienced by characters such as *Neuromancer*'s Case, *Count Zero*'s Newmark and Turner and *Mona Lisa Overdrive*'s Angie. Like these characters, she is confronted with a construct that feels disturbingly real and unreal – or indeed surreal – at once. Fantastic images crowd upon her as she explores Venice through the Sandbenders. What she sees is quite real but she has no way of grounding it in a world she has ever *really* experienced. The images encountered by Chia have their own reality but more often than not they come across as hallucinatory *déjà vus*.

Venice's status as the paradigm of the cybercity and of cyberspace itself rests on the proverbially loose character of its history and fabric. As the character of Villanelle states in Winterson's *The Passion*, Venice's spatial coordinates are eminently protean and flexible, amenable to transformations analogous to the ones endlessly undergone by the human body, and hence unsympathetic to concepts of linear progression and fixed destinations: Venice is 'the city of mazes. . . . Although wherever you are going is always in front of you, there is no such thing as straight ahead.'[42] As Villanelle later emphasizes:

> The city I come from is a changeable city. It is not always the same size. Streets appear and disappear overnight, new waterways force themselves over dry land. There are days when you cannot walk from one end to the other, so far is the journey, and there are days when a stroll will take you round your kingdom like a tin-pot Prince.[43]

Venice, like the matrix, defies mapping. This results not only from the fluidity of its urbanistic growth but also from the contrasting images associated with the city over the centuries. Venice has been alternately regarded as dreamy and pragmatic, romantic and cynical, progressive and conservative, the receptacle of high art and a gaudy display of souvenirs and trinkets. Above all, Venice has been repeatedly depicted as vaporous, ghostly, decadent and fragile. The city, it would seem, simply refuses to deliver a Platonic 'Shape' of the kind sought by Gentry in *Mona Lisa Overdrive*. It is the quintessentially hybrid character of Venice that makes it an ideal candidate as an ancestor of cyberspace. This feature of the ancient city is encapsulated by the somewhat *monstrous* character of its heraldic symbol: a lion constituted, like Frankenstein's creature, of various pieces of disparate origin assembled together. Moreover, as Richard Goy points out, Venice is 'half within and half out of the water, half eastern and half western, poised in that elusive zone between sea and sky',[44] just as the matrix itself constitutes a mobile threshold both connecting and separating incongruous domains. The liminal quality of Venice is clearly encapsulated by its lagoon, as a physical limit that is also, paradoxically, a denial of limits, given its literally fluid constitution. 'Reaching Venice by boat rather than from the mainland,' observes Elena Bianchi, 'means capturing the city's genuine essence.'[45] Cyberspace's navigators are, most famously, console cowboys and ancient spirits operating in both the literal night of the dystopian cybercity and the figurative night of the unknown. Venice has its own nocturnal breed of professional raiders, hunters and fishermen, to whom the lagoon is 'like a prairie where boats substitute horses and a different kind of cowboy ranges, especially at night'.[46]

Constantly planned and replanned from the Middle Ages to the present day, Venice resists formalization no less stubbornly than Gibson's matrix. Most of the plans put forward, since at least the Renaissance, with the intention of turning Venice into a *proper* city have been either unsuccessfully executed or not executed at all. One of the most spectacular attempts to remap Venice to make it look like a *real* city rather than a freaky phantom was made by Napoleon. His urbanistic interference altered certain physical aspects of the city but not its perception by its original inhabitants. Bonaparte intended to bring Venice 'into the modern era by some drastic interventions', including the filling in of several canals and the clearing and demolition of various quarters to establish the Public Gardens that survive today.[47] However, as Winterson's Villanelle ironically comments, Bonaparte's attempt to rationalize Venice achieved the opposite result: a magnification of its people's unbridled pursuit of 'pleasure' and 'excess'.[48] Venice may be remapped, modernized and rationalized, yet its fluid and hybrid spirit remains unabated, as does the nature of its people – what Winterson describes as a 'Siamese' soul, simultaneously 'holding hands with the Devil and God'.[49] The inconclusiveness of all attempts to restructure Venice – a phenomenon once more reminiscent of the open-endedness of any endeavour to discover the ultimate *form* of cyberspace – is confirmed by the inadequacy of the plans that have been drawn for decades in the hope of rescuing the city from collapse. As Adalberto Falletta reminds us, 'While Venice drowns, the State throws to the wind torrents of money for projects that are never completed.'[50] Although to date over 200 billion lira have been devoted to various studies and projects, it is expected that by 2050 Venice will be flooded for 100 days a year and by 2100 for up to 200.

The abortive nature of many an effort to alter Venice's baffling geography can be attributed to the fact that this prismatic city, like the matrix's ubiquitous datasphere, is built from *literally* fluid materials and that its architecture is accordingly plastic and airy. As Goy observes:

Few cities have been built in a physical environment quite so comprehensively lacking in the basic materials of building construction as Venice. . . . The difficult nature of the subsoil meant that it was necessary to minimize the load of a building on to the foundations . . . The second principle was to ensure that the design of a building incorporated flexibility. . . . Many towers have collapsed.[51]

Here Venice brings to mind not only the unstable geography of cyberspace but also the puzzling architecture of many of cyberpunk's cities. A paradagmatic example of such a location is supplied by Gibson's *Virtual Light*, where a whole city relentlessly and organically grows around the San Francisco Bridge after its semi-destruction by an earthquake and its appropriation by scores of dispossessed citizens. Gibson's bridge and its culture closely resemble the world of Venice as illusory, floating and fanciful, on the one hand, and practical and money-oriented, on the other. Like both Venice and the matrix, the bridge is an ever-proliferating construct without any obvious shape or clearly identifiable boundaries:

Its steel bones, in stranded tendons, were lost within an accretion of dreams: tattoo parlors, gaming arcades, dimly lit stalls stacked with decaying magazines, sellers of fireworks, of cut bait, betting shops, sushi bars, unlicensed pawnbrokers, herbalists, barbers, bars. Dreams of commerce, their locations generally corresponding with the decks that had once carried vehicular traffic; while above them, rising to the very peaks of the cable towers, lifted the intricately suspended barrio, with its unnumbered population and its zones of more private fantasy. . . . Everything ran together, blurring, melting in the fog.[52]

As in Venice, life on Gibson's bridge is driven by financial imperatives. Yet this accretional and amorphous world is also a 'Fairyland', a product of 'magic' and, most significantly, a 'patchwork carnival of scavenged surfaces'.[53]

Neuromancer's 'Night City' is also redolent of Venice. Defined by a compassionless profit-driven philosophy, this location also discloses a dreamlike atmosphere of mystery, a sense of stylishness and an obstinate commitment to convention: 'Biz here was a constant subliminal hum, and death the accepted punishment for laziness, carelessness, lack of grace, the failure to heed the demands of an intricate protocol.'[54] Furthermore, the fascination held by Venice in the context of cyberculture is testified by the city's use in adverts which, notes Chris Chesher, by means of computer animation take the 'virtual traveller on a journey down the canals of Venice'.[55]

Like Venice, cyberspace is ultimately enigmatic and perplexing *not* because it represents something that does not exist but rather because it maps out space in ways that its navigators cannot quite recognize – and yet know, intuitively and viscerally, they *should* be able to recognize. Two main factors incapacitate recognition: the incessant transformability of digital space and its intoxicating sense of excess. This is exemplified by Chia's total disorientation in the setting of Venice, 'facades and colonnades springing up around her' and 'the prows of black gondolas [bobbing] like marks in some lost system of musical notation'. By the time she is faced with the Carnival masks, 'Black, penis-nosed leather, empty eye-holes', she has definitely *had enough*.[56] The image of the mask, so unsettling for Gibson's young heroine, points to the elusive and disquieting world of the carnival, a world where anything may happen, where identities and roles are subverted and where, as in the matrix, reality and fiction are extremely difficult to separate.

SPACE AND NARRATIVE STRUCTURE

Gibson's Chiba City incarnates the concept of the postmodern cybercity by uniting digital hi tech and rampant decay. Indeed, corruption inhabits the very core of Chiba City, its innermost 'Zone'. Gibson's choice of a Japanese setting is especially apposite if one considers that Japan's population is about half the size of that of the United States yet packed into an area about the size of California alone. When Gibson speculates about the urban sprawl and cheap hotels providing sleeping spaces hardly larger than coffins, he is also portraying a cultural reality. At the same time, architectural bodies, unable to expand towards the outside by crammed urban conditions, proliferate internally like galloping cancers, as testified by Gibson's 'arcologies' – namely, whole cities enclosed in a single building. Though the pressures of demographic density are everywhere to be felt in the *Trilogy*, what is repeatedly emphasized is not so much the material reality of overcrowding as the dizzying frequency and overbearing intensity with which digital data are exchanged within the

city's body. As the ones and zeros furiously interact across the megalopolitan Sprawl, the rate of traffic becomes so dense as to resemble
a star 'about to go nova'.[57]

The map drawn by Gibson may depict a new civilization in which
physical constraints are marginalized by electronic communications
systems. Yet it also supplies a graphic reminder of the eminently
material conditions of all systems, the threat of implosion being
never far away. Moreover, although Chiba City is undoubtedly a
version of postmodern urbanology, Gibson does not turn to Japanese culture merely to paint pictures of the present or of the imminent future. He also adopts aspects of that culture to comment on
the enduring influence of the past and of ancient customs. Thus,
Gibson's appropriation of Japanese words associated with urban
culture should not be seen exclusively as a means of lending credibility to the portrait of a futuristic megalopolis. 'Pachinko' (a
popular gambling machine), 'yakitory' (a common street snack),
and 'gaijin' (a derogatory term for westerners) are some of the
words often used to add colour to images of urban existence. Other
words of Nipponic derivation simultaneously refer to the present,
and specifically to popular cultural products, and to time-honoured
traditions. For example, 'Manriki chains' and 'shuriken' (steel stars
with lethally sharp points) are associated with the contemporary
ninja movies that have made them familiar but also hark back to
ancient martial codes and practices. Other words prove even more
ambiguous: 'sarariman', for example, denotes a businessman
employed by a large corporation and is a paradigmatically postmodern portmanteau resulting from the combination of the English
words 'salary' and 'man'. But 'sarariman' also hints at a traditional
power figure of older standing. According to Darko Suvin, Gibson's ' "nipponizing" vocabulary' is 'centred on how strangely and
yet peculiarly appropriate Japanese feudal-style capitalism is as an
analog or, indeed, ideal template for the new feudalism of present-
day corporate monopolies'.[58] Gibson's urban spaces, then, are concurrently grounded in dystopian representations of the present and
the impending future, and in much older structures of power and
knowledge. This is attested not only by his lexical experiments but
also, as we have seen, by his revamping of primordial systems of
belief.

Owing to their emphasis on fragmentation and flux, on the one
hand, and to their interweaving of diverse temporal planes, on the

other, Gibson's cities are hard to *measure*, either spatially or historically. It would be quite pointless to try to rationalize them by
recourse to geometrical systems based on notions of regularity and
order. Had they to be measured, the only relevant tools would possibly be those supplied by *fractal geometry*, what Benoit Mandel-
brot describes as 'a way of measuring qualities that otherwise have
no clear definition: the degree of roughness or brokenness or
irregularity in an object', for example.[59] This geometry proposes
alternative ideations of space to the ones fostered by the Euclidean
system and pivots on ambiguity and paradox. Indeed, it deals with
the irregular but, in so far as it explores ways of measuring the
irregular, it is also committed to a logic of regularity: for example,
finding out whether irregularity manifests itself regularly and, if so,
in what guises. Fractal geometry has had a major impact on digital
forms of representation. As Brooks Landon observes, 'Mandel-
brot's work with fractal geometry both represents and helps drive a
new wave of computer imaging which allows the representation,
generation, and manipulation of images, viewing perspectives, and
degrees of realism never possible before.'[60] In *The Lost Dimension*,
Paul Virilio associates the revolutionary approach to measurement
brought about by fractal geometry with a radical displacement of
anthropocentrism and, concomitantly, of the dimension of absolute
referentiality. It is impossible to go on viewing *man* as the measure
of all things when the geometrical attributes of irregular entities
such as coastlines and snowflakes will change according to whether
they are measured by a human being or by an insect, say.[61] Gibson
offers an emblematic illustration of irregular, fractal space in
Idoru's 'City of Darkness', a space that grows indefinitely 'between
the walls of the world':

> ... building or biomass or cliff face looming there, in countless
> unplanned strata, nothing about it even or regular. Accreted
> patchwork of shallow random balconies, thousands of small win-
> dows throwing back blank silver rectangles of fog. Stretching
> either way to the periphery of vision, and on the high, uneven
> crest of that ragged facade, a black fur of twisted pipe, antennas
> sagging under vine growth of cable.... *Fractal filth*, bit-rot, the
> corridor of their passage tented with crazy swoops of faintly flick-
> ering lines of some kind.... Then they were ascending a maze of
> twisting stairwells.[62]

Fractal geometry has a correlative in narrative forms that juxtapose regularity and irregularity: patterns of recurrence, symmetries and parallelisms, on the one hand, and images assembled and related on the basis of random associations, on the other. Katherine Hayles describes these narrative formations as characterized by 'areas of clear symmetry intermixed with other areas of suggestive but fuzzy replication'.[63] Several cyberpunk narratives exhibit this feature. Just as its cities are hybrid in so far as they can be conceptualized as abstract networks of data and yet present intensely material scenarios, so cyberpunk's textual structures are hybrid by virtue of their commingling of pattern and randomness. Cyberpunk's texts are comparable to its cities. Indeed, exploring the structural and formal traits of several cyberpunk fictions is somewhat akin to embarking on a fantasy voyage down a sprawling continent of megacities. The reason for addressing the issue of narrative structure in the context of a discussion of cyberpunk's treatment of the city is precisely this: both the urban and the textual spaces constructed by cyberpunk thrive on a paradoxical fusion of order and disorder. Gibson's fiction clearly exemplifies this.

Gibson draws ambivalent maps that interweave symmetry and fuzziness through narrative structures and plots that combine carefully worked-out patterns of analogies and correspondences with a sense of random chance and coincidence. This paradoxical mix is largely a result of Gibson's approach to story-telling. He has suggested that, however skilful and successful a fiction writer may be, he or she may still feel a sense of uncertainty or even 'panic' in the face of the challenge posed by the blank page. However developed the writer's plotting techniques are, the sense of doubt still lingers. Gibson tells us:

> I always feel like one of the guys *inside* those incredible dragons you see snaking through the crowds in Chinatown. Very brightly coloured, but from the inside you know the whole thing is pretty flimsy – just a bunch of old newspapers and papier-mâché and balsa struts.[64]

Moreover, Gibson is aware that his central theme, cyberspace, allows a degree of freedom that is both exciting (characters can be situated 'in any sort of setting or against any backdrop') and 'dangerous', since it becomes tempting to let characters 'be sucked into apparent realities' and thus fail to tell a story.[65] A way of counteracting this sense of vulnerability is to construct plots that tightly cohere by virtue of internal connections. Gibson believes that this can be achieved only if the 'rhythm' of the narrative is sustained and that missing 'a *beat*' is enough to lose the overall tempo.[66]

One of the most distinctive features of Gibson's narrative rhythm consists precisely of the juxtaposition of structural balance and unpredictable changes of direction. This is perhaps not surprising, given cyberpunk's concern with the digital processing and transmission of data. Indeed, recent developments in information theory have stressed that pattern and randomness are not binarily opposed concepts but actually mutually complementing phenomena. When applied to the realm of narrative structure, this discovery throws into relief the twofold status of the fictional text. On the one hand, the text constitutes a blend of order and irregularity, pattern and randomness. On the other, it becomes a metaphor for the human body for, as Hayles has indicated:

> Just as the human body is understood in molecular biology as simultaneously a physical structure and an expression of genetic information, so the literary corpus is at once a physical object and a space of representation, a body and a message.[67]

The interprenetration of narrative and biological strands is likewise highlighted by Land, who maintains that what we find in *Neuromancer*, for example, is fundamentally a 'confluence of dispersed narrative threads' which mirrors the uncanny collusion of 'the biotic and the technical'.[68] If Gibson uses narrative structures in which symmetries, correspondences and parallelisms play a vital role, it is also the case that these are very gradually and almost surreptitiously set up. To begin with, the text of *Neuromancer* seems to encompass discrete – or only elliptically related – plots. Their interconnections become incrementally obvious and intricate, as incidents and complications multiply. Gibson *fuzzes*, so to speak, the geometry of his yarns by recourse to two central mechanisms: a delaying strategy that deliberately postpones the disclosure of internal linkages; and an acceleration technique whereby, once a few major connections have been indicated, more come hurtling through the narrative with increasing momentum.

A detailed analysis of the textual organization of *Count Zero* exemplifies this process. The chapter-by-chapter breakdown proposed below labels each section not by actual chapter titles but by reference to the name(s) of the character(s) that dominate it. Turner is the 'mercenary' employed by 'vast corporations warring covertly for the control of entire economies'[69] and, on this particular occasion, recruited to engineer the safe delivery of the head Maas-Biolabs designer Mitchell, who is reputed to want to defect to Hosaka. Turner's employer is Conroy, a dubious character playing double on behalf of both Hosaka and Herr Virek (see below). Bobby Newmark is a frustrated and ambitious youth from derelict Barrytown, aspiring to a career as a console cowboy and drawn into a nefarious intrigue by his testing of *hot* software. Marly, an ex-gallery owner whose business has folded as a result of a forgery produced by her lover Alain, is employed by Herr Virek to find the origins of a peculiar artwork, a box filled with unrelated objects of a nostalgic derivation. Virek is immensely rich but his body amounts to millions of vat-supported, rioting cells ravaged by multiple cancers. Virek is greedy for biosoft as his sole chance of redemption and knows that, in discovering the origins of the peculiar artwork, he will also find the origins of the invaluable chips. Chapters 1 to 9 display a balanced, geometrically regular pattern of repetition, by focusing on each of the main characters as follows:

1]   Turner
2]   Marly
3]   Bobby

4]   Turner
5]   Marly
6]   Bobby

7]   Turner
8]   Marly
9]   Bobby

The pattern is disrupted by the sequence of the next three chapters:

10]   Marly
11]   Turner
12]   Marly

At this juncture in the narrative, Bobby is temporarily left out, possibly to heighten the suspense created by the revelation, occurring at the end of Chapter 9, that he is 'chosen of Legba'.[70] Geometrical regularity is reinstated in the two sets of subsequent chapters, with the important addition to the Turner subplot of Angie, Mitchell's daughter, whom Turner ends up rescuing in place of her father after a monumental explosion on the Maas Arizona estate:

13]	Bobby
14]	Turner/Angie
15]	Marly
16]	Bobby
17]	Turner/Angie
18]	Marly

Chapters 19 to 30 alter the character order but the overall rhythm of recursiveness is maintained:

19]	Bobby
20]	Marly
21]	Turner/Angie
22]	Bobby
23]	Marly
24]	Turner/Angie
25]	Bobby
26]	Marly
27]	Turner/Angie
28]	Bobby
29]	Marly
30]	Turner/Angie

However, Chapter 30 is, in a sense, no more Turner's or Angie's than it is Bobby's. By this point, these two strands have become inseparable. Chapters 31 to 33 bring all three subplots together, Chapter 32 constituting the pivotal moment of their interweaving and Chapters 31 and 33 offering a conceptual explanation for their connections.

Chapters 34 to 36, by oscillating between images of the past and future premonitions, supply a provisional rounding off of the narrative whose open-endedness clearly creates scope for the sequel, *Mona Lisa Overdrive*.

This analysis hopefully shows that Gibson is concurrently committed to the construction of a geometrically tight structure and to its explosion by means of *fractal* variations, ruptures and changes of direction. The interconnections he sets up are, obviously, carefully worked out. Yet they are simultaneously surrounded by an aura of indeterminateness, for they are not explicitly spelled out. In fact, it is the reader's task to identify their possibility, and to pursue the clues provided by the text. In the absence of an omniscient author's instructions, there is every chance that these clues will – at least at first – lead the reader to incorrect assumptions or rushed conclusions. Much of the time, the reader can simply register the subliminal existence of connections without being able to ascertain their full import.

One of the first crucial links alluded to by the narrative in a characteristically *fuzzy* fashion is the one between the BOBBY and the MARLY plots. Bobby hears from the Finn about 'weird sculpture things' consisting of 'a bunch of garbage and shit, stuck together in a box'. The Finn admits to having purchased some of these works from the same agents who sell him software described as 'biosoft'.[71] The agents themselves are ostensibly sent by William Ludgate, once a great cowboy and now a doting old man living in orbit, sustained only by the conviction that the matrix is God. The boxes are, of course, the very same sculptures that Marly is employed by Herr Virek to find – and when she eventually does find them she finds Ludgate, too. Various clues previously dropped now merge into a coherent picture: Ludgate is the source of both the strange sculptures (produced by the Boxmaker in the same orbital venue that Ludgate inhabits) and of the precious biochips that Virek yearns for. At the same time, it turns out that the killer programme that has taken Bobby close to death is precisely a biosoft programme sent by Ludgate to the Finn, subsequently purchased by the voodoo men Lucas and Beauvoir, and then downloaded onto Two-a-Day so that he may find a test-driver for it – namely Bobby.

The next pivotal link, already mentioned in the previous chapter, is the one between the BOBBY and the TURNER/ANGIE plots. The young cowboy is rescued from a lethal programme by a girl's voice in the very early parts of the novel,[72] but it is only considerably later that Angie becomes identifiable as the owner of that voice: 'The other night I dreamed about a boy, and he'd reached out, picked up something, and it was hurting him, and he couldn't see that he was free, that he only needed to let go. So I told him.'[73] This connection is developed in Chapter 28, when Turner and Angie reach the Hypermart to which they have been led by the voices grafted in the girl's brain and Bobby is startled into a recognition of his saviour: 'Bobby stared, then gaped as the memory hit him. Girl voice, brown hair, dark eyes, the ice eating into him.'[74]

The MARLY plot is interwoven with the TURNER/ANGIE one by means of their shared involvement with Sense/Net (something of a simstim version of soap opera). First we discover that in a previous incarnation Turner has been recruited 'to provide security for a Sense/Net simstim team'.[75] Later Marly, while travelling to an orbital site where the famous boxes are supposed to originate, communicates with Herr Virek through the Sense/Net star Tally Isham, whom Angie will soon replace. Having 'found herself locked into Tally's . . . sensorium via a simstim cassette', Marly realizes that Tally is the vehicle through which Virek is manifesting himself to remind her of his limitless powers.[76]

From Chapter 25 onwards, correspondences and parallelisms proliferate. We find that Beauvoir (BOBBY plot) is aware of the peculiar events surrounding the explosion on the Maas Arizona estate and of the claim that Mitchell is dead.[77] Soon after, the link between the BOBBY and the MARLY plots is consolidated, as Marly encounters William Ludgate in orbit.[78] The climactic interweaving occurs in Chapter 32, appropriately entitled 'Count Zero'. Here Bobby and Jackie jack together into the matrix to reach Jaylene Slide, a character who has played a key role in the planning of Mitchell's escape, tell her that Conroy is responsible for her partner Ramirez's death (which Jaylene longs to avenge) and thus enlist her support. What Bobby and Jackie encounter, however, is a 'cybernetic megastructure'[79] of ice, which kills Jackie almost instantly. This unimaginably vast protective system has been erected by Virek's associates 'in an attempt to prevent Angela Mitchell's escape' since, in the absence of her father, Virek now covets the girl. Enraged at Jackie's death, Bobby confronts Virek and annihilates him. Significantly, Bobby is here sustained by voodoo energies that he himself has hitherto been unaware of possessing: ' "My name," a voice said, and Bobby wanted to scream when he realized that it came from his own mouth, "is Samedi, and you have slain my cousin's horse . . .". And Virek was running.'[80] Having dispatched Virek to the kingdom of shadows, Bobby finally meets Jaylene and informs her of Conroy's crime, whereupon she wreaks vengeance upon the double player.[81]

As suggested earlier, fuzzily symmetrical stories based on the interweaving of disparate yarns and discourses could be seen as narrative equivalents of the ambiguous, equivocal maps drawn by technoscience on both the body and the city. What is more, by underscoring the coexistence of the physical and the incorporeal, stability and disorder, symmetry and dissymmetry, Gibson's fictions exhibit points of contact with theories that attempt to account for the existence and state of large systems, their harmonies and disruptions, chances of endurance and prospects of collapse – namely, *catastrophe*, *crisis* and *chaos* theories. The relevance of these theories to everyday existence is overtly borne out by the urban experience as presented by cyberpunk. Cybercities undergo incessant transformations of a radical, albeit not always instantly visible, kind that hint at the dynamics of *catastrophe*. They manage to survive, in spite of repeated and often brutal assaults on their fabric, by forging a sense of stability out of a condition of constant *crisis*. Finally, they incorporate *chaos* into their texture as the principle that paradoxically disrupts them and holds them together at one and the same time. *Catastrophe*, *crisis* and *chaos* theories also bear on narrative space: the city-body of the text.

Narratives that underscore the coexistence of principles of stability and instability articulate metaphorically certain positions put forward by *catastrophe theory*, which, as Benjamin Woolley observes, emphasize the abrupt and discontinuous changes that cause a system to move 'from one state to another'.[82] The narrative process becomes analogous to the processes whereby the world unfolds through phenomena of 'ceaseless creation'.[83] The narrative exposure of the concept of stability as an inevitably precarious and rescindable achievement is also redolent of positions articulated by *crisis theory*, the principal concern of which lies with establishing:

> . . . why systems that are on the point of crisis somehow manage to persist. The universe is supposed to be headed in the direction of equilibrium . . . . Yet there are . . . all these structures, ourselves

included, teetering on the edge of crisis . . . that are nevertheless stable, and even self-sustaining.[84]

The texts examined in this study likewise spurn the tendency to equate order and form to rigid and immutable structures, opting instead for models wherein productive and destructive forces constantly interact. They highlight the ongoing tension between the attraction of ordering schemata and the propensity for self-explosion and self-implosion inherent in any ostensibly stable system. In so doing, they exhibit parallels to the insights provided by science into the inextricability of order from *chaos*:

> [C]haos does not just produce order, it *has* order: there is a deep structure . . . in the apparently random, chaotic behaviour that characterizes all natural and some social phenomena. This structure takes the form of . . . a 'strange attractor' . . . a state towards which a system is drawn. . . . [A]ll chaotic, apparently meaningless phenomena are drawn towards a strange attractor. . . . [T]hough chaotic systems may be stable at the level of the strange attractor, they are highly unstable at the level we experience them directly. . . . [They] fly off the handle at the slightest provocation. This is known as the 'butterfly effect'.[85]

In other words, *chaos theory* argues that even deterministic systems are capable of random behaviour and unpredictability. Though governed by certain laws, such systems are made unstable by the possibility of minute variations in their initial state, by the disruptive potential of as infinitesimal a factor as the flap of a butterfly's wing. When the initial conditions of a system alter, no matter how slightly, no matter how apparently flimsy the agent of change, there is no way of predicting how the situation may develop and be then calculated or measured.

As the theories of Ilya Prigogine and Isabelle Stengers have indicated, matter and energy do not constitute 'conservative systems' totally insulated from their surroundings. All systems are, in fact, subject to an incessant flow of matter and energy emanating from the outside. This flow cannot be absorbed in its entirety: it must also exit the system, be dissipated – hence the phrase 'dissipative systems'.[86] In such systems, forms of stability and equilibrium may be achieved but these are dynamic rather than static. The elements in the system are held together in a balance that, though stable, is intrinsically variable. These forms of stability are termed 'attractors' and the shifts that transmute one attractor into another are termed 'bifurcations'.[86] Essentialist and deterministic positions are radically dislocated by the possibility of thinking in terms of dissipative, rather than conservative, systems. Dissipative systems inaugurate unceasing forms of stabilization and diversification where the identity of a system is not reducible to one essence, or *centre*, and where there is nothing transcendentally *necessary* about a system's transition from one equilibrium to another.

As we saw in Chapters 3 and 4 of this volume, the bodies represented by cyberpunk are ambiguous entities, suspended between a fantasy of escape from the meat and an awareness of the inevitable materiality of embodiment. Cyberpunk's cities, as argued in this chapter, are no less ambiguous. Made hard and shiny by technology, they are none the less pervaded by corruption and evil; neatly charted by digital networks and grids, they none the less proliferate in all imaginable directions in ways that stubbornly defy any systematic management of space. The ambiguities exhibited by cyberpunk's bodies and cities are emblematically mirrored by the ambiguous status of the figures and constructs that are supposed to control cyberspace and turn out, in fact, to have only a limited knowledge and a slippery grasp of the matrix's mysteries. In *Neuromancer*, for instance, Wintermute features as a kind of Creation deity, able to access the catatonic body of Corto (an utterly dehumanized residue of war) and to turn him into Armitage, a cybernetic weapon. Wintermute constructs alternative life forms. He has control over Case and Molly and over Armitage/Corto and seems to have a clear idea of what he needs in order to fulfil his aim, namely to merge with Neuromancer. Yet Wintermute is neither omnipotent nor omniscient; most crucially, he does not know and indeed *cannot* know the 'magic word' that will activate the 'ceremonial terminal' by means of which Neuromancer could be accessed:

> You might say what I am is basically defined by the fact that I don't know, because I *can't* know. I am that which knoweth not the word. If you knew, man, and told me, I couldn't *know*. It's hardwired in.[88]

Mona Lisa Overdrive likewise stresses that AIs are simultaneously godlike and toylike. Their decisions are quite arbitrary and often whimsical. For example, Continuity is, among other things, a *writer* whose skills are not channelled into the interests of scientific knowledge but rather put to the service of circular self-entertainment:

> Continuity was writing a book. Robin Lanier had told her [Angie] about it. She'd asked what it was about. It wasn't like that, he'd said. It looped back into itself and constantly mutated; Continuity was *always* writing it. She asked why. But Robin had lost interest: because Continuity was an AI, and AIs did things like that.[89]

AIs may be construed as mighty gods but they themselves are sceptical – or, at any rate, non-committal and distressingly laconic – when it comes to commenting on such a possibility. When Angie manages to engage Continuity in a quasi-theological exchange about the relationship between the matrix and spiritualism, all she gets is evasive and often monosyllabic responses:

> 'If there were such a being [God],' she said, 'You'd be a part of it, wouldn't you?'
> 'Yes.'
> 'Would you know?'
> 'Not necessarily.'
> '*Do* you know?'
> 'No.'
> 'Do you rule out the possibility?'
> 'No.'
> 'Do you think this is a strange conversation, Continuity?'
> . . .
> 'No.'[90]

In conclusion, it could be argued that cyberpunk's cities are, to a significant degree, the product of technologies that pride themselves on their ability to penetrate the universe's darkest mysteries. However, the cryptic nature of digital technology's supreme representatives, namely artificial intelligences such as Wintermute and Continuity, casts a shadow of doubt on this assumption. AIs are ostensibly capable of running 'the whole show'. Yet their powers are restricted by the very nature of the 'show', that is, the matrix: an ambivalent space that concurrently signifies 'Nowhere' and

'Everywhere'.[91] Like its simulated constructs, cyberpunk's settings demonstrate than even in a world exhaustively explored and mapped out by technoscience, space retains obscurities and secrets. 'If there is no *terra incognita* today in the absolute sense,' John K. Wright writes, 'so also no *terra* is absolutely *cognita*.'[92] As long as cities, like human bodies, go on combining the features of 'a product of nature' and those of 'an artificial construction', to use Robert Park's formulation, they will never be totally mappable, let alone intelligible.[93]

CHAPTER 6

CYBERPUNK AND THE GOTHIC

What noun would 'Gothic' appropriately modify, then? I would suggest the term 'complex'. According to the *American Heritage Dictionary*, this word (like 'Gothic') may be both an adjective and a noun. As an adjective it means 'consisting of interconnected or interwoven parts'; 'involved or intricate, complicated'; and in grammar, 'pertaining to or designating a sentence consisting of an independent clause and one or more dependent clauses'. As a noun, it means 'a whole composed of interconnected parts', or (from psychiatry) 'a connected group of repressed ideas that compel characteristic or habitual patterns of thought, feeling, or action'. Informally, it is used to mean 'an exaggerated or obsessive concern or fear'. Also like Gothic, 'complex' denotes an intersection of grammar, architecture, and psychoanalysis. Like Gothic architecture and narrative, it denotes intricacy, 'complexity', and in different contexts it may refer to behavioural manifestations or to an unconscious structure that nevertheless has its 'real', that is, its material, effects.

(Anne Williams)[1]

As the preceding quotation from Anne Williams's *Art of Darkness* underlines, complexity is one of the Gothic's main features and it is not the aim of this chapter to simplify this prismatic discourse. However, given that the scope of the book precludes the possibility of examining the Gothic in *all* its complexity of forms and themes, it seems necessary to point out that, in the present context, the term Gothic is understood in two fundamental ways: first, as a fictional genre, encompassing the strands of historical romance, horror and tales of psychological obsession and haunting, ranging from the eighteenth century to the present; and second, as a discourse of wider resonance, utilizing images of disorder and monstrosity that embody cultural anxieties about the disintegration of traditional western values and social formations. A fascination with the transgression of cultural limits and with the fears and fantasies bred by transgression is, arguably, the Gothic's most pervasive motif across time and space. Taking these basic definitions as a working model, this chapter seeks to highlight the Gothic dimension of cyberpunk's aesthetics.

In both the eighteenth and the nineteenth centuries, it was common to associate the Gothic with tastelessness, with the consumption of pulp fiction by an unrefined (if economically ascendant) middle-class market, and particularly with the female portion thereof. Paradoxically, however, the Gothic's ideological function was implicitly recognized, in so far as the experience of terror was often endowed with cathartic powers: the genre was deemed capable of facilitating the reconstitution of a sense of normality and order by provoking extreme fear and hence encouraging the expulsion of the fearful object. Yet this ideological function remained hard to quantify, and this difficulty only served to reinforce the Gothic's suspect status. Indeed, fictions equipped with a moral, reparative finale could not automatically be regarded as moral in their entirety. The ending may simply be paying lip service to mainstream conceptions of right and wrong, good and evil, without really purging the body of the story of immoral or amoral contents.

A variety of writers from disparate historical and cultural backgrounds have been described as Gothic. Walpole, Radcliffe, Polidori, Maturin, Shelley, Godwin, the Brontë sisters, Sheridan Le Fanu, Stoker, Stevenson, Wilde, Bierce, Kafka, Poe, James, Faulkner, Tolkien, Peake, Rhys, Carter, Coover, Morrison, Ellis, Dinesen, Eco, Tennant and McGrath, for example, form *one* – by no means exhaustive – hybrid list of authors associated with the Gothic. The sheer diversity of texts and contexts evoked by these names (and the legion others that have been left out) testifies to the Gothic's protean nature. The Gothic, then, is not a unified literary form, movement or school. What justifies its usage as an umbrella term is the recursive articulation of themes of personal and collective decomposition, mental and physical disarray, and a view of the world as the playground for grotesque and absurd characters: namely, *human beings*.

In the twentieth century, cinema has steadily added momentum to the growth of a Gothic sensibility. From Murnau and Lang, through Browning and Mamoulian, to Hitchcock, De Palma, Lynch, Greenaway, Scorsese, Tarantino, Craven, Cronenberg, Fincher, Gilliam, Scott, Bigelow and Cameron (to mention but a handful of well-known directors), film has thrown into relief ongoing preoccupations with excess, transgression, horror, terror, images of psychological and bodily invasion, monstrosity and polymorphous sexuality. At the same time, science fiction (in both its literary and cinematic forms) has developed Gothic themes and modalities, often by foregrounding horror as a product of self-alienation and of the impenetrability of truth, thus supplying powerful critiques of modernity and humanism.

Even people who do not rank among the Gothic's most avid consumers would readily associate it with fantastic, mystical and supernatural discourses. There is every chance, however, that they would not quite so rapidly make a connection between the Gothic and technology. Nevertheless, it could be argued that the Gothic is no less technological than it is fantastic. Indeed, it is concerned with the ways in which beings, environments and histories are *made* – that is, *technologically* constructed in accordance with the belief systems of particular societies – and with the ways in which transgressive energies relentlessly threaten to *unmake* them. As cultural and ideological circumstances alter, so does the Gothic. Its recurring figures (vampires, monsters and ghosts, for example) subtly change over history and thus acquire novel connotations that reflect shifting social priorities and preoccupations. The Gothic, therefore, cannot be anchored either to one single space/time or to one single structure of values. It is inherent in its rhythms and themes that it should keep mutating, for, at the same time as it prophesies *the end*, it stubbornly *goes on*. The Gothic may be apocalyptic but its apocalypse keeps on disclosing new prospects no less emphatically than it announces a terminal *Dies Irae*. Cyberpunk is likewise impatient of facile notions of ultimate collapse. As Veronica Hollinger observes, cyberpunk 'displays a certain coolness, a kind of ironically detached approach to its subject matter' that 'discourages any recourse to the logic of apocalypse'. Like the Gothic, cyberpunk repeatedly toys with the idea of irreversible catastrophe, yet ironically postpones its realization; it is 'more engaged with historical processes than attracted by the jump-cuts of apocalyptic scenarios that evade such investment in historical change'.[2] Both the Gothic and cyberpunk remind us that, despite popular uses of the term 'apocalypse' to designate the end of the world and ultimate disaster, the word's Greek etymology actually points to notions of revelation and disclosure and hence to the prospect of new beginnings. The Greek word *apokalypsis* indeed means an 'uncovering' and the related verb *apo-kalyptein* means 'to uncover'. ('Apocalypse' is also, of course, the title of the last book of the New Testament, otherwise known as the 'Revelation' of St John.)

In its employment of Gothic motifs, cyberpunk shows that the Gothic is not a pure and uniform genre, set of themes, or corpus of literary conventions. In fact, it is a discourse, which encapsulates in very literal ways the sense of the original term *discursus* – an incessant back-and-forth motion that corrodes all aspirations to stability. The otherness of both the past and the future keeps on infiltrating the present with the obstinate regularity of a repetition compulsion, turning time and space into settings for the confrontation of ungraspable absences. It is in the idea of the *uncanny* that the Gothic's codification of spatial and temporal instability manifests itself most blatantly, as a troubling intermingling of the ordinary and the unfamiliar.

THE UNCANNY

Uncanny effects are produced through the collusion of familiarity and strangeness. The emotions they elicit are accordingly ambivalent: excitement and exhilaration, on the one hand, and revulsion and dread, on the other. By creating pockets of non-meaning in everyday worlds, rather than in distant or unearthly ones, the uncanny operates, as Victor Sage and Allan Lloyd Smith point out, as: 'not one code but a kind of gap between codes, a point at which representation itself appears to fail, displace, or diffuse itself'.[3] One of the first sustained theorizations of the uncanny is supplied by Sigmund Freud, who associates this feeling with a deeply unsettling sense of uncertainty. For example, it may be aroused by 'doubts whether an apparently animate being is really alive; or conversely, whether a lifeless object might not be in fact animate'.[4] Moreover, 'an uncanny effect is often and easily produced when the distinction between image and reality is effaced, as when something that we have hitherto regarded as imaginary appears before us in reality, or when a symbol takes over the full functions of the thing it symbolizes'.[5] Most importantly, uncanny experiences are so profoundly distressing

because their fundamental roots and origins lie *in us*, in those portions of our minds that shelter ancient and repressed fears. In the
face of an uncanny phenomenon – such as a being whose status we
are unable to ascertain – we may feel frightened and haunted. Yet the
spookiness of the experience is not so much to do with the phenomenon itself as with its ability to reawaken submerged aspects of our
psychic histories. In the confrontation with the uncanny, we find that
something 'familiar and old-established in the mind and which has
become alienated from it . . . through the process of repression'[6] has
metamorphosed into a troubling ghost. We feel haunted by something that, though it may seem alien, foreign and remote, is in fact
part of us.

The Gothic uncanny thrives on indeterminacy by capitalizing on
situations of suspense and not-knowing. To this extent, it is an epi-
stemological issue. Yet in problematizing the questions of knowledge, its constitution, dissemination and availability, it also throws
into relief ontological anxieties. What *is* reality, if the knowledge of
reality is always up for grabs? What *is* a familiar world, if familiarity
can be rescinded at any time?

Gibson throws these issues into relief by means of characters who
uncannily combine spectrality and *high resolution*. For instance,
'Colin', the 'ghost' emanating from a portable biochips unit in *Mona
Lisa Overdrive*, is not 'real', as his Aladdin-like master Kumiko 'stern-
ly' points out. Yet his appearance is 'uncomfortably sharp . . . the
nap on the lapels of his dark coat vibrating with hallucinatory clar-
ity'. What intensifies his ontological uncanniness is his ability to
conjure up images of a history he has never experienced and that
could, indeed, never have occurred: 'Kumiko closed her eyes and the
ghost began to whisper to her, something about the archaeology of
Heathrow, about the Neolithic and the Iron Ages, pottery and
tools.'[7] Gibson's cyberghost is uncanny essentially by virtue of his
indeterminate status. Like the entities cited by Freud, Colin is a creature of the border: animate and inanimate, imaginary and real, symbolic and embodied, at one and the same time. His role as a digital
recorder of historical events accentuates Colin's uncanny character.
As already mentioned, the uncanny is disquieting not because it
takes us into utterly foreign worlds but rather because it gives the
familiar an unexpected twist and thus reminds us that mystery dwells
in our very minds. Thus Colin's reconstruction of history is unsettling because it turns an ordinary present into a strange and

estranging narrative fabrication. Concurrently, Colin intimates that the past is an assemblage of buried or only partially unearthed objects and traces – just as human beings' personal histories consist largely of repressed materials.

History is the phantasmatic reconstruction, by an unreal body, of spaces and eras haunted by lifeless remains. The urge to weave speculative yarns about what *might have been* is irresistible, and continually fuelled by the uncanny indeterminateness of one's surroundings. This is borne out by Angie's struggle to make sense of her present life, a phantasmagoria of dreams, hallucinations and visions, by revisiting the hidden past of her environment: 'The house crouched, like its neighbours, on fragments of ruined foundations, and her walks along the beach . . . involved attempts at archaeological fantasy. She tried to imagine a past for the place, other houses, other voices.'[8]

Count Zero stresses that what is most harrowing about the uncanny is its intimacy, its ability to trigger reactions of extreme fear, anxiety and repugnance in ostensibly familiar and normal contexts. Turner has a typically uncanny experience when he accesses Mitchell's records by digital means:

> It was like waking from a nightmare. Not a screamer, where impacted fears took on simple, terrible shapes, but the sort of dream, infinitely more disturbing, where everything is perfectly and horribly normal, and where everything is utterly *wrong* . . . The *intimacy* of the thing was hideous![9]

In his analysis, Freud maintains that uncanny experiences fall into two main categories. Some result from the revival of 'repressed infantile complexes'[10] and, by extension, from *personal* experiences that have been pushed back into the unconscious because their reality would otherwise be intolerable. Others derive from a resurgence of 'primitive beliefs', such as fantasies, fears and superstitions associated with animism, magic and early mythologies, which modern civilization has only apparently 'surpassed'.[11] These lay emphasis on the *collective* dimension of uncanny experiences. Gibson often relates the uncanny to personal traumas suffered in childhood or early youth. For example, the chemical and biotechnological experiments inflicted on Angie, Slick, Mona and Laney as young people play a crucial role in the shaping of their personalities. When they find themselves in situations of uncertainty and potential danger, memories of those traumatic experiences return, thus arousing feelings of an uncanny nature. However, Gibson also associates the uncanny with a collective baggage of traditional beliefs and rituals. As argued in Chapter 2, his narratives consistently interweave technological images with mythological themes. The ultimate uncanny experience takes place when his characters, and indeed his readers, realize that the reality of scientific knowledge and of its technological applications is always liable to be infiltrated by vestiges of a fantasy world – a world repressed but never erased. The interpenetration of reality and fantasy radically questions the viability of any attempt to differentiate between the primitive and the civilized, or indeed between magic and science. This is attested by Gibson's employment of Faustian motifs and imagery. Harking back to Goethe's archetypal text, Gibson's *Count Zero* encodes knowledge and success as corollaries of a Mephistophelean pact: Mitchell, the unrivalled genius in the field of biotechnology, has excelled in spite of his initial lack of 'that certain signal curve of brilliance' through unholy alliances:

> Someone, something, had found Mitchell in his postgraduate slump and had started feeding him things. Clues, directions. And Mitchell had gone to the top, his arc hard and bright and perfect then, and it had carried him to the top . . . Who? What? . . . Faust. Mitchell had cut a deal.[12]

In building up uncanny effects based on both personal and collective experiences, cyberpunk, like the Gothic, subversively magnifies the very elements that classic realism endeavours to keep at bay: inhibited, ambiguous entities that simultaneously disgust and fascinate us. These entities are what western culture broadly designates as *taboo*. The opening pages of Gibson's *Mona Lisa Overdrive* supply a typical catalogue of quintessentially Gothic images evocative of a universe of taboos: haunting, death, madness and an ominous tenebrism. A spectral atmosphere is immediately conveyed by the picture of the young heroine Kumiko surrounded by 'vacant seats', with a cybernetic 'ghost' in her purse and 'her features composed in a small cold mask modelled after her dead mother's most characteristic expression', day-dreaming about 'bright stiff birds sailing the moonscape of her mother's madness' and remembering the 'black-suited company' imposed upon her by her father in the weeks following her mother's death.[13] Kumiko's father, we later learn, is himself a paradigmatic incarnation of the Gothic villain, a '*Kuromaku*', or 'black curtain', operating tacitly, tirelessly and with immense rewards in some indeterminate area 'behind the scenes'.[14] By compressing, in just a few sentences, some of the most distressing elements of the Gothic's image repertoire in a piece of cyberpunk, Gibson suggests that emptiness and darkness are no less relevant to contemporary science fiction than to traditional horror and ghost tales.

Both contemporary and traditional Gothic narratives are equally committed to conjuring up a universe of taboos, in which the *nonthings* that culture normally pushes into the interstices between one compartment and another are brought to the foreground. It is the liminality of tabooed objects that makes them especially attractive to a Gothic sensibility. In pulling to the surface unspeakable materials, the Gothic demonstrates that fantasy is not outside social reality but actually an *exposure* of social reality in inverted form. ('Monster' and 'monstrosity' indeed derive from the Latin word *monstrare*, meaning 'to show', 'to expose'.) The Gothic text and, by extension, cyberpunk narratives inspired by a Gothic aesthetic are representations of the world that capitalize on the dramatization of what consciousness represses and without which, however, it would not subsist. The Gothic, therefore, cannot be explained away merely as a form of escapism, if what is meant by escapism is a total retreat from society, for escapism is itself ideologically encoded. If one examines the socio-historical circumstances in which the Gothic found inception, it becomes clear that class tensions, uncertainties about the present's relation to a nebulously documented past, and anxieties about the future pervade its narrative fabric. Moreover, the fantasy worlds sought by its most avid readers were part of a rigidly mapped social calendar, namely the holiday realm of non-productive indulgence necessary to the preservation of a productive routine of efficiency and thrift. The dreamlike journey undertaken by many a Gothic hero or heroine as s/he descends into the Gothic building and hence into its owner's seedy secrets is also a descent into history – an attempt to understand and come to terms with social reality rendered urgently necessary by intimations of crisis and change.

The Gothic world painted by cyberpunk, and particularly by Gibson, is a world of chiaroscuro. Like the uncanny, it capitalizes on unrelieved feelings of suspense and uncertainty. It can never be a world of utter darkness, because without an element of light, however dim, there would be no tension, and hence no fear. In Gibson's Gothic environment, light falls and rises in subtle variations, suggesting the flickering dance of candle-flame and wisps of smoke, while juxtaposing the blaring illumination and spectral shadows of the post-industrial megalopolis. As shown in previous chapters, the bodies that populate these worlds are themselves intrinsically uncanny; they come across as threshold phenomena precariously suspended between materiality and immateriality and are, as a result, extremely hard to define. Like their environments, cyberpunk's bodies exhibit inherently Gothic traits. An intricate and befuddling incarnation of often repressed desires and fantasies, the Gothic body eludes labelling and its appeal is accordingly complex. Above all, it is boundless: this condition is most famously epitomized by the formless pulp of the unfinished female creature that Dr Frankenstein ends up scattering over the floor of his laboratory. Moreover, the skin that is conventionally presumed to contain the body is all too easily penetrated, perforated, dissolved. The dermal patchworks and face masks constructed by Buffalo Bill and Hannibal Lecter in Thomas Harris's *The Silence of the Lambs* vividly exemplify this redefinition of the skin's function. As pointed out by Stelarc, the body's penetrability cannot be regarded merely as a fictional theme, for it largely results from pressingly real technological developments:

> As surface, skin was once the beginning of the world and simultaneously the boundary of the self. . . . But now *stretched* and *penetrated* by machines, SKIN IS NO LONGER THE SMOOTH SENSUOUS SURFACE OF A SITE OR A SCREEN. Skin no longer signifies closure.[15]

LAYERING AND ARCHITECTURE

The connection between cyberpunk and the Gothic is not merely thematic but structural as well. This is borne out by striking similarities between digital technology's reconfiguration of space and the Gothic's own approach to spatial structures. The aim of this section is to show that technological and Gothic representations of space share an emphasis on principles of decentralization and layering, that these ideas are amply documented by Gothic architecture, and that cyberpunk's own architectural images are often overtly inspired by Gothic spaces and places.

As we have seen, current debates on the effects of technoscience both celebrate the possibility of a global community and deplore the loss of traditional threads of connection. Cyberculture is alternately construed as a liberating experience verging on the *sublime* and as a means of reinscribing conventional prejudices about identity and colonial fantasies of conquest. Leaving aside the polarizing trend, it may be possible to view digital technology not as a homogenizing phenomenon but rather as a set of practices capable of highlighting differences traditionally flattened by the rationalizing thrust of modernity and of destabilizing centralized systems of communication and control. This defiance of centralized control is parallelled by recent developments in the field of artificial intelligence. For a long time, scientists were interested in devising automata that imitated the structure of the human nervous system – a hierarchical network governed by a privileged centre. On the whole, it turned out that even the most sophisticated apparatus was rather primitive in comparison with the human brain. Over the last couple of decades, science has been moving away from the idea of the automaton as a centralized system of control and experimenting, instead, with *layering* (or *subsumption architecture*). The automaton is assembled through the layering of separate units, each corresponding to a specific behaviour system, without any dominating ruler *from above*. The principles of subsumption architecture exhibit intriguing points of contact with Gothic architecture in both its original form, in its eighteenth- and nineteenth-century Revivals, and in its dystopian interpretation by cyberpunk writers and artists.

Layering is a defining trait of Gothic architecture. Although the *ruin* is the architectural item most readily associated with the Gothic, the accumulation of layer upon layer of startlingly complex structures is no less crucial. The proliferation of halls, stairways and vaulted spaces to be found in the engravings of Piranesi (1720–78) collected under the title *Carceri d'invenzione* ('Imaginary Prisons') epitomizes the Gothic fascination with labyrinthine structures and an incremental layering reaching towards infinity. Horace Walpole was enthusiastic about Piranesi's achievements and particularly keen on his architectural daring. William Beckford, for his part, claimed to depict his settings, with their 'chasms, and subterranean hollows, the domain of fear and torture . . . in the style of Piranesi'.[16]In more recent times, a formal homology between Gothic aesthetics and imaginary architecture can be seen in the works of Maurits Cornelius Escher (1898–1972). As Miranda Fellows observes:

> Escher strove to achieve the impression of limitless space, to explore the transformation of one world into another, or others. Often we can follow the transformations as they occur and believe them, even though rationally we know they are impossible. . . . When approaching such works, it is best to suspend disbelief and join the artist on a journey into a world where even gravity does not seem capable of keeping our feet on the ground.[17]

This portrait of Escher's work could equally well serve to describe Gibson's cyberpunk. His characters' simulated journeys into the matrix indeed open up boundless vistas of interlocking worlds in which the laws of physics are repeatedly flaunted.

By fostering a radical decentralization of space, Gothic architecture often defies both gravity and logic. The most extreme exemplification of this programme is probably to be found in Fonthill Abbey, the 276-foot-high tower erected by William Beckford with the assistance of the neo-Gothic enthusiast James Wyatt. Fonthill Abbey, alas, turned out to be an impossible fantasy, the figment of a fervent but utterly impractical imagination. As Victor Sage points out, 'Its structure was insecure, the mason, who confessed the fact to Wyatt on his deathbed, having neglected to put in the foundations the architect had specified under the tower. The octagonal tower duly collapsed in 1825.'[18] Yet Fonthill's collapse was possibly not so much an accident as an integral part of its destiny from inception. Beckford, scornful of the classical style and fond of ruins from a young age, feasibly *wanted* Fonthill to be a ruin, a crumbling structure capable of supplying an appropriate stage setting for his Ossianic passions. As Kenneth Clark observes: 'in 1796 Beckford asked Wyatt to design him a ruined convent of which the chapel parlour, dormitory and part of a cloister alone should have survived'.[19] According to William Hazlitt, Beckford and Wyatt thus managed to contrive a spectacular admixture of the sublime and the ludic – if not exactly the ludicrous – in 'a desert of magnificence . . . a cathedral turned into a toyshop'.[20] Clark himself testifies, almost against his best intentions, to the eerie beauty of Fonthill's Gothic vision:

Fonthill can hardly be considered as more than stage scenery. As scenery it is superb. All the eighteenth century demanded from Gothic – unimpeded perspectives, immense height, the sublime, in short – was present in Fonthill, and present more lavishly, perhaps, than in real mediaeval buildings. Even we, who pride ourselves on classicism, cannot be quite dead to this sudden outburst of romantic rhetoric.[21]

Fonthill is also, of course, a telling commentary on the shortcomings of an architectural phallocentrism that Marie Mulvey-Roberts has dubbed 'Toweromania'.[22] The fate of Beckford's fictional hero/ villain Vathek, a famous designer of impossibly high towers, corroborates this reading.

Buildings erected on flimsy foundations or constructed so as to resemble ruins even before time has had a chance of impressing its passing upon them bear metaphorical similarities to Gibson's cyberspace. Indeed, the matrix is, in a basic sense, a foundationless space. The concept of foundations only makes sense as long as it is appropriate to think in terms of a *below* and an *above*, or of hierarchically related parts mutually sustaining one another. This is patently not the case in cyberspace, where data and images stretch over limitless surfaces without any one of them being ultimately any more real or solid than any other. Moreover, the virtual locations visited by Gibson's characters via simstim resemble ruins to the extent that they are always, by definition, fragmentary; no single location can ever represent the whole of the matrix as such. The dystopian cities depicted by cyberpunk, as argued in the previous chapter, are likewise dislocated and decrepit.

Fragmentary and foundationless spaces allude to cultural and ideological decay. Both cyberpunk's settings and Fonthill Abbey (as one of their most intriguing predecessors) typify the Gothic fascination with disintegrating structures as symbolic of the decomposition of consciousness and reason. Disintegration, in this respect, bears significant affinities with the Hegelian concept of *Zerrissenheit*, a term derived from *zerreissen* (meaning 'to tear, rend, lacerate, dismember, disconnect') and designed to describe, as Christoph Houswitschka stresses, the 'rent/lacerated consciousness' produced by personal and social alienation. This state is characteristic of the Enlightenment as 'the period after which the ethical and religious unity of medievalism and feudalism had been fragmented' and in

which 'the growing sense of specialization and limitation in indus-
trialized societies' created the feeling of the individual's unhealable
dissociation from both nature and culture.[23] Fantastic buildings
unable to either stand up or reach completion encapsulate this sense
of laceration and insinuate a vein of scepticism and doubt into
Enlightenment optimism. Cyberpunk amplifies this sense of personal and cultural displacement by setting its fictions in a dystopian
universe of unrelieved uncertainty. At the same time, as we have seen,
it uncompromisingly stresses that the present does not bear witness
to the triumph of reason because it is inextricable from past values
and beliefs, including superstitious ones. Similarly, Gothic architecture insistently emphasizes the infiltration of the present by the
past. Many of its buildings, in articulating a revivalist conversation
between disparate time zones, embody the ambiguous logic of the
counterfeit, a phenomenon described by Jerrold Hogle as intrinsically ambivalent:

> The counterfeit . . . is pulled in two directions at once: on the one
> hand, it includes a spectral longing for a fading 'natural' cor-
> respondence between sign and social status (the mediaeval 'bound
> sign'); on the other hand, that nostalgia is countered by the ten-
> dency to break signs of older status away from their earlier
> connections.[24]

The counterfeit is predicated on a desire to recuperate the past; yet
in so far as it edits and manipulates that past to forge novel configurations of meaning in the present, it concurrently dismantles and
reassembles history in the guise of pastiches. The counterfeits of
Gothic architecture, moreover, do not resuscitate the extinct by pre-
suming to uncover the *life* of bygone times (which is the objective of
traditional archaeology) but rather remind us that the past is only
ever experienced in the shape of a spectral ruin – that the past is
always already *dead* and that any present fabricated on its model
is likewise fashioned out of empty shells. The idea of space as a shell
is articulated by Gibson with reference to the Tessier-Ashpool dynasty. Its members construct intricate locations, meant to symbolize
the family's mythical power, and strive to insulate them from the
outside world by enclosing them within artificial vessels. These are
supposed to function as containers for a solid, richly textured and
homogeneous body. However, the Tessier-Ashpools' denial of the

external world ultimately amounts to a 'turning in', a pathological 'growing inward' that, far from consolidating their self-image, produces a 'void'. The inner space they have sought to create turns out to be an empty shell, its only promise of pleasure consisting of the superficial lustre of 'lapis' and 'pearl'.[25]

In its penchant for decomposition and flux, Gothic architecture is also comparable to Deleuze and Guattari's notion of *smooth* space, a term that denotes fluidity, boundlessness and the collapse of rationalizing grids, in contrast with *striated* space, the symbol of order, classification and categorization. Smooth space alludes to the strategies deployed by Gothic architecture in its tendency to synthesize 'a multiplicity of elements without effacing their heterogeneity or hindering their potential for future rearranging'.[26] Gibson's cyberspace is itself a smooth space, capable of integrating a bewildering array of heterogeneous data and of incessantly reconstellating them, which eludes rigid organization. Indeed, the stacks of data of which the matrix consists do not deliver any legible maps and 'trying to find your way to a particular piece of data'[27] is by and large a pointless exercise. Cyberspace is a dense mass of information that can be penetrated or cruised at random but cannot be grasped by attempting to isolate discrete strands of its fabric. Concomitantly, it does not have one single identifiable shape; to have a clear form it would have to be finite, which clearly it is not. The human body itself may be manipulated so as to resemble the architectonics of cyberspace. The Count, for example, is 'jacked' into 'a single solid lump of biochip' with 'virtually infinite', though untappable, 'storage capacity'. This makes him a multilayered and boundless agglomerate of 'any number of personality constructs'.[28] Smooth spaces of the kind represented by both the Gothic and cyberpunk inaugurate an 'anarchitecture' that confuses the conventional separation between inside and outside, challenges the codes of perspective and undermines the very foundations of Euclidean geometry – particularly, as Lebbeus Woods argues, its glorification of the pyramid as the supreme embodiment of 'intellectual, spiritual or political' hierarchies.[29]

At the same time, Gothic architecture is replete with psychoanalytical connotations. As Peter Brooks has commented, the layered map of many Gothic buildings bears affinities to the Freudian topology of the psyche:

The Gothic castle, with its pinnacles and dungeons, crenellations, moats, drawbridges, spiralling staircases and concealed doors, realizes an architectural approximation of the Freudian model of the mind, particularly the traps laid for the conscious by the unconscious and the repressed.[30]

Anne Williams elaborates the concept of 'the psyche as house' with an emphasis on the dynamics of infraction brought into play by architectural enclosures and demarcations:

> Building walls and declaring boundaries . . . creates both the possibility – and the desire – to transgress any or all of them. . . . A house makes secrets in merely being itself, for its function is to enclose spaces. And the larger, older, and more complex the structure becomes, the more likely it is to have secret or forgotten rooms.[31]

The codes and conventions associated with the Gothic building lend themselves to parodic exploits, as demonstrated by Robertson Davies's recipe for the designing of Haunted Houses:

> There are countless amenities which every house needs, for literary uses, and which have been allowed to disappear from modern domestic design. The attic, for instance – invaluable for nostalgia; it is a proven psychological fact that you can't be nostalgic on the ground floor. And the cellar – admirable for murders, for knife-fights in the dark, for the walling-up of wives who have not worn well. Your objection, I know, is that a house equipped with all these handsome comforts would be rather large. True, but when the owners have finished with it, no ingenuity at all is needed to convert it into a first-class Funeral home. The boudoir is of ample size for a chapel, you can garage the hearse in the Secret Passage, and the oubliette provides ample, cool accommodation for Unfinished Business.[32]

Although this kind of writing could be simply regarded as a mocking dismissal of Gothic clichés, it is also a vivid reminder of the affective import of architecture. The feelings and emotions that different places are capable of eliciting could be regarded as the fourth dimension of built space. According to Henri Lefebvre: 'Representational space is alive: it speaks. It has an affective kernel or centre: Ego, bed, bedroom, dwelling, house; or, square, church, graveyard. It embraces the loci of passion, of action and of lived situations.'[33]

The etymology of the word *matrix*, namely 'womb', is perhaps sufficient evidence for cyberpunk's engagement with the psychological import of constructed space. Like the buildings described by critics such as Brooks and Williams and parodied by Robertson Davies, the matrix appears to contain and systematize space (by incorporating into one single field the totality of computer-generated information) and at the same time demonstrates that space resists totalization. After all, wombs are only *temporary* containers. Moreover, there are always gaps in the chains of data delivered by the matrix that defy rational explanation, and the barriers used to protect specific sets of data from illicit incursions (primarily ICE) invariably stoke the urge to transgress them, even when death may be the most likely outcome.

The relationship between Gothic architecture and cyberpunk's approach to space can also be assessed by reference to two of the most popular terms of Gothic criticism: *terror* and *horror*. Terror is normally associated with the indefinite, with boundlessness, unnameable otherness and sliding signifiers, owing to its lack of a clear object. According to David Punter, it denotes the 'trembling, the liminal, the sense of waiting' as well as 'a limitless implication of the self in a series of actions which persuade us of their inexorability'.[34] Like the Sublime, Fred Botting observes, terror is 'linked to a sensation of awe and wonderment, to an individual's encounter with something breathtakingly incomprehensible'.[35] Horror, conversely, is tied to an object capable of eliciting either intense fear or revulsion and to the phenomenon of abjection as the violent expulsion of polluting agents. It 'is a stark transfixed staring', writes Punter, which 'provides us with shock and surprise'.[36] In one reading, terror is regarded as more intriguing than horror by virtue of its vagueness, its elusiveness and ability to conjure an unsettling sense of the unrepresentable. In another reading, horror is invested with a greater power to disturb than terror, due to its stark emphasis on the physical dimension and its related ability to intimate radical violations of humanity and embodiment. According to Botting, the bodiliness of horror stems from its association with 'encounters which are not so much threatening as taboo'[37] and point to the 'obliteration of the most solid distinctions between life and death, human and animal'.[38]

Gibson's (cyber)Gothic vividly illustrates the interpenetration of terror and horror in the spatial and architectural domains. Terror is evoked by multilayered and maze-like worlds that resist naming and mapping. Horror, on the other hand, is conjured up by the intensely corporeal qualities of Gibson's crumbling and dismembered megacities. If terror stems from an overwhelming sense of geographical instability and boundlessness, horror is elicited by the pervasiveness of tabooed forms that are attractive and repulsive at the same time. 'Villa Straylight', the extravagant structure created by the Tessier-Ashpools, combines these different elements and is explicitly described as 'a body grown in upon itself, a Gothic folly': 'Each space in Straylight is in some way secret, this endless series of chambers linked by passages, by stairways vaulted like intestines, where the eye is trapped in narrow curves, carried past ornate screens, empty alcoves.'[39] *Mona Lisa Overdrive* supplies another paradigmatic example of a Gothic space laden with psychological implications:

> The tunnel wound in on itself like a gut. The section with the mosaic floor was back there now, around however many curves and up and down short, curving stairwells. . . . Up another stairwell they hit a straight stretch that narrowed to nothing in the distance, either way you looked. It was broader than the curved part, and the floor was soft and humpy with little rugs, it looked like hundreds of them, rolled out layers deep over the concrete. . . . The ones on top, nearest the centre, were worn out to the weave, in patches. A trail, like somebody'd been walking up and down there for years. Sections of the overhead striplight were dark, and others pulsed weakly.[40]

'Sprawltown' itself is described by Lucas as 'a twisty place' capable of suspending all distinctions between the real and the illusory: 'Things are seldom what they seem.'[41] And the Hypermart, the epitome of Sprawl architecture, displays a Gothic map wherein 'there seemed to be no regularity to anything, no hint of any central planning agency. . . . There seemed to be no central source of lighting, either.'[42] Similarly, the 'bridge' in *Virtual Light* is portrayed as a quintessentially Gothic agglomeration – an 'amorphous' yet 'startlingly organic' architectural 'carnival' endowed with 'a queer medieval energy'[43]: 'This thing had just *grown* . . . one thing patched onto the next, until the whole span was wrapped in this formless mass of *stuff*, and no two pieces of it matched.'[44] These images suggest that, besides Fonthill Abbey, another possible ancestor of cyberpunk's Gothic settings is Walpole's Strawberry Hill. Like Gibson's locations, Strawberry Hill brings together a wide range of motifs and forms into a somewhat bewildering whole where the barrier between reality and illusion is easily crossed. Walpole's construct is a picturesque instance of Gothic collage in which details from disparate sources, mainly ecclesiastical ones, are faithfully replicated. Nevertheless, its overall structure is decidedly surreal for it is based on eclectic juxtaposition, not on the imitation of one particular Gothic building. Quintessentially Gothic, Strawberry Hill is *like* no Gothic building ever erected or even planned. What makes Fonthill Abbey and Strawberry Hill ideal candidates as forerunners of cyberpunk's extravagant conglomerates is the fact that, in Victor Sage's words, they share one basic factor: 'Both houses are essentially jokes.'[45]

Gibson's architectural *follies* hark back to the spirit of Gothic Revival as eclectic pastiche and, more specifically, to its early phases where, as Sage observes, 'a proliferation of sham and copied detail' far exceeds in importance 'structural principles of building'.[46] The 'Chateau' portrayed in *Idoru* embodies these features as a parodic feat of disproportioned Gothicity: 'Concrete beams overhead had been hand-painted to vaguely resemble blond oak. The chairs, like the rest of the furniture in the Chateau's lobby, were oversized to the extent that whoever sat in them seemed built to a smaller scale.'[47] Gibson's Gothic also embodies the paradox of revivalist style as an admixture of blatant artificiality and presumed naturalism. As Sage points out: 'alongside the self-confessed artifice, lies the appeal of the style to nature: the more theatrical it actually becomes, the "purer" it is claimed to be'. Central to the appeal to nature is the encoding of the 'pointed arch' as immediately related to 'the "natural" world'. According to Sage, 'the pointed arch reproduces semiotically the *Ur-Wald* [primeval forest]. There was even one experiment in the eighteenth century which attempted to prove this proposition by "growing" Gothic arches from wands of ash.'[48] It is tempting, though perhaps preposterous, to interpret this kind of experiment as a progenitor of Gibson's *vat-grown* flesh. A less extravagant connection could, however, be made between the revivalist experiment and Gibson's ideation of architectural forms that, though generated by nanotechnology, appear to *grow* analogously to living, organic species. In the Tokyo depicted in *Idoru*, buildings can be seen in the process of 'growing', especially at night, at an eerie pace comparable to that of candle-melting, 'but in reverse'.[49] Miraculous structures capable of being 'banal', 'sinister' and 'annoying' at one and the same time,[50] the nanotech buildings have a Gothic knack of entering the minds of their observers by crossing the boundary between the conscious and the unconscious planes in a typically uncanny fashion:

> He [Laney] closed his eyes, not wanting to see the new buildings. But they were still there, in the darkness and the light behind his eyelids. And as he watched, they slid apart, deliquesced, and trickled away, down into the mazes of the older city.
> He slid down with them.[51]

That cyberpunk shares with the Gothic a fascination with fragments, ruins and spatial disorder is attested by the important role played in its settings by *gomi*, namely: 'garbage, kipple, refuse, the sea of cast-off goods', as Gibson describes it in 'The Winter Market', which 'our century floats on'.[52] Not only is gomi unstoppable, there also comes a point when it is no longer clear where the gomi ends and the rest of the world begins, as testified by Japanese history:

> The Japanese, a century ago, had already run out of gomi space around Tokyo, so they came up with a plan for creating space out of gomi. By the year 1969 they had built themselves a little island in Tokyo Bay, out of gomi, and christened it Dream Island. But the city was still pouring out its nine thousand tons per day, so they went on to build New Dream Island.[53]

Gibson presents three main attitudes to gomi through Kumiko's reflections. The museological and archaelogical mentality endeavours to harness it to a taxonomic logic: in Japan, gomi 'was a resource to be managed, to be collected, sorted, carefully plowed under'. The Gothic mentality incorporates gomi and dwells in its intertextual yarn. This is exemplified by the architecture of London: 'In Kumiko's eyes, the bulk of the city *consisted* of gomi ... each wall patched by generations of hands in an ongoing task of restoration. The English valued their gomi in its own right ... they inhabited it.' A third mentality, that of the Sprawl, goes even further than the Gothic one by taking gomi's permutational possibilities to hyperreal extremes: 'Gomi in the Sprawl was something else: a rich humus, a decay that sprouted prodigies in steel and polymer. The apparent lack of planning alone was enough to dizzy her.'[54] Here the *terror* aroused by sprawling forms and spaces coexists with the *horror* evoked by inexplicably disquieting visions: the Sprawl is a cabinet of curiosities.

Gibson's revival of Gothic architecture undermines Clark's claim that 'modern architecture, street architecture, is flat' and that it has wholly supplanted medieval configurations of built space: 'One could walk all around the mediaeval cathedral, watching an endless interplay of spires and buttresses, but the street front has to depend entirely on a façade.' In fact, Gibson's hypermarts and streets – by taking to extremes the architecture of the postmodern shopping mall – evoke a sense of unfathomable depth and reinstate 'irregularity' as the dominant, thus producing results akin to those ascribed by Clark to revivalist architecture: 'a series of erosions and excrescences, breaking the line of our streets'.[55]

The Gothic, in conclusion, harbours an architectural sensibility based on haunting of the present by the past, of civilization by barbarism, of reason by irrationality, of progress by regression. This is no less true of the desolate post-industrial wastelands portrayed by cyberpunk than of bleak castles and their concealed passageways, of dilapidated abbeys and graveyards, old mansions, and labyrinthine streets. In all these locations, a sense of limitlessness and the practice of over-ornamentation debunk the classical dream of symmetry and purity. At the same time, the desire to maximize spatially alienating effects overrides the imperative of stylistic consistency. Gothic spaces and places tend to transgress physical laws and, in so far as they are the fictional settings for diabolical intrigues and voracious passions, they automatically exceed and subvert conventional notions of sanity and propriety. Furthermore, the secrets that haunt the Gothic building are not purely *mythical* phantoms. In fact, they are also, as Williams underlines, cultural phenomena produced by the complex *technology* of family structures, dynastic conflicts, and 'the anxieties, tensions, and imbalances' spawned by iniquitous allocations of political, economic and sexual power.[56]

FAMILIES

From its earliest employment in the language of architecture, which is where it finds its inception, the term Gothic has been associated with vandalism and barbarity – the buildings classed as 'Gothic' being the ones erected in the Dark Ages over the wrecks of classical civilizations. Significantly, the architectural term 'Gothic' entered the western vocabulary in the eighteenth century, precisely at the time when ethical conceptualizations and material configurations of *home* were beginning to reflect the values of the rising middle class. At this point, Gothic architecture came to signify everything that the bourgeois residence should disdain: discomfort, coldness, extravagance, unclear boundaries between inside and outside, and, above all, sprawling structures suggestive of lack of control over one's space. In using outlandish castles and labyrinthian mansions as the stage sets for fiction, Gothic literature was simultaneously challenging the bourgeois ideal of the sheltering home and supporting its claims to moral superiority – after all, the inhabitants of those accursed places were *aristocrats*. As we shall see, Gibson's own Gothic spaces are the haunt of a peculiar aristocracy, defined by the economic imperatives of cyberculture but still quite traditional in its attachment to the symbolic significance of lineage and blood. This section outlines some of the central issues raised by fictional representations of the Gothic family and examines their contemporary adaptations in cyberpunk.

Early Gothic settings contributed to the problematization of space not only in the domain of class politics but also in the sphere of family and gender politics. Indeed, the bourgeois promotion of an architectural code of comfort, privacy and control went hand in hand with the advancement of an ethos of domesticity that pivoted on the feminization of space: namely, the relegation of woman to the walled-in realm of the home, hypocritically dubbed as a celebration of woman's domestic (maternal, matrimonial) authority. Ironically, while the aristocratic, barbarian Gothic seemed to embody women's oppression by presenting its female characters as victims and captives of male persecutors, it was the bourgeois home itself that did its best to devalue women by confining them to the claustrophobic environment of *civilized* housing. Arguably, Gothic fiction is neither an attack against the evils of archaic, feudal buildings nor a celebration of bourgeois architecture (and ideology) by implication. Rather, it could be said to comment, in a displaced fashion, on the perpetuation by new regimes of the infamies of the old. According to Avril Horner:

> The heroine's attempts to escape [from the Gothic prison] indicate a desire to subvert a domestic ideology which was beginning to tyrannize the lives of middle-class women within a capitalist, newly-industrialized society; in such a society the bourgeois home was becoming uncomfortably like the castle or prison of the Gothic text in the way it constrained its female inhabitants.[57]

Woman, then, is the archetypal victim of the Gothic building and of its villainous master but she is also victimized by the bourgeois home and by the imperative to perform the role of *angel in the house*: how is the Gothic heroine to deal with space if space is always male-dominated? She may reject the space that incarcerates her and thus defy patriarchal domination – what Alison Milbank describes as: 'the Oedipal father, who in incest would imprison the daughter in cycles of uncanny repetition which, in Freudian theory, have more to do with the death-drives, with *thanatos* rather than *eros*'. But what is the alternative to the Oedipal father? What authority is the struggling heroine delivering herself to upon her rejection of the patriarchal master? According to Milbank, the only alternative authority available is that of the 'pre-Oedipal mother from whom one must separate in order to be a desiring subject at all'.[58] This is hardly a palatable alternative, as it amounts to the subject's alienation from the adult world of language, morality and responsibility. It would seem that the Gothic heroine ultimately has no choice but to come to terms with the walls that encircle her, to learn to negotiate them and the crimes and traumas they secrete, while also making the most of those weak spots where the stone unexpectedly yields or shifts to reveal concealed passages or openings.

The family, as a social, economic and psychosexual organization, plays a central role in Gothic fiction. Arguably, the vagaries and intricacies of traditional family structures have gained novel urgency in recent times as a result of technological developments. As Donna Haraway argues, 'the practices which bind the global family together ... are the simultaneously fiercely material and irreducibly imaginary, world-destroying and world-building processes of technoscience'.[59] However, the hybrid family concocted by technoscience is not a wholly contemporary phenomenon, for its juxtaposition of creative and destructive discourses bears affinities to the archetypal Gothic family, as a structure – always dominant, always precarious – predicated upon conflicting configurations of legitimacy and power. Gothic families abound with illegitimate children and accordingly unlawful claims to power; with semi-legitimate or even legitimate, yet deviant, members; and with aberrant acquired relations (often wives) likely to plant the seeds of disorder and eventual catastrophe. As Anne Williams has shown, the Gothic discourse itself has been critically categorized by recourse to familial metaphors. First, it has been branded as an illegitimate offspring, relegated to the status of 'a skeleton in the closet' by the Leavisite canon.[60] Second, it has been dismissed as a 'black sheep' throwing the spanner into the works of High Romanticism by failing to engage with profound philosophical and ethical issues. Third, it has been equated to a 'madwoman' contaminating the patriarchal home and the House of Fiction alike.[61]

Like the global family engendered by technoscience, the Gothic family is inherently ambiguous because it combines productive and devastating forces. Both the actual families depicted in Gothic fiction and the familial metaphors associated with the Gothic as a discourse point to 'an indeterminate realm of moral ambiguity'.[62] Some critics deplore this ambiguity. Robert Hume, for instance, views it as symptomatic of a total lack of 'faith in the ability of man to transcend or transform' everyday experience 'imaginatively'.[63] Others commend it as a healthy form of nihilism, comparable to surrealist and deconstructive practices. A third approach evinces an obsessive desire to invest the Gothic with origins, with a *family* of its own. This trend is testified by many a critic's insistent attempts to trace the Gothic back to Horace Walpole's dream-inspired composition of *The Castle of Otranto*, and thus grant an aesthetically and ethically dubious discourse with a father, an ancestry and hence a modicum of legitimacy. The 'Myth of Walpole', writes Williams, is fundamentally 'a patriarchal creation story',[64] which, like many of its kind, envisages the *origin* in metaphysical and supernatural terms and hence endeavours to efface the culturally specific and discursively constructed status of all fiction – no less than of social and familial hierarchies. After all, the Walpoles themselves 'had not been born aristocrats, but elevated to the peerage within living memory, just as Strawberry Hill was made, not born, a Gothic "castle"'.[65]

Gibson's cyberpunk articulates distinctively Gothic motifs in its treatment of the family and of the related topos of the trapped female. Gibson problematizes the concept of family in an eminently Gothic fashion by relating different types of family-like conglomerates to varying economic and class imperatives. *Count Zero* underscores the uncanny processes through which dynastic identities are preserved and emphasizes the interplay, within familial structures, of past, present and future. The 'high orbit clans', people like the Tessier-Ashpools and the Vireks, are described as 'a very late variant on traditional patterns of aristocracy, late because the corporate mode doesn't really allow for an aristocracy':

> The clans are trans-generational, and there's usually a fair bit of medicine involved: cryogenics, genetic manipulation, various ways to combat ageing. The death of a given clan-member, even a founding member, usually wouldn't bring the clan, as a business entity, to a crisis point. There's always someone to step in, someone waiting. The difference between a clan and a corporation, however, is that you don't literally need to marry into a corporation.[66]

Old familial modalities persist, in the dystopian fields of futuristic fiction, because, even though the aristocracy may seem antiquated or even obsolete, it is only the very wealthy who enjoy opportunities for virtually limitless survival by means of biotechnological enhancement. (Cyber)Gothic families are highly sophisticated cyborgs, as evinced by the Tessier-Ashpools' ability to clone their offspring – yet their motivations resonate with mythical, even superstitious, fantasies and fears, such as an ancestral *horror vacui*: they spawn their descendants 'in the compulsive effort to fill space, to replicate some family image of self'.[67] Traditional structures and ideologies will perpetuate themselves as long as they are able to go on treading the narrow path between the threat of extinction and the prospect of metamorphosis. The Tessier-Ashpools and the Virek clans are, therefore, 'fascinating anachronisms', neither annihilated nor left intact by change but rather compelled by 'evolutionary pressures'[68] to mutate. Gibson's family is a Gothic 'labyrinth of blood', a hybrid monster akin to 'a chimera with two wildly dissimilar heads'.[69] The transformations undergone by these old families as a result of the emergence of alternative forms of association are analogous to those experienced by the matrix (itself a family of sorts) when, having acquired self-consciousness, it simultaneously becomes aware of its coexistence with a non-human *other*. Ultimately, the history of a family like the Tessier-Ashpools delivers an impalpable record of 'ghost ships, lost cities. . . . Pure Gothic.'[70]

What roles are played specifically by women in this (cyber)Gothic world? Gibson's fiction features a number of tough, intelligent, resourceful and resilient female characters: most notably Molly/Sally in *Neuromancer* and *Mona Lisa Overdrive*, Marly in *Count Zero*, Chevette in *Virtual Light* and Chia in *Idoru*. However, like many traditional Gothic heroines before them, Gibson's females are often victimized, trapped and denied any real freedom of movement or choice. Angie and Mona Lisa in *Mona Lisa Overdrive* are possibly the most obvious examples. Like the Gothic, Gibson's cyberpunk does not portray these abused women out of a sadistic urge to indulge in scenarios of sexual oppression but rather in order to foreground the iniquity of the power structures that define all individuals and are most likely to prey upon dispossessed and defenceless people. Among such structures, the family is one of the most powerful and exerts its authority, paradoxically, not only through its presence but also through its absence. Indeed, while at times the predicaments faced by Gibson's heroines result from their manipulation by unscrupulous parents, at others their isolation and vulnerability derive from their status as rootless orphans. Thus Angie's life is shaped by her father's Faustian deal and Kumiko (in *Mona Lisa Overdrive*) is little more than a puppet in the hands of a ruthless patriarch. On the other hand, Molly, Mona Lisa and Chevette are moulded by parental absence, by families they never had, cannot remember or do not wish to remember. Over and above any nuclear family, present or absent, looms the technological family of multinational corporations, a structure capable of endlessly perpetuating itself, determined to shape 'the course of human history'[71] and, above all, bent on engulfing its members with all the malign zeal ever exhibited by traditional Gothic villains.

Mona Lisa Overdrive supplies a paradigmatic example of a Gothic plot based on the manipulation of women from various social ranks, in the interests of both a traditional family (the Tessier-Ashpools) and the global family of the corporational economy. Swain (executive of the Special Force) and Robin Lanier (Sense/Net co-star with Angie Mitchell) are recruited by the dead – yet active in the matrix – 3Jane Tessier-Ashpool to destroy two women she hates: Angie and

Sally (the Molly of *Neuromancer* provisionally renamed). Swain blackmails Sally into kidnapping Angie, the idea being that once the two women have been thus brought together they may be annihilated in one fell swoop. Sally teams up with Kumiko, the daughter of the Japanese magnate Yanuka whom Swain is forced to host in London. In the meantime, Mona Lisa's body is surgically reconstructed to look exactly like Angie's body and hence provide a replica of the Sense/Net star that may be used to simulate Angie's death. Eventually Sally, with Kumiko's aid, gets hold of both Angie and Mona, Angie is delivered into the matrix, Mona becomes her substitute, Kumiko is allowed to go back to Japan and Sally wanders off with a more or less clean sheet. This ending offers very mixed blessings for the novel's women, in so far as they are both released from their life-threatening ordeals and reinscribed into existing structures of power. Moreover, the novel as a whole emphasizes that all its female characters are in varying degrees vulnerable. 3Jane is a member of the aristocracy with a legendary dynastic past, Kumiko belongs to a traditional Japanese family, Angie is a commercial icon deprived of parents at a relatively early age, Sally is a rootless mercenary and Mona is an illiterate whore. However, regardless of their widely different social positions and family backgrounds, these five women are all liable to being ruthlessly handled as pawns in an intricate power game.

A pervasive mood of filial deprivation characterizes Gibson's work, where the bereft status of many a central character (such as Mona and Molly) is epitomized by their SINlessness, that is, their lack of a 'Single Identification Number' and concomitant marginalization by 'most official systems'.[72] The ghosts of dead parents litter the scene and the dire circumstances of their demise lend a sinister twist to their personalities and to their offspring's memories. In *Mona Lisa Overdrive*, for example, Kumiko's mother is said to have committed suicide, driven insane by her husband's unscrupulousness and greed. Although Kumiko treasures her reminiscences of the dead woman, especially when she associates her with story-telling and the bewitching figures of Northern European mythology,[73] she also exhibits a subliminal resentment against the departed parent – a feeling that is graphically visualized by the virtual merging of Kumiko's mother and the lethal, deranged character of Lady 3Jane Tessier-Ashpool towards the end of the novel.[74] Angie, for her part, perceives herself essentially as an orphan (indeed, there is something of the changeling in her presentation). She holds no certitudes and the only thing she knows, with scarcely any comfort to glean from it, is that she has been handled by her father as a tool for obtaining some special knowledge and that she cannot share her fate with anybody else. The pervasive sense of isolation and rootlessness that characterizes Gibson's portrayal of Angie is brought into relief by the description of her relationship with Bobby Newmark. This amounts to a brief spell of 'love' following the training meant to disclose to her the meaning of her voodoo dreams: 'They were well-matched, Angie and Bobby, born out of vacuums, Angie from the clean bank kingdom of Maas Biolab and Bobby from the boredom of Barrytown.'[75]

As suggested earlier, an important theme, in the context of the Gothic's handling of family sagas, intrigues, secrets and crimes, is that of the enclosed heroine. This theme also features quite prominently in cyberpunk's adaptation of Gothic concerns and imagery. Some examples of trapped female characters whose predicaments are redolent of those of traditional Gothic heroines have already been mentioned. Molly (*Neuromancer*) and Rikki ('Burning Chrome') are imprisoned in a Gothic labyrinth of necrophiliac fantasies. Angie (*Mona Lisa Overdrive*) is enclosed in her Miami villa and relentlessly surveyed through various technological devices. Kumiko and her mother (*Mona Lisa Overdrive*) are caged within the cultural conventions of both Japan and England. Mona (*Mona Lisa Overdrive*) knows little freedom – except for fleeting moments of release enabled by drugs – outside the boundaries of an ominous series of flats, hotels and hospitals in which she is all the time subjected to corporational and patriarchal authority. Lisa ('The Winter Market') is likewise confined to the recording studios where her visions are translated into lucrative commodities. Her very body is commodified, surrounded on all sides and without any hope of escape by media-led teams of 'medics', 'hairdressers and makeup artists', 'wardrobe people and image builders'. Like Mona, she only finds momentary freedom in drugs. Yet these too end up forming one more prison, a dreary trap reminiscent of the conventional Gothic dungeon and its ghostly inhabitants: 'The wizz was eating her, under the stuff the makeup team kept smoothing on, and sometimes it was like seeing a death's-head surface beneath the face of a not very handsome teenager.'[76]

Idoru presents one of the most harrowing examples of entrapment in an artificial world of secrets and lies. Zona Rosa is ostensibly the powerful leader of a world-wide digital network of rock fans. By the end of the narrative, it turns out that the charismatic and protean Zona Rosa repeatedly encountered by the protagonist Chia and by many others in a kaleidoscopic variety of simulated settings is actually 'the victim of an environmental syndrome' that has 'severely deformed' her and forced her into confinement: she 'has lived for the past five years in almost complete denial of her physical self'.[77] Chevette, in *Virtual Light*, is not as literally trapped as some of Gibson's other heroines. However, she is substantially restricted in her moves and hardly able to influence the course of events. Tenacious, clever and plucky, she is none the less caught in a relationship and in an environment over which she has only very limited control. The old man Skinner with whom Chevette shares a shelter on the San Francisco Bridge is not a Gothic patriarch. He has actually rescued her after her escape from the 'Juvenile Center', cured her potentially lethal illness and offered her food and accommodation. Chevette has every reason to be grateful to Skinner. Yet there is also a sense in which she is symbiotically bound to the old man: 'she'd stayed with Skinner, doing what he said to get them food and keep things working up in his room'.[78] The shelter Chevette shares with Skinner is itself a subliminally oppressive Gothic space, crammed with a bewildering range of objects, materials and textures, most of them in an advanced state of decay or eerily reminiscent of obsolete worlds: broken glass, greasy tools, frayed rags, spare mechanical parts, useless furniture, plastic toys.

The Gothic heroine's plight is most vividly exemplified by *Neuromancer*'s Lady 3Jane and it is to her case that the closing paragraphs of this section are devoted. The narrative links that lead to this character can help us understand her role and function. Case and Molly's initial task consists of appropriating the 'Dixie Flatline construct', an electronic recording of the mind of the dead computer hacker 'McCoy Pauley'.[79] The construct is locked in a vault in the Sense/Net quarters in Atlanta, which Molly penetrates remotely assisted by Case. In the course of this operation, a crucial clue – 'Wintermute'[80] – is disclosed and this leads Case and Molly to the AI's parent corporation, the Tessier-Ashpools. With the Finn's help, Case gains virtual access to Villa Straylight. This is 3Jane's Gothic haunt, as well as the home of the terminal that, were it to receive the right message, could fulfil Wintermute's desire: merging with

Neuromancer and thus achieving Godlike status in cyberspace. It is up to Molly to enter Villa Straylight, availing herself of the clues supplied by 3Jane to Armitage – a construct, as already mentioned, produced by Wintermute out of the 'catatonic fortress' of 'Colonel Willie Corto',[81] the *Screaming Fist* soldier who, having tried to escape Russia for Finland, finds himself hurled into the ultimate void of both space and insanity. Case rides 'Molly's broadcast sensory input through the corridors of Straylight' and finally, they reach 3Jane's world – to find that, despite its apparent imperviousness to alien intrusions, it has 'no door'.[82]

The absence of a structurally recognizable means of access to, or departure from, 3Jane's environment is highly symbolic. It alludes to a lack of boundaries and a spatial amorphousness that could signify freedom but also, spookily, ultimate entrapment: doors are irrelevant to 3Jane's fate. Doors are things one opens in order to get out and, figuratively, explore alternative worlds, and closes in order to gain privacy or protect a system of values. But 3Jane has nowhere to go, nothing to explore, no possessions that she could realistically call her own. As the latest descendant of 'an old family' whose age is reflected by the architectural and ornamental 'convolutions'[83] of their abode, 3Jane has no choice but carry, like a casualty of Nemesis, the burden of her dynasty's sinful past. Her lack of options makes her one of cyberpunk's most intriguing variations on the Gothic theme of the enclosed female. Like many Gothic heroines before her, 3Jane is a keeper of family secrets. She is the only character who knows the *magic word* meant to serve Wintermute's purpose. Both the AI's powers and Case's and the Dixie Flatline construct's flair for cutting ICE are, by themselves, inadequate. This vital knowledge makes 3Jane potentially very powerful. However, she is simultaneously weakened and passified by circumstances and emotions analogous to those experienced by traditional Gothic heroines: namely, physical confinement, loneliness, and the subjection to a long history of patriarchal oppression, haunting ghosts and repressed sexual longings.

A foreboding atmosphere of isolation surrounds 3Jane and this is concisely conveyed by the revelation that she is 'the only Tessier-Ashpool awake in Straylight'.[84] Moreover, she is physically caged within a 'single room', the amazing breadth and depth of which do not alleviate the feeling of entrapment but actually evoke the disconcertingly surreal impression of 'an inverse horizon'.[85] At the same time, 3Jane is constrained by the legacy of a paternal tyranny based on utterly arbitrary and whimsical rules. There are still areas of the Villa she is unable to enter: 'I don't have a key to the room you want,' she confesses to Molly. 'I never had one. One of my father's Victorian awkwardnesses.'[86] Beset by 'terror and lust',[87] 3Jane is trapped in a history of mysogynism. This is encapsulated by her father's brutal murder of her mother, an act inspired by the patriarch's intolerance towards his spouse's 'visionary' plans, namely the creation of artificial intelligences.[88] The Gothic flavour of 3Jane's experiences is intensified by her childhood recollections of a spectral world in which the AIs themselves are compared to dreams, apparitions, disembodied 'voices'. The cyber-reality of the Tessier-Ashpool family is furtively traversed by Gothic phantoms: 'there were ghosts in the corporate cores'.[89]

FASHION

Cyberpunk's fascination with the Gothic voices ongoing cultural anxieties but it also alludes to a fashion, posturing or style. This is borne out by Gibson's interest in clothes, accessories, decor and interior design. Gibson does not propose any *one* uniform Gothic style, for on the one hand, we see the Gothic being associated with black, paleness, stark contrasts and severe lines, and on the other, with eccentricity, chromatic extravagance, and sartorial and decorative excess. Gibson plays repeatedly with these stylistic contrasts.

In *Count Zero*, the image of the computer cowboy is crystallized in Bobby's outfit: a 'black t-shirt' bearing 'the square of holo-decal of cyberspace', 'tight black jeans' and a 'black leather garrison belt trimmed with twin lines of pyramidal chrome studs'.[90] This version of Gothic fashion capitalizes on minimalism in its choice of cuts, colours and sizes and brings them into relief through the inclusion of a typically punk accessory. In *Mona Lisa Overdrive*, Gibson supplies a veritable gallery of Gothic styles and the peculiarities of each are highlighted by means of contrasts. Thus Gentry, like Bobby, opts for the minimalist approach, for close-fitting and starkly constructed clothes: he 'dressed sharp and tight . . . black leather trimmed with jet black beads'.[91] Cherry, by contrast, is clad in 'at least four leather jackets, all of them several sizes too big'.[92] At the same time, the relative simplicity of these outfits is contrasted with ostentatious sartorial pastiches: the Kid, for example, is 'draped in a mink coat that [brushes] the immaculate tips of his yellow ostrich boots'[93] and Porphyre wears 'a long loose coat cut from tissue-thin black leather; rhinestone spurs [glittering] above the heels of black patent boots'.[94] Characters are defined by both their vestimentary preferences and by decorative motifs that render them instantly identifiable. The Kid, for instance, is virtually indissociable from his Dodge and the 'row of chrome-plated skulls welded to the massive front bumper'.[95]

Equally pronounced are the stylistic oppositions embodied by the various subcultures presented in *Count Zero*:

> At least twenty Gothicks postured in the main room like a herd of baby dinosaurs, their crests of lacquered hair bobbing and twitching. The majority approached the Gothick idea: tall, lean, muscular, but touched by a certain gaunt restlessness, young athletes in the early stages of consumption. The graveyard pallor was mandatory, and Gothick hair was by definition black.[96]

In 'sharp contrast with Gothick monochrome' is the 'baroque finery' of the 'Projects girls':

> Long black frock coats opened over tight red vests in silk brocade, the tails of enormous white shirts hanging well beneath their knees. Their dark features were concealed beneath the brims of fedoras pinned and hung with fragments of antique gold: stickpins, charms, teeth, mechanical watches.[97]

The Girls' clothes and accessories may appear to be less overtly Gothic than those of the Gothicks but this is not actually the case. The Gothicks embody many of the stylistic conventions that our culture has come to associate with the Gothic and that the subculture of punk has in various ways consolidated. However, the Girls' style is no less Gothic when one considers the affinities it bears with the multilayered complexity of medieval costume and with the proliferating richness of many items of Gothic architecture.

Moving from cyberpunk to the broader fashion scene of the 1990s, we find an intriguing confluence of contrasting Gothic styles in the creations of Thierry Mugler, with an emphasis, felicitously appropriate to the present project, on the interpenetration of mythological and technological elements. Capitalizing simultaneously on strategies of maximization and strategies of minimization, Mugler's photographs often stage the human body in ways that make it appear heroic and triumphant, on the one hand, and dwarfed by its surroundings, on the other. The body is both hard, sculpted, metallic, and soft, unbounded, velvety. This coexistence of apparently incompatible discourses is encapsulated by a paradoxical image drawn from the insectile realm, that of 'armoured fragility'.[98] Mugler's styles juxtapose mythological and technological motifs in an eminently Gothic vein, his collections encompassing sober city suits with chrome embellishments and velvet capes lined with satin; uniform-like outfits designed to emphasize the architecture of the human anatomy and a luxuriant proliferation of feathers, furs, sequins, gold lamé and chiffon; aerodynamic jumpsuits and draped frocks; cyborgian themes and mythological elements of medieval inspiration such as breastplates and bodices (*Astral Bodies, Gothic, Dracula Suit, Galactic Sirens, Rubber Robots*). Mythology and technology are not simply juxtaposed; in many a creation they actually meet and merge. In the four *stages* of the sequence *Robotic Couture*, for instance, the body is first displayed as wearing a long coat of violet satin and an extravagantly large black hat with floral ornaments; there is nothing explicitly technological about this image. Yet subsequent stages reveal a hybrid corporeality: beneath the violet coat lies a black chiffon dress, and beneath the dress a 'robot' body consisting of a silver and Plexiglass suit sheathing the entire body, head included.

Throughout the 1990s, a number of designers have been incorporating Gothic elements into their creations. Claude Montana, Jean-Paul Gaultier and John Galliano are some of the most prominent representatives of this trend. As a surprising variety of *shades* of black, rendered in a wide range of both natural fibres and technofabrics, flows along the international catwalks – counterpointed by accordingly Gothic accessories and make-up (for example, Dior's Autumn 1998 *Les Tenebreuses* collection) – some designers also capitalize on the Gothic's connection with sciencefiction imagery of robotic and cyborgian orientation: for example, Gianni Versace, Veronique Branqhino and Alexander McQueen. Gianfranco Ferre and Ghost, for their part, juxtapose the romantic tone of flowing lines and diaphanous materials, medieval motifs, and a *hard* imagery inspired by industrial technology and computer circuitry.

The sartorial code is not merely a source of descriptive detail for

Gothic-oriented writers, artists and designers. The Gothic as a discourse is itself implicated in the rhetoric of clothing, particularly on the stylistic plane. Henry James explicitly indicates the convergence of vestimentary and literary codes in the Gothic when he describes Robert Louis Stevenson's landmark as 'an amplitude of costume'. This amplitude is best understood by comparison with the 'decency' of writers who avoid sartorial excess, by presenting themselves before the critic 'with just the right amount of drapery that is necessary'.[99] Extrapolating from James's assessment of Stevenson's archetypal Gothic *gnome*, Judith Halberstam suggests that 'amplitude' denotes the Gothic's stylistic 'excess' in opposition to classic realism's sartorial/rhetorical discipline: 'Gothic seems to denote the clothed word as opposed to the near nakedness of supposed realist writing which hesitates to call attention to its costume.' Paradoxically, amplitude of *style* does not entail amplitude of *size* for, as is well known, Gothic novels such as *Dr Jekyll and Mr Hyde*, *Frankenstein* and even *Dracula*, to some extent, do not quite fit the recipe for excellence expected by nineteenth-century realists, namely exorbitant length. Twentieth-century Gothic fictions, for their part, confuse these already hazy parameters by oscillating between monumentality (for example, Anne Rice's *Chronicles*) and capsulation (for example, Angela Carter's short stories) – between the full-length gown and the miniskirt, as it were. However, the clothed theatricality of the Gothic remains a dominant, as 'grotesque' effects are consistently achieved 'through a kind of transvestism, a dressing up that reveals itself as costume. Gothic is a cross-dressing, drag, a performance of textuality.'[100]

Gibson is also interested in the relationship between the Gothic and superficial trends. This is confirmed, in *Virtual Light*, by the dubious agenda of 'NIGHTMARE FOLK ART – SOUTHERN GOTHIC',[101] an enterprise keen on exploiting the commercial potentialities of the cultural myth putatively inspired by William Faulkner. The firm's manager, Ms Cooper, describes her programme as follows:

> What we offer people here is a certain *vision* . . . . A certain *darkness* as well. A Gothic quality. . . . I'm hoping to find someone who can help to *convey* that very darkness. . . . The *mind* of the South. A *fever dream* of sensuality.

Paradoxically, Ms Cooper turns out to come from 'New Hampshire'.[102]

While it is undeniable that the Gothic is a fashion, or rather a set of fashions, a number of critics have stressed that it is also an ambiguous phenomenon that combines dread and excitement and cannot be automatically interpreted as a fairground syndrome. Whether we follow William Patrick Day's line, according to which the Gothic transforms 'the anxiety of fear' into 'pleasure',[103] or whether we follow Judith Halberstam's approach and see the Gothic as a translation of desire into fear triggered by libidinal anxieties,[104] what seems obvious is that the Gothic is based on the interrelation of pleasurable and detestable emotions. This paradox is what connects it most explicitly with an apocalyptic ethos wherein baleful and hopeful visions coexist, prospects of doom and rebirth being indissolubly entangled in the concept and etymology of apocalypse, no less than in the Gothic mentality. Arguably, we go on revisiting the Gothic realms of aberration and darkness in order to name the spectres that scare us most. According to the German film-maker Fred Kelemen, our attraction to many an incarnation of physical, psychological, geographical and historical Gothicity results from a desire 'to put a spell on the demons', comparable to cave-people's attempts to 'capture the demons' (what they feared most acutely) by painting pictures of them in animal form in the eerie depths of the earth.[105]

If the Gothic can be described as a fashion, then, this is not only because of its collusion with trends and styles of a fundamentally commercial kind. It is also because the Gothic *fashions*, or *gives form* to, powerful but often amorphous emotions and to both desires and fears that western culture has construed as taboo. In its deployment of a Gothic aesthetic, cyberpunk stresses an enduring fascination with darkness, mystery and monstrosity that cannot be regarded as a merely superficial attitude. In fact, it speaks volumes about our unceasing efforts to come to terms with horrors that are very real indeed. Like earlier Gothic narratives, Gothic cyberpunk presents political, social and economic evils in a displaced fashion: that is, through fictional beings and hypothetical worlds. Some may be tempted to think that, in doing so, cyberpunk exempts its readers from the responsibility of facing up to actual afflictions, thus pandering to the requirements of those people who are still reluctant to confront horror in its documentary forms: bodies disfigured by hunger, torture, rape, mutilation and the sinister machinery of war crimes committed by tyrants and abetted by putatively democratic dispensations. Nevertheless, by articulating abuse and injustice in fictional form, cyberpunk does not obfuscate their political significance, let alone sublimate their impact. In fact, cyberpunk makes it abundantly clear that the violence perpetrated on defenceless human beings by the governments and economies that *fashion* their lives is not a futuristic fantasy but is actually embedded in the here-and-now. Moreover, cyberpunk's Gothic scenarios emphasize the dilemmas that attend our inevitable confrontation of the experience of *loss*.

TIME ZONES

Gibson's Gothic aesthetic is epitomized by *Agrippa: A Book of the Dead*, a text that addresses the themes of loss, death and mourning not only through its content but also through its structure. An art book produced through the collaboration between Gibson and the New York-based painter Dennis Ashbrough, *Agrippa* consists of a floppy disk containing Gibson's text and of etched pictures related to the text's themes. The main peculiarity of this artefact is that, once the text recorded on the floppy is read, it is automatically erased by the program built into it. *Agrippa* is a self-destructive text that graphically encapsulates the Gothic attraction to dissolution and transience. At the same time, its design mirrors the character of the cyberculture presented in all of Gibson's other works, as a scenario of permanent irresolution. In *Agrippa*, as in cyberculture generally, experience is coded as data that are easily accessible and thus foster in the reader/user an illusion of control. However, the data are also presented as precarious and ghostly; they do not form a solid body of knowledge, for they disappear in sequence at the same pace as they are consumed. Cyberculture makes vast amounts of information readily available by means of computer networks and related virtual technologies, thus conveying a sense of reality and presence. Yet that information is inevitably caught into circuits so complex that they can only go on functioning by shifting and redistributing their data in variable patterns. As a result, a piece of information that is available one minute may well disappear the next, and a piece of information the existence of which one did not even suspect may unexpectedly become accessible. Presence and absence are *virtually* inseparable.

This (cyber)Gothic picture comes vividly to life in *Agrippa*. The project was inspired by Gibson's discovery of an album belonging to his dad, who died when the writer was little. The images contained in the album become a means of reconstituting childhood memories and of singling them out from the adult's body of accumulated recollections. In a Gothic vein, *Agrippa* thus suggests that death is never final, that the dead go on inhabiting our lives and indeed haunting them not only in scary but also in comforting and illuminating ways. The album is symbolic of the interplay of presence and absence. It is present as an object evocative of myriad memories, yet its presence gains significance from the physical absence of its owner.

Like many Gothic settings and like many of cyberpunk's cities, the album is a *ruin*: 'A Kodak album of time-burned / black construction paper' hinting at 'some later demolition'. It is an ensemble of *fragments* in which intelligible data are disjointed by illegible gaps:

> Inside the cover he inscribed something in soft graphite
> Now lost
> Then his name
> W.F. Gibson Jr.
> and something, comma,
> 1924.

The pictures then follow in a sequence that would no doubt have seemed logical to Gibson's dad but that Gibson himself and the reader have to make sense of in a tentative fashion, lacking the benefit of shared experience. The number of links one could establish among images such as the following, for example, is unthinkably large: 'a flat-roofed shack', 'the spaniel Moko', 'a horse named Dixie', 'moma . . . beside the pond / in white big city shoes'. The album's design and its readings are comparable to the shapes and possible interpretations of the data supplied by the matrix. Cyberspace gives us data but it does not provide obvious instructions as to how they should be organized and read, let alone understood.

One of *Agrippa*'s recurring motifs is a sense of spatial dislocation that mirrors both Gothic and cyberpunk sensibilities. Empty spaces haunted by ghostly traces, decaying cities, overly decorated buildings, dispiritingly anonymous venues and industrial wastelands are prominent in the text. We are invited to visualize 'high-ceiling bedrooms, / unoccupied, unvisited' that hold 'commemorative montages of the country's World War dead' in 'cold chemical darkness'; a 'city' peopled by 'pimps' who go about 'their business / on the sidewalks of a lost world', dubiously beautified by a 'corner of carpenter's Gothic'; an Ohio river bank clouded by 'smoke foul and dark ... overgrown with factories'; a 'heavy, unattractive' house 'sheathed in stucco'; a 'dimestore floored with wooden planks'; an 'all night bus station'. All these settings are smothered by a blanket of intolerable quietness, a 'silence / spreading out' that evokes both the silence of the grave and the unsettling awareness of a 'mystery untold'.[106] In many ways, the past presented by Gibson's father's album antici- pates the present and the future situations and settings depicted by cyberpunk. At the same time, Gibson attempts to make sense of that past by reference to the present he knows and the future he is inclined to imagine. It is hard to determine which tense comes first; the past can be read as a premonition of subsequent developments, yet, simultaneously, the present and the future can be projected onto the past and used to reshape it in the light of the now or the near-now.

Gibson and Sterling's collaboration, *The Difference Engine*, elab- orates on this theme. Given this novel's revivalistic character, an examination of its themes seems an appropriate conclusion for this discussion of the relationship between cyberpunk and the Gothic as a discourse that, as we have seen, is deeply implicated in the rhetoric of Revival. One of the novel's most intriguingly revivalistic traits is its prose style: a minutely calculated parody, or even pastiche, of nineteenth-century narrative techniques, imagery and idioms. Like *Agrippa*, *The Difference Engine* explores the complex interrelations of past, present and future. The novel does not merely project the present onto the future (as cyberpunk generally tends to do) but actually takes the present and the future back into the past, by pro- jecting the cybernetic age onto the cultural reality of the nineteenth century. A work of science fiction, the novel is also, however, some- thing of a documentary record of momentous events: the Industrial Revolution, the Luddite movement and the radical transformations of the social fabric triggered by technological development. More- over, the cybernetic machinery described in the novel is not wholly imaginary. In fact, it stems from a real project revolving around the nineteenth-century inventions of Charles Babbage, to whom the character of Mick refers as 'the Newton of our modern age'.[107] Bab- bage's ideas have come down to us largely through the words of Ada

Lovelace, Lady Byron's daughter, who, like her mother, was enthusiastic about new technologies and highly proficient in mathematics. *The Difference Engine* explicitly refers to 'Lady Ada Byron' as 'the very Queen of Engines'[108] and 'Enchantress of Number',[109] and to 'Byron and his Industrial Radicals' as the technophiliacs that Luddism was committed to eliminating.[110] The 'Rads' are also associated with Darwin's evolutionary theories and their faith in the new is deflatingly described as a passion for 'dinosaurs'.[111]

Babbage's inventions, neither of them developed to his full satisfaction, were the Difference Engine and the Analytical Engine. Both machines were designed to synthesize data and can therefore be considered ancestors of the modern computer. Yet, as Lovelace shows, there are important distinctions between the two models: the Difference Engine is a machine that can simply perform the most basic mathematical operation, while the Analytical Engine is capable of encapsulating the *principles* of mathematics:

> The Difference Engine can in reality . . . do nothing but *add*; and any other processes, not excepting those of simple subtraction, multiplication and division, can be performed by it only just to that extent in which it is possible, by judicious mathematical arrangement and artifices, to reduce them to a *series of additions*.[112]

The Analytical Engine, by contrast, was intended to be able not just to add but also to embody the whole 'science of operations'.[113] According to Sadie Plant:

> Such an undertaking required the mechanization not merely of each mathematical operation, but the systematic bases of their functioning, and it was this imperative to transcribe the rules of the game itself which made the Analytical Engine a universal machine.[114]

The Analytical Engine is akin to a Jacquard loom, the first automated weaving machine. *The Difference Engine* makes reference to this revolutionary apparatus in its opening page, where the sick and ageing Sybil is portrayed resting 'her arthritic hands upon fabric woven by a Jacquard loom',[115] and again in the description of a fabric 'woven in a dizzy mosaic' of minute squares in a pattern that

Ada is said to have created 'by programming a Jacquard loom to weave pure algebra'.[116] What is most strikingly innovative about Jacquard's design is its similarity to computer technology. Indeed, the machine operated by stringing together a large number of punch cards, comparable to present-day software, and was hence capable of storing and processing data at unprecedented speed and volume.[117] Babbage, keen on developing the Jacquard loom model, focused on the possibility of producing complex interactions among the punch cards that could simulate human memory. Lovelace informs us that Babbage explored means of 'backing the cards in certain groups according to certain laws' so as to ensure that 'any particular card or set of cards' could be brought 'onto use any number of times successively in the solution of one problem'.[118] (In *The Difference Engine*, punch cards also play a vital role in its authors' imaginative reworking of magic-lantern shows, a crucial component of the nineteenth-century entertainment industry.[119])

As Plant points out:

> [M]ore than one hundred years passed before it [the Analytical Engine] was put to use, and it is this remarkable timelag which inspires Gibson and Sterling to explore what might have happened if it had been taken up in the 1840s rather than the 1940s.[120]

In this respect, *The Difference Engine* overtly exhibits affinities with the Gothic's revivalistic ethos. The Gothic's return to putatively primitive ages is often a means of highlighting what things *might have been* like had western civilization taken a different course. Concurrently, it draws attention to what history has marginalized or ostracized. Gothic Revivals have time and again sought to question the past by suggesting that its *pastness* does not make it obsolete but actually compels us to address its relevance to the present, especially if conspicuous parts of the past have been censored and hence prevented from coming to fruition. *The Difference Engine* has much in common with this programme. It speculates about the opportunities that past ages have repressed or failed to pursue and about the uncanny resurgence of such opportunities in contemporary culture. Like the Gothic generally, the novel typifies an unwillingness to *leave things alone* and an inclination to keep on haunting the past by which it is, in turn, haunted.

One of the most strikingly Gothic features of Gibson and

Sterling's collaboration is its ironical debunking of the philosophy of Rationalism. The novel teems with both real and imaginary Societies and institutions (the Royal Society, the Royal Geographical Society, the Royal Society's Commission on Free Trade, the Department of Quantitative Criminology, the Section of Criminal Anthropometry, and so on) that are intent on systematizing knowledge and thus testify to the Victorian passion for taxonomies as a means of exorcizing the threat of cultural instability. The Societies presented in *The Difference Engine* often consist of unprofessional enthusiasts whose 'curiosity' is no less 'shallow' than it is 'broad' and makes them a clownish body of 'zealots' and 'amateurs'.[121] The Enlightenment is called into question not only by such allusions to his champions' euphoric ingenuousness but also by the novel's consistent emphasis on a Gothic reality of corruption, espionage, racial discrimination and savage murders, saturated by 'a cloacal reek' of 'subterranean intensity'.[122] In the typically anti-idealistic spirit of cyberpunk, *The Difference Engine* portrays a world of rootlessness, dispossession and greed in which even the loftiest ideals are bound 'to be crushed again and again and again, like the carcass of a mongrel dog under the racketing wheels of an express train'.[123]

EPILOGUE

CYBER PUNK AND MEMORY

Computers in my books are simply a metaphor for
human memory: I'm interested in the hows and whys of
memory, the way it defines who and what we are, in how
easily memory is subject to revision.

(William Gibson)[1]

I think it's difficult for us to know what we lose. We are
constantly losing things, and often, as we lose them, we
can't remember what they were. They go, they really do;
we lose them totally as we move forward in this increasingly mediated existence. I think that's probably one of
the tasks of the contemporary poet: to try to capture that
sense of constant loss.

(William Gibson)[2]

This closing section sums up the main themes and issues explored in
the body of the book, using as a leading thread the idea that cyberpunk and cyberculture reconfigure radically our grasp of history and
time, with profound repercussions on both individual and collective
memories. As we have seen, cyberculture articulates a deep sense of
instability. Definitions of cyberculture itself are fundamentally
unstable due to their openness to a sometimes baffling variety of
interpretations. Additionally, our understanding of both cyberculture and its fictional constellations in cyberpunk is unremittingly
destabilized by intimations that technology, despite its scientific
matrices, is steeped in fantasy and myth. The Gothic precariousness
and ambiguity of biological and urban bodies alike typify the general atmosphere of impermanence evoked by cyberculture. This
sense of impermanence is further fuelled by radical redefinitions of
the relationship between identity and memory. In both cyberculture
generally and cyberpunk specifically, memories tend to take an
increasingly *prosthetic* form, as images that do not result from personal experience but are actually implanted in our brains by the
constant flow of mass information. These images evoke the picture
of history as something of a massive data-bank with no clear
boundaries, dimensions or proportions. In Gibson's cyberpunk,

moreover, memories are prosthetic data that characters acquire when they jack into simstim.

Gibson's notion that computers are a metaphor for human memory and that memory is easily subject to revision is also a central preoccupation of Philip K .Dick's short story 'We can remember it for you wholesale' and of Paul Verhoeven's film *Total Recall* based on Dick's text. Both question radically the idea that human identities are defined by personal memories by suggesting that recollections can actually be artificially grafted. Bruce Sterling's *The Artificial Kid* likewise undermines the notion that personal memories are the guarantee of people's humanity: its central character is constructed on the basis of mnemonic transfer. There is something deeply unsettling about the dissevering of identity from the baggage of individual reminiscences. The assertion, made by the mutant Quarto in *Total Recall*, that 'a man is defined by his actions, not by his memories', may well fit in with a mutant's philosophy but does not quite tally with human expectations. Of course, it could be argued that memory implants may allow people to experience interesting and exciting worlds and situations that would not otherwise be within their reach. This may initially seem to be the burden of *Total Recall*, as Doug Quade buys a set of artificial memories of a journey to Mars that enable him to make the journey himself as any fictional persona he fancies. Yet it soon turns out that memory implants do not grant total freedom. Quade takes his trip in the guise of a secret agent, a role he has deliberately chosen for himself. However, the recollections he is flooded with fall out of his control, as it becomes clear that they have been grafted by an agency based on Mars. Quade's whole identity has been erased, transformed into a dream or illusion. He is not who he thinks he is and cannot really make sense of his artificial identity, much as he struggles to impart coherence to his shattered personality. Quade has no authentic identity, for anything he may regard as a self is actually a product of the microchip implanted in his head. His sense of alienation is fuelled by constant attacks that threaten to fragment further his splintered personality. One of his fiercest enemies is a wife who is not really his wife, the marriage being 'just a memory implant'. In the end, Quade stands out as a hero, having saved the Mutants of Mars from the threat of utter destruction caused by oxygen deprivation. This act, guided by a sense of moral obligation to his fellow beings, may finally make him authentic and human. Yet a margin of doubt remains as to the *reality* of his heroic exploits or indeed of the *memories* evoked by them.

The theme of memory is also famously central to Ridley Scott's *Blade Runner*. On the one hand, the film emphasizes the dependence of both human beings and genetically engineered replicants on material vestiges of the past: photographs that, by supplying them with memories, are concurrently supposed to supply them with a sense of identity. On the other hand, *Blade Runner* shows that memories are not necessarily evidence for lived experiences or for the possession of an individually unique past. The replicant Rachel, for instance, takes the images of her childhood with which she is provided as evidence for her humanity. In fact, those images and the memories they evoke do not belong to Rachel but to her creator's niece. The idea that memories may be simulated, revised and artificially implanted calls seriously into question the traditional western notion that mnemonic powers are a personal possession, that the pictures they conjure up are unique and that this uniqueness is the measure of our humanity. In quizzing conventional approaches to the relationship between the individual and memory, the real and the simulated, the human and the other, *Blade Runner* encapsulates what Gabriele Schwab terms the 'dark side of a culture of cyborgs':

Technology, meant to extend our organs and our senses or even to support our phantasms of immortality and transcendence, seems to threaten what we wanted to preserve by destroying us as the subjects we thought ourselves to be when we took refuge in technological projects and dreams.[3]

Cyberpunk insistently shows that human memories are neither impregnable nor reliable. They can be accessed by computers, edited and manipulated, as testified by Gibson's *Neuromancer*. Here Wintermute penetrates Case's memory storehouse and translates some of its data into holograms to be further reorganized to his own advantage. This scenario presents rather a bleak denial of people's right to remember and save their memories as individual markers of identity. At the same time, it alludes to a repressive conception of history that is not purely futuristic, for it actually reflects traditional approaches to the recording and storing of past events. This version of history is based on the suppression of personal memories and on their transformation into official *facts*. Humanist models of history and memory have traditionally capitalized on these strategies, by repressing actual and fluid recollections and by crystallizing them into theoretical data. Memories are thus divorced from lived experience and enclosed in the lifeless space of the *archive*. Kathleen Biddick has commented on the import of humanist approaches to history and memory thus: 'Humanist history deterritorializes memory as remembering and reterritorializes it as archive. It has served as the institutional discipline of memory, marking and remarking who is remembered, what is remembered and in what way.'[4] Cyberpunk exposes the repressive and violent character of the humanist regulation of memory by emphasizing sustained violations of the individual's memory-bank.

At the same time, cyberpunk challenges the humanist commitment to the colonizing logic of the archive by undermining the possibility of organizing information and memories in any permanent and systematic way. The cybernetic data-bank can hardly be visualized in spatial terms; it is not ultimately locatable because it belongs in a realm that qualifies as space and non-space at the same time. Indeed, in exploring any one portion of the matrix, 'you could get this funny sense that you were leaning out, over the edge of the world, and the space beyond that sort of fell away, forever' in a 'cloud or fog or sky that was no colour and every colour at once, just sort of seething'.[5] In cyberspace, the discrete identity of any one set of data is continually called into question by its interpenetration with an unthinkable number of other data: 'data so dense you suffered sensory over-load if you tried to apprehend more than the merest outline'.[6] Furthermore, the notion of the archive as a neatly mapped construct in which knowledge is systematically recorded is radically dislocated by Gibson's depiction of hallucinatory spaces in which robots, androids, mutants, cyborgs and AIs constantly interact with phantoms, vampires, centaurs and voodoo spirits. The present is relentlessly open to a process of Gothic infiltration by both the past and the future which turns history into 'the plot of a multi-headed narrative tapeworm',[7] a palimpsest in which each tense invokes the other in a transactional continuum.

If the sprawling geography and hybrid population of the matrix defy mapping and classification, so does its temporal dimension. As argued in the closing section of the preceding chapter, Gibson repeatedly problematizes time by interweaving past, present and future dimensions in his yarns. This point is vividly emphasized by Nick Clark:

> While a number of recent writers of fiction – Gibson included – have offered vivid depictions of cities layered with obsolete signifying objects and images, it is not always certain that their most futuristic constructions escape the imprint of the past. Afterimages and premonitions often seem indistinguishable.[8]

The picture painted by Clark evokes a postmodern conception of history in which linearity is drastically undermined and the present becomes the always provisional meeting-place of the past and the future. The idea that the present, in both its actual and its futuristically distorted manifestations, is all the time traversed by past traces also echoes Walter Benjamin's assertion that the 'angel of history' cannot look at the future without all the time beholding the waste that fills the present and the past. History may seem to move forward but this movement is rendered non-linear and unprogressive by an indomitably retroactive pull.[9] As Jean Baudrillard puts it, 'reality loops around itself', as 'each phase of value integrates into its own apparatus the anterior apparatus as a phantom reference, a puppet or simulation reference'.[10]

The present, the future and the past are as inextricably intertwined in cyberpunk as are technology and mythology. This is clearly exemplified by Gibson's interpretation of history, in *Mona Lisa Overdrive*, as the high-resolution dream of a digital apparition, namely the 'ghost' Colin emanating from a portable biochips unit. Colin is a state-of-the-art incarnation of futuristic high tech, yet he is programmed, paradoxically, to divulge information about the obscure, submerged past. As Colin pedantically lectures his Aladdin-like owner Kumiko about London's hidden past, history comes across as a fictional reconstruction, by a simulated body, of spaces and eras haunted by mysterious traces that may ultimately prove just as virtual.[11] The idea of history as a synthetic construct with an ultimately unverifiable authenticity suggests that the past may be fantasized about in myriad ways but never retrieved. Relatedly, both individual and collective memories are objects of endless speculation that preclude the possibility of ever ascertaining to what extent the images we recall encapsulate lived experiences and to what extent they embody unfulfilled longings or repressed fears.

Gibson's work consistently underscores the uncertain nature of memory and the elusiveness of the past by intimating that neither closure nor disclosure are viable projects. His plots are by and large open-ended and his characters often have to live with impenetrable secrets. Even when mysteries are solved and crimes are punished, we are left with an overall sense of incertitude and doubt. The ending of *Neuromancer* records the breakdown of the relationship between Molly and Case. The closing pages of *Count Zero* portray Angie and Bobby in an idyllic setting but the spiteful assessment of Bobby's behaviour by Angie's producer makes it quite clear that the idyll is not to last. In *Mona Lisa Overdrive*, the finale registers some of the main characters' dissolution into the unbounded matrix: a playground that is also, however, something of a limbo. *Virtual Light* comes close to supplying a compensatory rounding off of the fictional experience in hinting at the possibility of Rydell and Chevette being reunited. Yet the reader does not obtain any incontrovertible evidence of this felicitous conclusion. As for *Idoru*, the ending sees its young heroine restored to the relative safety of home, yet burdened by disillusionment and loneliness. What is more, Gibson's plots abound with characters whose minds have been tampered with in a variety of brutal and sinister ways and who struggle to regain a modicum of control over their mental faculties. On the whole, what their efforts allow them to resurrect is not a rational, orderly and authentic past but a wrenching sense of loss. Case, Angie, Slick and Laney are arguably the most obvious illustrations of split identities that no amount of psychoanalytical working-out would feasibly endow with a sense of wholeness.

Gibson's stories patently shun the idea that by digging into the past we may unveil hidden truths, allow the repressed to manifest itself freely, and thus inculcate a sense of order on the chaotic jumble of both personal recollections and historical events. In this respect, Gibson's version of history is inspired by a Gothic aesthetic that rejects orthodox notions of archaeology as a recovery of the past and stresses instead images of irreparable devastation. The Gothic ruin is eminently non-archaeological, for it foregrounds death rather than life; it points to the disintegration of the present rather than to the life of a past culture. In psychoanalytical terms, archaeology is a symbolic practice that allows the subject to cover over its own roots while focusing on the unveiling of those of a dead culture, in order to bring it back to life. The Gothic ruin, on the other hand, forces the subject to confront its own fragmentary status and the pervasiveness of irreversible decay across time and space. Gibson offers as radical a demystification of archaeological pretensions. On the facetious level, this debunking is typified by the character of 'Mr. Paleologos'.[12] Although his name is overtly reminiscent of the study of the buried past, his professional occupation as a travel agent arranging holidays in orbit serves to confuse the relationship between past and present, present and future. Where is he *really* taking his clients? Back to the future? Forward into the past? Furthermore, throughout Gibson's output vestiges and remnants gleaned from the past fail to yield a harmonious picture of *life-as-it-was*, for all they supply is a discontinuous and splintered assemblage of haphazardly selected objects that may well testify to *life-as-it-might-have-been* more than to any ascertainable epoch. In *Count Zero*, as we have seen, the past is Gothically documented by 'boxes' containing an array of disconnected mementoes. The boxes are most definitely attempts to deal with the past but they do not presume to function as ways of recuperating a vision of wholeness. In fact, they are born of a painful recognition of the futility of all claims to coherence. There may have been 'a brilliant time . . . without duration' where everything existed everywhere in blissful undifferentiation, but this is merely a speculation for what we *know* in the present is a state of disunity and 'scattered fragments'. The boxes contain promiscuous collections of 'traces of memory' and it is precisely by virtue of their jumbled gesture that they may bear witness to 'all the worn sad evidence of a family's humanity'[13] – not by virtue of a commitment to the restorative ambitions of official archaeology. Gibson's cyberpunk shows that the past is concurrently irretrievable, if what we seek in it is a logical chain of causes and effects, and unerasable, owing to its magical knack for infiltrating the present and the future.

Gibson's work is by no means the sole expression of cyberpunk's preoccupation with the vagaries of time and memory. To date, the genre in practically its entirety has consistently displayed an unflinching focus on the dilemmas engendered by the web of individual and communal memories that shape our understanding of history and simultaneously complicate our grasp of the relationship between reality and illusion. These issues are vividly dramatized by the Wachowsky Brothers' film *The Matrix*, which, as a recent work of science fiction, seems to supply an appropriate exit point for this study. The most salient affinities between *The Matrix* and cyberpunk fiction can be observed in the film's handling of time, in its settings, in its character types and stereotypes and in its articulation of motifs made popular by Gibson and his contemporaries. Among these motifs, some of the most prominent are electronically simulated stimulation, technological modifications of the body, the use of elements of Japanese tradition (such as martial arts), the collapse of the boundary between the human and the non-human, the coalescence of technology and mythology and, most importantly, the interplay of reality and hallucination. This last theme provides the structural axes on which the film hinges and the underpinning for its definition of the concept of the matrix.

Like Gibson, Larry and Andy Wachowsky ideate the matrix as the totality of the data surrounding us at all times. If in Gibson it is already hard to establish whether such data are in any sense real, in the film it is graphically stressed that reality is an 'illusion' – a fantasy, a dream or, more likely, a nightmare. *The Matrix* describes the apparently real world that surrounds us (the buildings, the machines and people themselves) as a 'simulated world'. The film's ideas and vocabulary are overtly inspired by the writings of Jean Baudrillard (whose name is actually mentioned in an early draft of the script) and specifically by his theories regarding simulation. Baudrillard's influence is visually brought home by the appearance of one of his most famous books, *Simulacra and Simulations*. The hero, Neo/Thomas Anderson, keeps the illegal computer programs that he sells for large amounts of money in a hollowed-out copy of that text. The only extant page of which the spectator is allowed a glimpse is, intriguingly, the opening of the chapter 'On Nihilism'. The fact that the book itself is hollow, a pretence of the real book, can be taken as a comment on the emptiness and deceptiveness of the reality depicted by *The Matrix*. Baudrillard argues that in postmodern culture, images, copies and simulacra do not imitate a pre-existing reality but rather *replace* reality. Simulation has become reality. Signs no longer bear any resemblance or correspondence to the so-called real world. In fact, they produce their own *hyperreality*: an order of representation capable of engulfing our bodies and minds because it neither looks nor feels unreal but, if anything, *more* than real.[14] In hyperreality, there is no reality behind the flux of codes that generate it. These codes, moreover, are not visible in themselves. We only see them in their simulated manifestations: clothes, furniture, weapons, popular icons and food, for example. *The Matrix* highlights the notion of hyperreality by presenting, scene after scene, very physical and indeed violent confrontations among people who are not actually people but digital representations of bodies passively lying on simstim chairs. However, like Gibson's cyberpunk, the film emphasizes that the physical body is not transcended by such means: one can *die* in an electronically simulated scenario as easily as in a dark alley. If the sensorium is shattered by a simstim experience, the body accordingly collapses, for mind and body, it is maintained, cannot survive without each other.

In his analysis of simulation, Baudrillard argues that hyperreality serves specific ideological purposes. It is an illusion, yet its principal aim is to make us forget that this is the case. It constructs us as passive consumers of assorted false promises and manages to keep us in its thrall by making us forget that we are the world's inmates rather than free agents. *The Matrix* dramatizes this point in its definition of the matrix itself: namely, what is uncritically taken as real but is, in fact, a 'computer-generated world' produced 'to keep us under control'. The matrix is a sprawling network of data that is 'everywhere' and whose very pervasiveness is designed to 'keep you a slave'. A 'neural interactive simulation', strongly reminiscent of Gibson's definition of cyberspace as a *consensual hallucination*, the matrix/reality is constructed so as to prevent its inhabitants from realizing that the world is a 'prison' and that 'humankind' itself, to quote Ian Nathan, 'vegetates in billions of gloop-filled tanks. Mere battery packs for the machineworld.'[15]

In order to expose the illusory nature of reality, *The Matrix* radically unsettles conventional perceptions of time and memory. The year in which the story takes place is not, as the inhabitants of the matrix naively assume, 1999 but rather some year approximately close to 2199. The matrix itself, we are told, was created in 2197. Two hundred years prior to the events presented in the film, the earth was reduced to ashes and heaps of ruins by a lethal conflict between humans and artificial intelligences. Only one city has survived at the centre of the earth and this, tantalizingly, is called 'Zion'. The world that people deem real is actually a simulacrum of the spaces destroyed by the conflict, a virtual reality run by a technocracy of AIs that farm human beings, in Adam Smith's words, 'as living Duracells'.[16] The keepers of law and order in this synthetic world are an artificial body of technomutants and their enemies are a resistance group of rebel computer hackers, situated in a rickety hovercraft unrelentingly threatened by bio-mechanoid octopuses and taran-tulas. (The ship is named 'Nebuchadnezzar', after the king who vanquished Jerusalem and created the Hanging Gardens of Babylon – an image, as we have seen, also used by Gibson.) The renegades hold on to the possibility of setting people 'free' by making them recognize the illusions they live through. The group's leader, Morpheus, believes that 'one' chosen being must be capable of carry-ing out this consciousness-raising mission. After a few blunders, he hits on Neo. Convinced of Neo's extraordinary potential, Morpheus proceeds to reprogram him, train him and raise his powers to unimaginable levels.

Morpheus's project may sound utopian. However, in *The Matrix*, as in much cyberpunk fiction, utopias and dystopias – idealized real-ities and 'the desert of the real' – are closely interwoven. At the same time, the realm of technology is continuously crisscrossed by mytho-logical images. Morpheus can never be certain, in the course of the action, whether Neo is truly the 'One'. In this atmosphere of doubt, mysticism and fantasy come to play an important role: what high technology cannot rationalize must be explained by a sibylline 'Oracle'. Laurence Fishburn (who plays the character of Morpheus in the film) has commented on the interweaving of cybertechnology and mysticism in *The Matrix* thus: 'the film . . . does several things at one time. . . . It introduces you to this really amazing concept about alternate realities. It deals with a great many spiritual teachings which have run through human consciousness for centuries.'[17] Jerry Glover has likewise stressed the multilayered character of *The Matrix* as a text 'stacked with references' to diverse discourses and media: 'From television to classical mythology, from cyberpunk to Oriental philosophy.'[18]

The esoteric is also brought into play by the film's recourse to numerology. The numerical symbolism implied by the name 'Neo' is fairly basic, the hacker Thomas Anderson's pseudonym amounting to an anagram of 'One'. However, the film uses numerology more subtly on several occasions. For example, the number of the heroine Trinity's flat is 303, and both her name and the number carry overtly religious connotations. At the same time, it is worth recalling that 'Trinity' is also the town in New Mexico where the first nuclear weapon test was carried out and hence a location symbolically related to the theme of global annihilation. Further, the number that the viewer zooms into in the opening frames is 555, which symbolically denotes the Messiah, another chosen 'One'. The collusion of technological and fantastic motifs is confirmed by the film's equation of Neo to two imaginary characters famously associated with spatial and temporal dislocation: the 'Alice' of Lewis Carroll's *Alice in Wonderland*, following 'the white rabbit' and tumbling down 'the rabbit hole', and the 'Dorothy' of Frank Baum's *The Wizard of Oz*. Immediately prior to his first trip into reality, Neo is told: 'Buckle your seat belt, Dorothy, "cause Kansas is going bye-bye.'

Like much cyberpunk fiction, *The Matrix* problematizes the concept of the real by suggesting that apparently solid worlds may ultimately amount to impalpable illusions and that such worlds are concurrently technological and mythological. Products of sophisticated electronic devices and apparatuses, they are nevertheless incessantly traversed by the traces of legend, mysticism and fantasy. The ambivalence of these worlds is symbolically encapsulated, in *The Matrix*, by the duplicity of the character of Morpheus. The resistance leader aims at freeing people by exposing the evils of the technologies that have created and maintain the matrix through his own technologies. However, Morpheus's strategies also involve wresting his trainees into often gruesome visions and hallucinations that hark back to a submerged world of primal fantasies. If the matrix is a fictitious world, there is a sense in which Morpheus, too, peddles fictions and dreams. Morpheus was, after all, the classical god of sleep responsible for giving shape to dreams, and little can be predicted about what sleep and dreams will bring, either tonight or tomorrow.

REFERENCES

PREFACE

1 W. Gibson, *Neuromancer*, London: HarperCollins, [1984] 1995, p. 67.
2 N. Land, 'Travels in cyber-reality', *Guardian*, 18 March 1995, p. 17.
3 D. Punter, 'Problems of recollection and construction: Stephen King', in V. Sage and L. Smith (eds), *Modern Gothic*, Manchester: Manchester University Press, 1996, p. 138.
4 B. Sterling, 'Preface' to *Mirrorshades*, New York: Arbor House, 1986, p. ii.
5 J. Dyson, 'Spellbound', *Vogue* (British edition), May 1999, p. 30.
6 I. Csicsery-Ronay Jr., 'Cyberpunk and neuromanticism', in L. McCaffery (ed.), *Storming the Reality Studio: A Casebook of Cyberpunk and Postmodern Fiction*, London and Durham, NC: Duke University Press, 1991, p. 187.
7 C. Raven, 'From zero to it-boy', *Guardian*, 19 August 1998, pp. 4–5.
8 J. Kristeva, *The Powers of Horror*, trans. L. Roudiez, New York: Columbia University Press, 1982.

INTRODUCTION: SCIENCE FICTION AND CYBERPUNK

1 B. Sterling, from 'License to Dream', a contribution to the Convocation on Technology and Education, National Academy of Sciences, Washington, DC, 10 May 1993: http://www.uflib.ufl.edu/sterling.license.html.
2 In G. Salza, 'Interview with William Gibson', 1994: http://www.maxheadroom.com/gibson_interview.html. A slightly different version of this interview was incorporated in Giuseppe Salza's book *Che cosa ci faccio in Internet*, Rome: Theoria Edizioni, 1995.
3 I. Calvino, *Six Memos for the Next Millennium*, trans. P. Creagh, London: Vintage, 1996, p. 20.
4 This definition of science fiction is derived from an editorial by Hugo Gernsback published in *Amazing Stories* in 1926, quoted in M.

Wynne-Davies (ed.), *The Bloomsbury Guide to English Literature*, London: Bloomsbury, 1989, p. 897.

5 'Science Fiction', *Grolier Multimedia Encyclopedia*, version 7.0, Grolier Electronic Publishing, 1995, p. 1.

6 Ibid., p. 2.

7 K. Amis, *New Maps of Hell*, New York: Columbia University Press, 1960.

8 D. Suvin, *Metamorphoses of Science Fiction*, New Haven and London: Yale University Press, 1979.

9 J.G. Ballard, *Crash*, London: Vintage, 1995, p. 4.

10 F. Botting, *Gothic*, London and New York: Routledge, 1996, p. 157.

11 D. Punter, *The Literature of Terror*, vol. 2, New York: Longman, 1996, p. 120.

12 Ibid., p. 136.

13 J. G. Ballard, *Crash*, p. 151 (see note 9).

14 S. Metcalf, 'Autogeddon', in J. Broadhurst Dixon and E.J. Cassidy (eds), *Virtual Futures: Cyberotics, Technology and Post-Human Pragmatism*, London and New York: Routledge, 1998, p. 112.

15 J.G. Ballard, *Crash*, p. 134 (see note 9).

16 Ibid., p. 172.

17 I. Ousby, *The Crime and Mystery Book: A Reader's Companion*, London: Thames & Hudson, 1997, p. 91.

18 B. McHale, 'POSTcyberMODERNpunkISM', in L. McCaffery (ed.), *Storming the Reality Studio: A Casebook of Cyberpunk and Postmodern Fiction*, London and Durham, NC: Duke University Press, 1991, p. 316.

19 T. Mooney, *Easy Travel to Other Planets*, New York: Farrar, Strauss & Giraux, 1981, p. 24.

20 D. Porush, 'Frothing the synaptic bath: what puts the punk in cyberpunk?', in G. Slusser and T. Shippey (eds), *Fiction 2000*, Athens, Georgia: University of Georgia Press, 1992, p. 258.

21 K. McCarron, 'The body and cyberpunk', in M. Featherstone and R. Burrows (eds), *Cyberspace/Cyberbodies/Cyberpunk: Cultures of Technological Embodiment*, London: Sage, 1995, p. 265.

22 R. Rucker, *Software*, New York: Ace, 1982, p. 30.

23 V. Sobchack, *Screening Space*, New York: Ungar, 1987, p. 225.

24 L. McCaffery, 'Introduction: the desert of the real', in *Storming the Reality Studio*, p. 16 (see note 18).

25 H. Moravec, *MIND Children: The Future of Robot and Human Intelligence*, Cambridge, Mass.: Harvard University Press, 1988.

26 W.J. Williams, *Hardwired*, New York: T. Doherty Associates, 1986, p. 293.

27 R. Rucker, *Software*, p. 15 (see note 22).

28 B. Sterling, 'Preface' to *Mirrorshades*, New York: Arbor House, 1986, p. ix.

29 C. Springer, *Electronic Eros*, Austin: Texas University Press, 1996, p. 36.

30 B. Sterling, 'Twenty evocations', originally published in *Mississippi Review* 47/48, 1988; reprinted in *Storming the Reality Studio*, p. 154 (see note 18).

31 Ibid., p. 156.

32 Ibid., pp. 159–61.
33 B. Sterling, *Schismatrix*, New York: Ace Science Fiction, 1985, p. 44.
34 L. McCaffery, 'Introduction: the desert of the real', p. 12 (see note 24).
35 S. Brown, 'Before the lights came on', in *Storming the Reality Studio*, p. 177 (see note 18).
36 I. Csicsery-Ronay Jr., 'Cyberpunk and neuromanticism', in *Storming the Reality Studio*, p. 186.
37 D. Hebdige, *Subculture: The Meaning of Style*, London and New York: Methuen, 1988, p. 151.
38 Ibid., p. 64.
39 Ibid., pp. 66–7.
40 Ibid., p. 65.
41 Ibid., p. 66.
42 L. McCaffery, 'Cutting-up: cyberpunk, punk music, and urban decontextualizations', in *Storming the Reality Studio*, p. 289 (see note 18).
43 Ibid., pp. 290–1.
44 L. McCaffery, note on 'Contributors', in *Storming the Reality Studio*, p. 387.
45 J. Shirley, 'Wolves of the plateau', in *Storming the Reality Studio*, pp. 138–43.
46 L. Shiner, 'Stoked', *Re: Artes Liberales*, Spring/Fall 1988, p. 198.
47 J. O'Barr, 'Frame 137', in *Storming the Reality Studio*, p. 118 (see note 18).
48 Ibid., p. 120.
49 M. Leyner, 'I was an infinitely hot and dense dot', from *My Cousin, My Gastroenterologist*, New York: Harmony/Crown, 1990, p. 3.
50 Ibid.

1: CYBERPUNK AND VIRTUAL TECHNOLOGIES

1 H.W. Targowsky, *Mark/Space* 1994: http://www.euro.net/mark-space/; M. Heim, *The Metaphysics of Virtual Reality*, Oxford: Oxford University Press, 1993, p. 150; L. Person, personal e-mail to H.W. Targowsky, August 1997; B. Sterling, 'Preface' to *Mirrorshades*, New York: Arbor House, 1986; F. Jameson, *Postmodernism, or, The Cultural Logic of Late Capitalism*, London: Verso, 1991, p. 419; W. Jeschke, 'Three points of no return – glimpses of the future?', Guest of Honour Speech, Confiction 1990 (48th World Science Fiction Convention), The Hague, 25 August 1990; P. Cadigan, quoted in M. Brace, 'Virtual celebrity', *Guardian*, 16 March 1994.
2 J. Winterson, *Gut Symmetries*, London: Granta, 1997, p. 6.
3 Ibid., p. 72.
4 Ibid., p. 73.
5 N.K. Hayles, 'Virtual bodies and flickering signifiers', in T. Druckrey (ed.), *Electronic Culture*, New York: Aperture, 1996, p. 269.
6 A. Kroker and M. Weinstein, 'The hyper-texted body, or Nietzsche gets a modem', 1997: http://www.aec.at/ctheory/e-hyper-texted.html. From

Data Trash: The Theory of the Virtual Class, New York: St Martin's Press, and Montreal: New World Perspectives, 1994.

7 B. Laurel, *Computers as Theatre*, Reading, Mass.: Addison Wesley, 1991.
8 S. Cubitt, *Digital Aesthetics*, London: Sage, 1998, p. 3.
9 H. Besser, 'From Internet to Information Superhighway', in J. Brook and I.A. Boal (eds), *Resisting the Virtual Life: The Culture and Politics of Information*, San Francisco: City Lights, 1995, p. 63.
10 A.L. Shapiro, 'Street corners in cyberspace', *The Nation*, 3 July 1995, p. 10.
11 S. Pfohl, 'Theses on the cyberotics of HIStory: Venus in Microsoft, remix', in J. Broadhurst Dixon and E.J. Cassidy (eds), *Virtual Futures: Cyberotics, Technology and Post-Human Pragmatism*, London and New York: Routledge, 1998, p. 27.
12 C. Chesher, 'The ontology of digital domains', in D. Holmes (ed.), *Virtual Politics: Identity and Community in Cyberspace*, London: Sage, 1997, p. 82.
13 B. Sterling, from 'License to Dream', a contribution to the Convocation on Technology and Education, National Academy of Sciences, Washington, DC, 10 May 1993: http://www.uflib.ufl.edu/sterling.license.html.
14 A. Bruckman, 'Finding one's own space in cyberspace', *Technology Review* 99.1, January 1996, pp. 48–54.
15 N. Negroponte, *Being Digital*, New York: Alfred A. Knopf, 1995, p. 4.
16 R. Shields, *Cultures of Internet: Virtual Spaces, Real Histories, Living Bodies*, London: Sage, 1996.
17 J. Wood, 'Curvatures in space-time-truth', in J. Wood (ed.), *The Virtual Embodied: Presence/Practice/Technology*, London and New York: Routledge, 1998, p. 4.
18 M. Poster, 'Cyberdemocracy', in *Virtual Politics*, p. 224 (see note 11).
19 S. Turkle, 'Constructions and reconstructions of the self in Virtual Reality', in *Electronic Culture*, p. 355 (see note 4).
20 Ibid., pp. 355–6.
21 S. Turkle, *Life on the Screen*, London: Weidenfeld & Nicolson, 1996, p. 22.
22 V. Seidler, 'Embodied knowledge and virtual space', in *The Virtual Embodied*, pp. 27–8 (see note 16).
23 L.M. Blackman, 'Culture, technology and subjectivity', in *The Virtual Embodied*, p. 143.
24 J. Lanier and F. Bocca, 'An insider view of the future of Virtual Reality', *Journal of Communication* 42.4, 1992, pp. 150–72.
25 M. Heim, *The Metaphysics of Virtual Reality*, Oxford: Oxford University Press, 1993, p. 7.
26 W. Gibson, *Neuromancer*, London: HarperCollins, [1984] 1995, p. 26.
27 V. Margolin, 'The politics of the artificial', ISAST 1997, LEONARDO ON-LINE, world wide web site of Leonardo / the International Society for the Arts, Sciences and Technology: http://mitpress.mit.edu/e-journals/Leonardo/isast/articles/margolin.html.
28 G. Vattimo, *The End of Modernity: Nihilism and Hermeneutics in Post-modern Culture*, trans. J.R. Snyder, Cambridge: Polity Press, 1988.

29 V. Margolin, 'The politics of the artificial' (see note 25).
30 M. Heim, *The Metaphysics of Virtual Reality*, p. 92 (see note 23).
31 W. Gibson, *Count Zero*, London: HarperCollins, [1986] 1995, p. 197.
32 I. Csicsery-Ronay Jr., 'Cyberpunk and neuromanticism', in L. McCaffery (ed.), *Storming the Reality Studio: A Casebook of Cyberpunk and Postmodern Fiction*, London and Durham, NC: Duke University Press, 1991, p. 187.
33 J. Lacan, 'The mirror stage as formative of the function of the I as revealed in psychoanalytic experience', in *Ecrits: A Selection*, trans. A. Sheridan, London: Tavistock, 1977, pp. 1–7.
34 L. Althusser, *Lenin and Philosophy and Other Essays*, London: New Left Books, 1971.
35 W. Gibson, *Neuromancer*, p. 39 (see note 24).
36 W. Gibson, *Virtual Light*, London: Penguin, [1993] 1994, pp. 125, 155.

2: CYBERPUNK, TECHNOLOGY AND MYTHOLOGY

1 W. Gibson, *Count Zero*, London: HarperCollins, [1986] 1995, pp. 9–10.
2 C. Fredericks, *The Future of Eternity: Mythologies of Science Fiction and Fantasy*, Bloomington: Indiana University Press, 1982, p. 153.
3 M. Foucault, *Discipline and Punish*, trans. A. Sheridan, New York: Vintage, 1979.
4 A. Kroker, *Spasm*, New York: St. Martin's Press, 1993, pp. 43, 39.
5 G.L. Downey, J. Dumit and S. Williams, 'Cyborg anthropology', in C.H. Gray (ed.), *The Cyborg Handbook*, London and New York: Routledge, 1995, p. 343.
6 M.E. Clynes and N.S. Kline, 'Cyborgs and space', in *The Cyborg Handbook*, p. 29; originally in *Astronautics* 14 (9), pp. 26–7, 74–5, September, 1960.
7 R.W. Driscoll, 'Engineering man for space: the Cyborg Study' [1963 Report to NASA Biotechnology and Human Research], in *The Cyborg Handbook*, p. 76.
8 C.H. Gray, S. Mentor and H.J. Figueroa-Sarriera, 'Cyborgology', in *The Cyborg Handbook*, p. 3.
9 Ibid., p. 2.
10 N.K. Hayles, 'The life cycle of cyborgs', in *The Cyborg Handbook*, p. 322.
11 H. Moravec, *MIND Children: The Future of Robot and Human Intelligence*, Cambridge, Mass.: Harvard University Press, 1988.
12 H.J. Figueroa-Sarriera, 'Children of the mind with disposable bodies', in *The Cyborg Handbook*, p. 133 (see note 6).
13 A. Balsamo, *Technologies of the Gendered Body: Reading Cyborg Women*, London and Durham, NC: Duke University Press, 1997, p. 18.
14 L. Levidow and K. Robins, 'Socializing the cyborg self', in *The Cyborg Handbook*, p. 119 (see note 6).
15 C.J. Fuchs, 'Death is irrelevant: cyborgs, reproduction, and the future of male hysteria', in *The Cyborg Handbook*, p. 282.

16 J. Goldberg, 'Recalling totalities: The Mirrored Stages of Arnold Schwarzenegger', in *The Cyborg Handbook*, pp. 235–6.

17 A. Balsamo, *Technologies of the Gendered Body*, p. 11 (see note 13).

18 G. Bateson, *Steps to an Ecology of Mind*, New York: Ballantine, 1972, p. 319.

19 D. Haraway, 'A manifesto for cyborgs', *Socialist Review* 80.2, 1985, p. 96.

20 Ibid., p. 175.

21 Ibid., p. 197.

22 Ibid., p. 179.

23 C.H. Gray and S. Mentor, 'The cyborg body politic', in *The Cyborg Handbook*, p. 459.

24 G. Deleuze, *Difference and Repetition*, trans. P. Patton, London: Athlone, 1994, pp. 264–5.

25 Ibid., p. xix.

26 Ibid., p. 66.

27 C.J. Fuchs, 'Death is irrelevant: cyborgs, reproduction, and the future of male hysteria', in *The Cyborg Handbook*, p. 285 (see note 6).

28 C. Fredericks, *The Future of Eternity*, p. 170 (see note 2).

29 J. Shirley, 'Wolves of the plateau', in L. McCaffery (ed.), *Storming the Reality Studio: A Casebook of Cyberpunk and Postmodern Fiction*, London and Durham, NC: Duke University Press, 1991, pp. 148–9; emphasis added.

30 W. Gibson, *Neuromancer*, London: HarperCollins, [1984] 1995, pp. 127, 148.

31 W. Gibson, *Count Zero*, p. 33 (see note 1).

32 Ibid., p. 88.

33 Ibid., p. 64.

34 Ibid., pp. 103–4.

35 Ibid., p. 111.

36 Ibid., p. 113.

37 Ibid., p. 114.

38 Ibid., p. 116.

39 Ibid., p. 162.

40 Ibid., p. 163.

41 Ibid., p. 173.

42 Ibid., pp. 234–5.

43 Ibid., p. 179.

44 W. Gibson, *Mona Lisa Overdrive*, London: HarperCollins, [1988] 1995, p. 28.

45 W. Gibson, *Count Zero*, p. 189 (see note 1).

46 Ibid., p. 192.

47 W. Gibson, *Mona Lisa Overdrive*, p. 196.

48 W. Gibson, *Count Zero*, p. 284.

49 Ibid., p. 294.

50 Ibid., p. 319.

51 W. Gibson, *Mona Lisa Overdrive*, p. 29 (see note 44).

52 Ibid., pp. 49, 90.

53 Ibid., p. 168.

54 Ibid., p. 239.
55 Ibid., p. 34.
56 Ibid., p. 316.
57 W. Gibson, *Virtual Light*, London: Penguin, [1993] 1994, pp. 266–7.
58 D. Suvin, 'On Gibson and cyberpunk SF', in *Storming the Reality Studio*, p. 358 (see note 29).
59 S. Delany, 'Is cyberpunk a good thing or a bad thing?', *Mississippi Review* 47/48, 1988, p. 33.
60 L. McCaffery, 'Introduction: the desert of the real', in *Storming the Reality Studio*, pp. 12, 15 (see note 29).
61 W. Gibson, *Virtual Light*, p. 258 (see note 57).
62 G. Lovink, 'Contemporary nihilism: About organized innocence', in T. Druckrey (ed.), *Electronic Culture*, New York: Aperture, 1996, p. 388.
63 P. Cadigan, *Tea from an Empty Cup*, London: HarperCollins, 1998, p. 2.
64 Ibid., pp. 4–5.
65 Ibid., p. 13.
66 W. Gibson, *Count Zero*, pp. 169–70 (see note 1).
67 W. Gibson, *Mona Lisa Overdrive*, p. 315 (see note 44).
68 W. Gibson, *Count Zero*, p. 223.
69 W. Gibson, *Mona Lisa Overdrive*, p. 316.
70 W. Gibson, *Count Zero*, pp. 299–300.
71 W. Gibson, *Idoru*, London: Penguin, [1996] 1997, p. 138.
72 T. Hawkes, *Structuralism and Semiotics*, London and New York: Methuen, 1977, p. 51.
73 In L. McCaffery, 'An Interview with William Gibson', in *Storming the Reality Studio*, p. 274 (see note 29).
74 Ibid., p. 272.
75 D. Nelkin, 'Perspectives on the evolution of Science Studies', in S. Aronowitz, B. Martinsons and M. Menser (eds), *Technoscience and Cyberculture*, London and New York: Routledge, 1996, p. 31.
76 P. Gross and N. Levitt, *Higher Superstition*, Baltimore: Johns Hopkins University Press, 1995.
77 D. Nelkin, 'Perspectives on the evolution of Science Studies', pp. 32–3; emphasis added (see note 75).
78 See, for example, P. Proctor, *Value Free Science?*, Cambridge, Mass.: Harvard University Press, 1991.
79 See, for example, T. Hughes, *Networks of Power*, Baltimore: Johns Hopkins University Press, 1983.
80 S. Aronowitz and M. Menser, 'On Cultural Studies, science and technology', in *Technoscience and Cyberculture*, pp. 7–8 (see note 75).
81 D. Haraway, *Simians, Cyborgs, Women*, London and New York: Routledge, 1991, p. 249.
82 A. Sokal and J. Bricmont, *Intellectual Impostures*, London: Profile Books, 1998, pp. ix–x.
83 Ibid., p. 4.
84 Ibid., p. 9.
85 Ibid., p. 47.
86 Ibid., p. 150.

87 Ibid., p. 165.
88 Ibid., p. 194.
89 B. Woolley, *Virtual Worlds*, London: Penguin, 1993, p. 15.
90 Quoted in ibid., p. 36.
91 Quoted in T. Carpenter, 'Slouching toward cyberspace', *Village Voice*, 12 March 1991, p. 37.
92 C. Chesher, 'The ontology of digital domains', in D. Holmes (ed.), *Virtual Politics: Identity and Community in Cyberspace*, London: Sage, 1997, p. 81.
93 A. Sokal and J. Bricmont, *Intellectual Impostures*, p. 9 (see note 82).
94 Ibid., p. 176.
95 E. Spenser, *The Faerie Queene*, ed. T. Roche Jr., Harmondsworth: Penguin, 1978, p. 15.
96 A. Sokal and J. Bricmont, *Intellectual Impostures*, p. 8 (see note 82).
97 In L. McCaffery, 'An Interview with William Gibson', p. 281 (see note 73).
98 Ibid., p. 269.
99 Ibid., p. 270.
100 In G. Salza, 'Interview with William Gibson', 1994: http://www.maxheadroom.com/gibson_interview.html. A slightly different version of this interview was incorporated in Giuseppe Salza's book *Che cosa ci faccio in Internet*, Rome: Theoria Edizioni, 1995.
101 In L. McCaffery, 'An Interview with William Gibson', p. 281 (see note 73).
102 S. Delany, 'Among the Blobs', in *Storming the Reality Studio*, p. 58 (see note 29).
103 Ibid., p. 60.
104 C. Fredericks, *The Future of Eternity*, p. 170 (see note 2).
105 I. Calvino, *The Literature Machine*, trans. P. Creagh, London: Secker & Warburg, 1987, pp. 32, 38.
106 J. Willett, *Brecht on Theatre*, New York: Hill & Wang, 1964, p. 96.

3: CYBERPUNK AND THE BODY

1 P.L. Wilson, 'Boundary violations', in S. Aronowitz, B. Martinsons and M. Menser (eds), *Technoscience and Cyberculture*, London and New York: Routledge, 1996, p. 227.
2 F. Jacob, *The Possible and the Actual*, New York: Pantheon, 1982, p. 39. A detailed examination of the concept of 'biosociality' can be found in P. Rabinow's essay, 'Artificiality and Enlightenment: from sociobiology to biosociality', in J. Crary and S. Kwinter (eds), *Incorporations*, New York: Zone, 1992, pp. 34–53.
3 A.R. Stone, 'Virtual systems', in *Incorporations*, pp. 609–11.
4 R. Hardin, 'Penetrabit: Slime-Temples'; 'nerve terminals'; 'Fistic Hermaphrodites', *Mississippi Review* 47/48, 1988; reprinted in L. McCaffery (ed.), *Storming the Reality Studio: A Casebook of Cyberpunk and Postmodern Fiction*, London and Durham, NC: Duke University Press, 1991, pp. 75–9.

5 M. Feher, 'Of bodies and technologies', in H. Foster (ed.), *Discussions in Contemporary Culture*, DIA Art Foundation, Seattle, Wash.: Bay Press, 1987:159.

6 J. Wajcman, *Feminism Confronts Technology*, University Park: Pennsylvania State University Press, 1991, p. 149.

7 A. Balsamo, *Technologies of the Gendered Body: Reading Cyborg Women*, London and Durham, NC: Duke University Press, 1997, p. 5.

8 J. Hoshen, J. Sennott and M. Winkler, 'Keeping tabs on criminals', *IEEE Spectrum* 32.2, 1995, p. 28.

9 C. Cookson, 'A brave new olfactory world', *Financial Times*, 8 June 1995, p. 22.

10 W. Gibson, *Idoru*, London: Penguin, [1996] 1997, p. 18.

11 C. Boyer, *CyberCities*, New York: Princeton Architectural Press, 1996, p. 74.

12 R. Braidotti, 'Cyberfeminism with a difference', *New Formations* 29, Autumn 1996, p. 23.

13 N. Land, 'Cybergothic', in J. Broadhurst Dixon and E.J. Cassidy (eds), *Virtual Futures: Cyberotics, Technology and Post-Human Pragmatism*, London and New York: Routledge, 1998, p. 82.

14 W. Gibson, *Virtual Light*, London: Penguin, [1993] 1994, p. 60.

15 V. Hollinger, 'Cybernetic deconstructions', in *Storming the Reality Studio*, p. 212 (see note 4).

16 In L. McCaffery, 'An Interview with William Gibson', in *Storming the Reality Studio*, p. 277.

17 B. Sterling, 'Preface' to *Burning Chrome*, London: HarperCollins, 1995, p. 11.

18 G. Benford, 'Is something going on?', *Mississippi Review* 47/48, 1988, p. 19.

19 D. Suvin, 'On Gibson and cyberpunk SF', in *Storming the Reality Studio*, p. 352 (see note 4).

20 P. Cadigan, *Tea from an Empty Cup*, London: HarperCollins, 1998, pp. 16–17.

21 Ibid., p. 22.

22 Ibid., pp. 23, 26.

23 Ibid., p. 25.

24 W. Gibson, *Neuromancer*, London: HarperCollins, [1984] 1995, p. 11.

25 M. Piercy, *Body of Glass*, London: Penguin, 1991, p. 203.

26 R. Barthes, 'The death of the author', in *Image, Music, Text*, trans. S. Heath, Glasgow: Fontana, 1977, p. 142.

27 J. Monk, 'The digital unconscious', in J. Wood (ed.), *The Virtual Embodied: Presence/Practice/Technology*, London and New York: Routledge, 1998, p. 32.

28 W. Gibson, *Idoru*, p. 92 (see note 10).

29 Ibid., pp. 175–6.

30 The Technology Page, 'Nanotechnology', © 1996, 1997 Developmental Technologies, Inc., http://www.dvtech.com/pages/pages/TecNANO.htm.

31 W. Gibson, *Virtual Light*, p. 273 (see note 14).

32 W. Gibson, *Idoru*, p. 202 (see note 10).

33 Ibid., p. 178.

34 G. Deleuze and F. Guattari, *Anti-Oedipus: Capitalism and Schizophrenia*, trans. R. Hurley, M. Seem and H.R. Lane, London: Athlone, 1984, p. 2.

35 Ibid., p. 5.

36 W. Gibson, *Idoru*, p. 237 (see note 10).

37 G. Deleuze and F. Guattari, *Anti-Oedipus*, pp. 8–9 (see note 34).

38 C. Vasseleu, 'Virtual bodies, virtual worlds', in D. Holmes (ed.), *Virtual Politics: Identity and Community in Cyberspace*, London: Sage, 1997, p. 55.

39 W. Gibson, *Idoru*, p. 38 (see note 10).

40 Ibid., p. 25.

41 Ibid., p. 132.

42 Ibid., p. 148.

43 A. Gordon, *Ghostly Matters: Haunting and the Sociological Imagination*, London and Minneapolis: Minnesota University Press, 1997, p. 31.

44 M. Blanchot, 'The two versions of the imaginary', in *The Space of Literature*, trans. A. Smock, Nebraska: Nebraska University Press, 1982:11.

45 W. Gibson, *Mona Lisa Overdrive*, London: HarperCollins, [1988] 1995, p. 24.

46 Ibid., p. 77.

47 Ibid., p. 83.

48 Ibid., p. 50.

49 M. Laidlaw, 'Office of the future', in *Dad's Nuke*, New York: Lorevan, 1984, pp. 194–7.

50 A. Gordon, *Ghostly Matters*, p. 16 (see note 43).

51 Ibid., p. 7.

52 R.M. Rilke, 'Letter to Witold von Hulewicz', *Selected Letters 1902–26*, trans. R.F.C. Hull, quoted in M. Warner, *The Inner Eye*, London: National Touring Exhibitions/The South Bank Centre, 1996, p. 48.

53 M. Heidegger, *Basic Writings*, ed. D.F. Krell, New York: Columbia University Press, 1977.

54 W. Gibson, *Mona Lisa Overdrive*, p. 55 (see note 45).

55 T. Eagleton, *The Ideology of the Aesthetic*, Oxford: Blackwell, 1990, pp. 288–9.

56 J. Baudrillard, *The Transparency of Evil*, trans. J. Benedict, London: Verso, 1993, p. 174.

57 T. Leary, 'Foreword' to *HR Giger ARh=*, Cologne: Taschen, 1996, p. 4.

58 W. Gibson, *Virtual Light*, p. 201 (see note 14).

59 W. Gibson, *Idoru*, p. 81 (see note 10).

60 Ibid., pp. 2–3.

61 M. Warner, *The Inner Eye*, p. 9 (see note 52).

62 D. Haraway, 'The promise of monsters: a regenerative politics of inappropriate/d others', in L. Grossberg (ed.), *Cultural Studies*, London and New York: Routledge, 1992, p. 320.

63 W.A. Ewing, *Inside Information*, London: Thames & Hudson, 1996, p. 7.

64 Ibid., p. 9.
65 Ibid., p. 14.
66 M. Kemp and K. Arnold, *Materia Medica: A New Cabinet of Medicine and Art*, London: The Wellcome Institute for the History of Medicine, 1995, p. 13.
67 W.A. Ewing, *Inside Information*, p. 15 (see note 63).
68 M. Warner, *The Inner Eye*, p. 10 (see note 52).
69 J. Winterson, *Gut Symmetries*, London: Granta, 1997, p. 3.
70 S. Cubitt, *Digital Aesthetics*, London: Sage, 1998, p. 88.
71 Ibid., pp. 90–1.
72 Critical Art Ensemble, 'The coming of age of the flesh machine', in T. Druckrey (ed.), *Electronic Culture*, New York: Aperture, 1996, p. 397.
73 Ibid.
74 W. Gibson, 'Johnny Mnemonic', in *Burning Chrome*, p. 36 (see note 17).
75 Ibid., pp. 23–4.
76 Ibid., p. 31.
77 Ibid., p. 36.
78 In G. Salza, 'Interview with William Gibson', 1994: http://www.maxheadroom.com/gibson_interview.html. A slightly different version of this interview was incorporated in Giuseppe Salza's book *Che cosa ci faccio in Internet*, Rome: Theoria Edizioni, 1995.
79 W. Gibson, 'The Belonging Kind', in *Burning Chrome*, p. 62 (see note 17).
80 Ibid., p. 65.
81 Ibid., p. 71.
82 W. Gibson, 'The Gernsback Continuum', in *Burning Chrome*, pp. 39–40.
83 Ibid., p. 42.
84 Ibid., p. 48.
85 Ibid., p. 41.
86 Ibid., pp. 40–1.
87 Ibid., p. 40.
88 Ibid., p. 47.
89 W. Gibson, 'The Winter Market', in *Burning Chrome*, p. 164.
90 Ibid., p. 140.
91 Ibid., pp. 146–7.
92 Ibid., p. 164.
93 P. Cadigan, 'Rock On', in *Storming the Reality Studio*, p. 53 (see note 4).
94 W. Gibson, 'Hinterlands', in *Burning Chrome*, p. 76 (see note 17).
95 Ibid., pp. 81–2.
96 Ibid., p. 80.
97 W. Gibson, 'Burning Chrome', in *Burning Chrome*, p. 197.
98 Ibid., p. 198.
99 Ibid., p. 211.
100 Ibid., p. 216.
101 B. Turner, *The Body and Society*, Oxford: Blackwell, 1984, p. 8.
102 W. Gibson, *Mona Lisa Overdrive*, p. 37 (see note 45).
103 Ibid., pp. 127–8.
104 Ibid., p. 158.

105 Ibid., p. 47.
106 Ibid., p. 84.
107 Ibid., p. 132.
108 Ibid., pp. 134–5.
109 W. Gibson, *Neuromancer*, p. 95 (see note 24).
110 W. Gibson, *Mona Lisa Overdrive*, pp. 84–5 (see note 45).
111 Ibid., p. 83.
112 V. Flusser, 'Digital apparition', in *Electronic Culture*, p. 245 (see note 72).
113 Ibid., p. 242.
114 M. Heim, *The Metaphysics of Virtual Reality*, Oxford: Oxford University Press, 1993, p. 83.
115 Plato, *The Symposium*, trans. W. Hamilton, Harmondsworth: Penguin, 1951.
116 R. Barthes, *A Lover's Discourse*, trans. R. Howard, London: Penguin, 1990, pp. 5–7.
117 W. Gibson, *Mona Lisa Overdrive*, p. 62 (see note 45).
118 Ibid., p. 105.
119 Ibid., p. 283.
120 Ibid., p. 294.
121 Ibid., p. 8.
122 bid., p. 187.
123 W. Mosley, *Gone Fishin'*, London: Serpent's Tail, 1997, p. 54.
124 G. Wood, *The Smallest of All Persons Mentioned in the Records of Littleness*, London: Profile Books, 1998, pp. 7–8.
125 Ibid., p. 13.
126 Ibid., p. 20.
127 W. Gibson, *Neuromancer*, pp. 166–8 (see note 24).
128 C. Boyer, *CyberCities*, p. 108 (see note 11).
129 A. Hewitt, *Fascist Modernism: Aesthetics, Politics, and the Avant-Garde*, Stanford: Stanford University Press, 1993, p. 146.

4: CYBERPUNK, GENDER AND SEXUALITY

1 A. Balsamo, *Technologies of the Gendered Body: Reading Cyborg Women*, London and Durham, NC: Duke University Press, 1997, p. 9.
2 B. Woolley, *Virtual Worlds*, London: Penguin, 1993, p. 125.
3 A. Kroker and M. Kroker, *Body Invaders*, New York: St. Martin's Press, 1987.
4 A. Balsamo, *Technologies of the Gendered Body*, p. 15 (see note 1).
5 Ibid., p. 13.
6 Ibid., p. 58.
7 W. Gibson, *Idoru*, London: Penguin, [1996] 1997, p. 3.
8 W. Gibson, *Neuromancer*, London: HarperCollins, [1984] 1995, p. 74.
9 R.T. Farrior and R.C. Jarchow, 'Surgical principles in face lift', in P.H. Ward and W.E. Berman (eds), *Aesthetic Surgery*, St. Louis: C.V. Mosby, 1984, p. 298.

10 S. Irvine, 'Will you? won't you?', *Vogue* (British edition), September 1998, pp. 334–6.

11 B. Sterling, *Schismatrix*, New York: Arbor House, 1985, p. 44.

12 W. Gibson, *Mona Lisa Overdrive*, London: HarperCollins, [1988] 1995, p. 153.

13 Ibid., p. 181.

14 Ibid., p. 185.

15 E. Martin, 'Anthropological knowledge', in M. Jacobus, S. Shuttleworth and E. Fox Keller (eds), *Body'Politics: Women and the Discourse of Science*, London: Routledge, 1990.

16 C. Springer, *Electronic Eros*, Austin: Texas University Press, 1996, p. 9.

17 Ibid., p. 51.

18 Ibid., p. 104.

19 B. Sterling, 'CATscan: cyber-superstition', *Science Fiction Eye* 8, Winter 1991, p. 11.

20 A. Clarke, 'Modernity, postmodernity and reproductive processes ca. 1890–1990', in C.H. Gray (ed.), *The Cyborg Handbook*, London and New York: Routledge, 1995, p. 146.

21 Ibid., p. 148.

22 M.J. Casper, 'Fetal cyborgs and technomoms on the reproductive frontier', in *The Cyborg Handbook*, p. 185.

23 Ibid., p. 187.

24 M.R. Harrison, 'The fetus as patient', in M.R. Harrison, M.S. Golbus and R.A. Filly (eds), *The Unborn Patient*, Philadelphia: W.B. Saunders Company, 1991, p. 3.

25 M.J. Casper, 'Fetal cyborgs and technomoms . . .', p. 187 (see note 22).

26 A.L.R. Findlay, *Reproduction and the Fetus*, London: Edward Arnold, 1984, p. 96.

27 C. Merchant, *The Death of Nature*, San Francisco: Harper & Row, 1980, p. xix.

28 S. Mies and V. Shiva, *Ecofeminism*, London: Zed Books, 1993, p. 14.

29 Y. King, 'The eco-feminist perspective', in L. Caldecott and S. Leland (eds), *Reclaiming the Earth*, London: The Women's Press, 1983, pp. 10–11.

30 P. Gunn Allen, *The Sacred Hoop*, Boston: Beacon Press, 1986. C. Christ, 'Rethinking technology and nature', in J. Plant (ed.), *Healing the Wounds*, Philadelphia: New Society, 1989.

31 V. Margolin, 'The politics of the artificial', ISAST 1997, LEONARDO ON-LINE, world wide web site of Leonardo / the International Society for the Arts, Sciences and Technology: http://mitpress.mit.edu/e-journals/Leonardo/isast/articles/margolin.html.

32 J. Gordon, 'Yin and yang duke it out', in L. McCaffery (ed.), *Storming the Reality Studio: A Casebook of Cyberpunk and Postmodern Fiction*, London and Durham, NC: Duke University Press, 1991, p. 199.

33 J. Slonczewski, *A Door Into Ocean*, New York: Arbor House, 1986.

34 J. Russ, *The Female Man*, Boston: Gregg, 1975, p. 2.

35 R. Braidotti, 'Cyberfeminism with a difference', *New Formations* 29, Autumn 1996, p. 25.

36 M. Strathern, *After Nature*, Cambridge: Cambridge University Press, 1992, p. 43.
37 M. Stanworth, *Reproductive Technologies*, Cambridge: Polity Press, 1987, p. 34.
38 S. Franklin, 'Fetal fascinations', in S. Franklin, C. Lury and J. Stacey (eds), *Off-Centre: Feminism and Cultural Studies*, London: HarperCollins Academic, 1991, pp. 190–204.
39 N. Nixon, 'Cyberpunk: preparing the ground for revolution or keeping the boys satisfied?', *Science Fiction Studies* 57, July 1992, p. 222.
40 T. Leary, 'Quark of the decade?', *Mondo 2000* 1, 1989, p. 56.
41 J. Gordon, 'Yin and yang duke it out', p. 196 (see note 32).
42 W. Gibson, *Virtual Light*, London: Penguin, [1993] 1994, p. 265.
43 Ibid., pp. 3–4.
44 Ibid., p. 37.
45 W. Gibson, *Neuromancer*, p. 21 (see note 8).
46 Ibid., p. 37.
47 Ibid., p. 41.
48 R. Binion, *Love Beyond Death: The Anatomy of a Myth in the Arts*, New York: New York University Press, 1993, p. 9.
49 E. Bronfen, *Over Her Dead Body*, Manchester: Manchester University Press, 1992, p. xiii.
50 W. Gibson, *Neuromancer*, pp. 43–5 (see note 8).
51 Ibid., p. 45.
52 Ibid., pp. 90–1.
53 Ibid., p. 219.
54 F. Miller and B. Sienkiewicz, *Elektra Assassin*, New York: Epic Books, 1986/1987.
55 K. Acker, *Empire of the Senseless*, New York: Grove, 1988, pp. 31–7.
56 A. Ross, *Strange Weather: Culture, Science, and Technology in the Age of Limits*, London: Verso, 1991, p. 158.
57 J. Shirley, 'Wolves of the plateau', in *Storming the Reality Studio*, p. 151 (see note 32).
58 W.J. Williams, *Hardwired*, New York: T. Doherty Associates, 1986, p. 16.
59 W. Gibson, 'The Belonging Kind', in *Burning Chrome*, London: HarperCollins, 1995, pp. 74–5.
60 W. Gibson, 'Burning Chrome', in *Burning Chrome*, pp. 204–5.
61 J.G. Ballard, 'Interview by Lynn Barber', *Penthouse* September 1970; reprinted in *Re/Search* 8–9, 1984, p. 164.
62 C. Springer, *Electronic Eros*, pp. 50–1 (see note 16).
63 S. Bright, *Susie Bright's Sexual Reality: A Virtual Sex Reader*, Pittsburgh: Cleis Press, 1992, p. 65.
64 H. Rheingold, *Virtual Reality*, New York: Summit, 1991, p. 346.
65 K. Lillington, 'Surfing for sex', *Guardian ONLINE*, 14 May 1998, pp. 1–3.
66 P. Cadigan, *Tea from an Empty Cup*, London: HarperCollins, 1998, p. 25.
67 R. Baker, 'PDF™ – the digital hostess', in J. Wood (ed.), *The Virtual Embodied: Presence/Practice/Technology*, London and New York: Routledge, 1998, p. 206.
68 Ibid., pp. 208–11.

69 S. Plant, 'Coming across the future', in J. Broadhurst Dixon and E.J. Cassidy (eds), *Virtual Futures: Cyberotics, Technology and Post-Human Pragmatism*, London and New York: Routledge, 1998, p. 30.

70 W. Gibson, *Neuromancer*, pp. 284–5 (see note 8).

71 Ibid., pp. 70–2.

72 D. Lupton, 'The embodied computer/user', in M. Featherstone and R. Burrows (eds), *Cyberspace/Cyberbodies/Cyberpunk: Cultures of Technological Embodiment*, London: Sage, 1995, pp. 110–11.

73 C. Davies, 'Osmose: Notes on "BEING" in Immersive Virtual Space', ISEA Conference Proceedings (Sixth International Symposium on Electronic Arts), Montreal, September 1995: http://www.softimage.com/Projects/Osmose/notes.htm.

5: CYBERPUNK AND THE CITY

1 T. Jurek, *Straight Fiction*, from an extract reprinted in L. McCaffery (ed.), *Storming the Reality Studio: A Casebook of Cyberpunk and Post-modern Fiction*, London and Durham, NC: Duke University Press, 1991, p. 86.

2 N. Clark, 'Rear-view mirrorshades: The Recursive Generation of the Cyberbody', in M. Featherstone and R. Burrows (eds), *Cyberspace/Cyberbodies/Cyberpunk: Cultures of Technological Embodiment*, London: Sage, 1995, p. 121.

3 J. Christie, 'Of AIs and others: William Gibson's transit', in G. Slusser and T. Shippey (eds), *Fiction 2000*, Athens, Georgia: University of Georgia Press, 1992, p. 173.

4 F. Jameson, *The Seeds of Time*, New York: Columbia University Press, 1994, p. 157.

5 D. Haraway, *Modest_Witness @ Second_Millennium*, London and New York: Routledge, 1997, pp. 135–6.

6 G. Metzger, 'The artist in the eye of the storm', in J. Wood (ed.), *The Virtual Embodied: Presence/Practice/Technology*, London and New York: Routledge, 1998, p. 107.

7 D.R.F. Taylor, 'Postmodernism, deconstruction and cartography', *Cartographica* 26.3–4, 1989, p. 115.

8 D. Haraway, *Modest_Witness @ Second_Millennium*, p. 134 (see note 5).

9 N. Land, 'Cybergothic', in J. Broadhurst Dixon and E.J. Cassidy (eds), *Virtual Futures: Cyberotics, Technology and Post-Human Pragmatism*, London and New York: Routledge, 1998, p. 81.

10 C. Blake, 'In the shadow of cybernetic minorities: life, death and delirium in the capitalist imaginary', *Angelaki* 1.1, 1993, p. 133.

11 J. Winterson, *Gut Symmetries*, London: Granta, 1997, p. 82.

12 J-F. Lyotard, *The Postmodern Condition: A Report on Knowledge*, trans. G. Bennington and B. Massumi, Manchester: Manchester University Press, 1984, p. 57.

13 E. de Bono, 'Lateral thinking and science fiction', in P. Nicholls (ed.), *Explorations of the Marvellous*, Glasgow: Fontana/Collins, 1978, p. 39.

14 F. Guattari, 'Regimes, pathways, subjects', in J. Crary and S. Kwinter (eds), *Incorporations*, New York: Zone, 1992, p. 18.

15 T. Johnson, 'When worlds collide', *Guardian*, 19 November 1998, p. 9.

16 E. Martin, 'Citadels, rhizomes, and string figures', in S. Aronowitz, B. Martinsons and M. Menser (eds), *Technoscience and Cyberculture*, London and New York: Routledge, 1996, p. 100.

17 Ibid., p. 103.

18 J. Rich and M. Menser, 'Introduction', in *Technoscience and Cyberculture*, p. 2.

19 J.D. Barrow, 'Strings', in A. Bullock, O. Stallybrass and S. Trombley (eds), *The Fontana Dictionary of Modern Thought*, 2nd edn, London: Fontana Press, 1990, p. 820.

20 M. Green, 'Superstrings', *Scientific American*, September 1986.

21 J.D. Barrow, 'Superstrings', in *The Fontana Dictionary of Modern Thought*, p. 829.

22 J. Winterson, *Gut Symmetries*, p. 159.

23 Ibid., p. 98.

24 S. Plant, 'Beyond the screens: film, cyberpunk and cyberfeminism', in S. Kemp and J. Squires (eds), *Feminisms*, Oxford and New York: Oxford University Press, 1997, pp. 506–7.

25 H. Jaffe, 'Max Headroom', in *Storming the Reality Studio*, p. 83 (see note 1).

26 J. Buick and Z. Jevtic, *Cyberspace for Beginners*, Cambridge: Icon, 1995, p. 56.

27 N. Land, 'Cybergothic', p. 85 (see note 9).

28 W.J. Mitchell, *City of Bits: Space, Place, and the Infobahn*, Cambridge, Mass.: MIT Press, 1995, p. 5.

29 J. Raban, *Soft City*, London: Hamish Hamilton, 1974, p. 245.

30 Ibid., p. 10.

31 S. Cubitt, *Digital Aesthetics*, London: Sage, 1998, p. 47.

32 C. Boyer, *CyberCities*, New York: Princeton Architectural Press, 1996, p. 11.

33 R. Braidotti, 'Cyberfeminism with a difference', *New Formations* 29, Autumn 1996, p. 9.

34 F. Rotzer, 'Between nodes and data packets', in T. Druckrey (ed.), *Electronic Culture*, New York: Aperture, 1996, p. 249.

35 P. Cadigan, *Tea from an Empty Cup*, London: HarperCollins, 1998, p. 22.

36 K. Piper, 'The dis-orderly city: a nigger in cyberspace', *Actes: 6e Symposium des arts electroniques*, Montreal, 1995, p. 234.

37 W. Gibson, *Neuromancer*, London: HarperCollins, [1984] 1995, p. 51.

38 Quoted in K. Lucic, *Charles Sheeler and the Cult of the Machine*, Cambridge, Mass.: Harvard University Press, 1991, p. 16.

39 S. Cubitt, *Digital Aesthetics*, pp. 64–5 (see note 31).

40 W. Gibson, *Mona Lisa Overdrive*, London: HarperCollins, [1988] 1995, pp. 11–12.

41 W. Gibson, *Idoru*, London: Penguin, [1996] 1997, p. 36.

42 J. Winterson, *The Passion*, London: Penguin, 1988, p. 49.

43 Ibid., p. 97.
44 R. Goy, *Venice: The City and its Architecture*, London: Phaidon, 1998, p. 14.
45 E. Bianchi, 'Dalla parte del mare', *Meridiani* XII.75, Milan: Editoriale Domus, 1999, p. 39.
46 Ibid., p. 46.
47 R. Goy, *Venice*, p. 296 (see note 44).
48 J. Winterson, *The Passion*, p. 52 (see note 42).
49 Ibid., p. 57.
50 A. Falletta, 'Acqua, miliardi, e parole', *Meridiani* XII.75, pp. 48–9.
51 R. Goy, *Venice*, pp. 46, 49, 51 (see note 44).
52 W. Gibson, *Virtual Light*, London: Penguin, [1993] 1994, pp. 58–9.
53 Ibid., p. 59.
54 W. Gibson, *Neuromancer*, p. 14 (see note 37).
55 C. Chesher, 'The ontology of digital domains', in D. Holmes (ed.), *Virtual Politics: Identity and Community in Cyberspace*, London: Sage, 1997, p. 81.
56 W. Gibson, *Idoru*, p. 186 (see note 41).
57 W. Gibson, *Neuromancer*, p. 57 (see note 37).
58 D. Suvin, 'On Gibson and cyberpunk SF', in *Storming the Reality Studio*, p. 353 (see note 1).
59 Quoted in J. Gleick, *Chaos*, London: Heinemann, 1988, p. 98.
60 B. Landon, 'Bet on it', in *Storming the Reality Studio*, p. 240 (see note 1).
61 P. Virilio, *The Lost Dimension*, trans. D. Mashenberg, New York: Autonomedia, 1991.
62 W. Gibson, *Idoru*, pp. 181–2 (see note 41); emphasis added.
63 N.K. Hayles, *Chaos Unbound: Orderly Disorder in Contemporary Literature and Science*, Ithaca: Cornell University Press, 1995, p. 247.
64 In L. McCaffery, 'An Interview with William Gibson', in *Storming the Reality Studio*, p. 268 (see note 1).
65 Ibid., pp. 272–3.
66 Ibid., p. 271.
67 N.K. Hayles, 'Virtual bodies and flickering signifiers', in *Electronic Culture*, p. 262 (see note 34).
68 N. Land, 'Cybergothic', p. 82 (see note 9).
69 W. Gibson, *Count Zero*, London: HarperCollins, [1986] 1995, p. 14.
70 Ibid., p. 88.
71 Ibid., pp. 175–6.
72 Ibid., p. 33.
73 Ibid., p. 222.
74 Ibid., p. 294.
75 Ibid., p. 129.
76 Ibid., p. 240.
77 Ibid., p. 261.
78 Ibid., p. 268.
79 Ibid., p. 316.
80 Ibid., p. 319.
81 Ibid., p. 321.

82 B. Woolley, *Virtual Worlds: A Journey in Hype and Hyperreality*, London: Penguin, 1993, p. 91.
83 Ibid., p. 90.
84 Ibid., p. 94.
85 Ibid., p. 88.
86 I. Prigogine and I. Stengers, *Order Out of Chaos*, New York: Bantam Books, 1984.
87 I. Stewart, *Does God Play Dice: The Mathematics of Chaos*, Oxford: Blackwell, 1989, pp. 95–100.
88 W. Gibson, *Neuromancer*, p. 207 (see note 37).
89 W. Gibson, *Mona Lisa Overdrive*, p. 59 (see note 40).
90 Ibid., p. 139.
91 W. Gibson, *Neuromancer*, p. 315 (see note 37).
92 J.K. Wright, 'Terrae incognitae: the place of the imagination in geography', *Annals of the Association of American Geographers* 37.1, 1947, p. 4.
93 R.E. Park, 'The city: suggestions for investigation of human behaviour in the urban environment', in R.E. Park, E.W. Burgess, R.D. McKenzie and L. Wirth (eds), *The City: Suggestions for Investigation of Human Behaviour in the Urban Environment*, Chicago and London: Chicago University Press, 1984, p. 1.

6: CYBERPUNK AND THE GOTHIC

1 A. Williams, *Art of Darkness*, London and Chicago: Chicago University Press, 1995, pp. 23–4.
2 V. Hollinger, 'Cybernetic deconstructions', in L. McCaffery (ed.), *Storming the Reality Studio: A Casebook of Cyberpunk and Postmodern Fiction*, London and Durham, NC: Duke University Press, 1991, pp. 213–14.
3 V. Sage and A.L. Smith, 'Introduction', in V. Sage and A.L. Smith (eds), *Modern Gothic*, Manchester: Manchester University Press, 1996, p. 2.
4 S. Freud, 'The uncanny', *The Standard Edition of the Complete Works of Sigmund Freud*, vol. 17, trans. J. Strachey, London: Hogarth Press and the Institute of Psychoanalysis, 1919, p. 226.
5 Ibid., p. 244.
6 Ibid., p. 241.
7 W. Gibson, *Mona Lisa Overdrive*, London: HarperCollins, [1988] 1995, p. 10.
8 Ibid., p. 24.
9 W. Gibson, *Count Zero*, London: HarperCollins, [1986] 1995, pp. 40–1.
10 S. Freud, 'The uncanny', p. 248 (see note 4).
11 Ibid., p. 249.
12 W. Gibson, *Count Zero*, p. 282 (see note 9).
13 W. Gibson, *Mona Lisa Overdrive*, pp. 7–8 (see note 7).
14 Ibid., p. 79.
15 Stelarc, 'From psycho-body to cyber-systems: images as post-human

entities', in J. Broadhurst Dixon and E.J. Cassidy (eds), *Virtual Futures: Cyberotics, Technology and Post-Human Pragmatism*, London and New York: Routledge, 1998, p. 118.

16 Quoted in 'Piranesi', in S. West (ed.), *Guide to Art*, London: Bloomsbury, 1996, p. 708.

17 M. Fellows, *The Life and Works of Maurits Cornelius Escher*, Bristol: Parragon, 1995, pp. 5–6.

18 V. Sage, 'Gothic Revival', in M. Mulvey-Roberts (ed.), *The Handbook to Gothic Literature*, London: Mamillan, 1998, p. 94.

19 K. Clark, *The Gothic Revival*, London: Thames & Hudson, 1995, p. 87.

20 Quoted in M. Franklin, 'Beckford', in *The Handbook to Gothic Literature*, p. 23.

21 K. Clark, *The Gothic Revival*, p. 89.

22 M. Mulvey-Roberts, 'Introduction', in *The Handbook to Gothic Literature*, xvi.

23 C. Houswitschka, '*Zerrissenheit*', in *The Handbook to Gothic Literature*, p. 258.

24 J.E. Hogle, 'Counterfeit', in *The Handbook to Gothic Literature*, p. 263.

25 W. Gibson, *Neuromancer*, London: HarperCollins, [1984] 1995, p. 207.

26 G. Deleuze and F. Guattari, *A Thousand Plateaus: Capitalism and Schizophrenia*, trans. B. Massumi, London: Athlone, 1988, pp. xii—xiii.

27 W. Gibson, *Mona Lisa Overdrive*, p. 22 (see note 7).

28 Ibid., pp. 162–3.

29 L. Woods, *Anarchitecture*, New York: St Martin's Press, 1992, p. 46.

30 P. Brooks, *The Melodramatic Imagination*, New Haven and London: Yale University Press, 1976, p. 19.

31 A. Williams, *Art of Darkness*, p. 44 (see note 1).

32 Quoted in G. Turcotte, 'English-Canadian Gothic', in *The Handbook to Gothic Literature*, pp. 52–3 (see note 18).

33 H. Lefebvre, *The Production of Space*, Oxford: Blackwell, 1991, p. 42.

34 D. Punter, 'Terror', in *The Handbook to Gothic Literature*, pp. 236–7.

35 F. Botting, *Gothic*, London and New York: Routledge, 1996, p. 123.

36 D. Punter, 'Terror', pp. 236–7.

37 F. Botting, *Gothic*, p. 124.

38 Ibid., p. 127.

39 W. Gibson, *Neuromancer*, p. 206 (see note 25).

40 W. Gibson, *Mona Lisa Overdrive*, pp. 232–3 (see note 7).

41 W. Gibson, *Count Zero*, p. 205 (see note 9).

42 Ibid., pp. 206–7.

43 W. Gibson, *Virtual Light*, London: Penguin, [1993] 1994, pp. 58–9.

44 Ibid., p. 163.

45 V. Sage, 'Gothic Revival', p. 93 (see note 18).

46 Ibid., p. 91.

47 W. Gibson, *Idoru*, London: Penguin, [1996] 1997, p. 1.

48 V. Sage, 'Gothic Revival', p. 91.

49 W. Gibson, *Idoru*, p. 46.

50 Ibid., p. 81.

51 Ibid., pp. 81–3.

52 W. Gibson, 'The Winter Market', in *Burning Chrome*, London: Harper-Collins, 1995, p. 141.
53 Ibid., pp. 142–3.
54 W. Gibson, *Mona Lisa Overdrive*, p. 168 (see note 7).
55 K. Clark, *The Gothic Revival*, p. 215 (see note 19).
56 A. Williams, *Art of Darkness*, p. 46 (see note 1).
57 A. Horner, 'Heroine', in *The Handbook to Gothic Literature*, pp. 116–17 (see note 18).
58 A. Milbank, 'Female Gothic', in *The Handbook to Gothic Literature*, p. 56.
59 D. Haraway, 'Cyborgs and Symbionts', in C.H. Gray (ed.), *The Cyborg Handbook*, London and New York: Routledge, 1995, p. xii.
60 A. Williams, *Art of Darkness*, p. 2 (see note 1).
61 Ibid., p. 8.
62 Ibid., p. 6.
63 R.D. Hume, 'Gothic versus Romantic', *PMLA* 84, 1969, p. 289.
64 A. Williams, *Art of Darkness*, p. 11.
65 Ibid., p. 9.
66 W. Gibson, *Count Zero*, pp. 144–5 (see note 9).
67 W. Gibson, *Neuromancer*, p. 200 (see note 25).
68 W. Gibson, *Count Zero*, p. 196.
69 W. Gibson, *Mona Lisa Overdrive*, pp. 132–3 (see note 7).
70 Ibid., p. 111.
71 W. Gibson, *Neuromancer*, p. 242 (see note 25).
72 W. Gibson, *Mona Lisa Overdrive*, p. 64.
73 Ibid., p. 78.
74 Ibid., pp. 274–5.
75 Ibid., p. 29.
76 W. Gibson, 'The Winter Market', in *Burning Chrome*, p. 156 (see note 52).
77 W. Gibson, *Idoru*, p. 285 (see note 47).
78 W. Gibson, *Virtual Light*, p. 126 (see note 43).
79 W. Gibson, *Neuromancer*, pp. 65–6 (see note 25).
80 Ibid., p. 88.
81 Ibid., pp. 231–2.
82 Ibid., p. 252.
83 Ibid., p. 206.
84 Ibid., p. 231.
85 Ibid., p. 253.
86 Ibid., p. 300.
87 Ibid., p. 307.
88 Ibid., p. 271.
89 Ibid., p. 272.
90 W. Gibson, *Count Zero*, pp. 209–10 (see note 9).
91 W. Gibson, *Mona Lisa Overdrive*, p. 86 (see note 7).
92 Ibid., p. 20.
93 Ibid., p. 19.
94 Ibid., p. 192.

95 Ibid., p. 17.
96 W. Gibson, *Count Zero*, p. 57 (see note 9).
97 Ibid., p. 59.
98 F. Baudot, *Thierry Mugler*, London: Thames & Hudson, 1998, p. 8.
99 H. James, 'Robert Louis Stevenson', in *Partial Portraits by Henry James*, Ann Arbor: University of Michigan Press, 1970, p. 139.
100 J. Halberstam, *Skin Shows*, London and Durham, NC: Duke University Press, 1995, p. 60.
101 W. Gibson, *Virtual Light*, p. 50 (see note 43).
102 Ibid., pp. 53–4.
103 W.P. Day, *In the Circles of Fear and Desire*, Chicago: Chicago University Press, 1985, pp. 10–11.
104 This argument is put forward by Halberstam in *Skin Shows* (see note 100).
105 F. Kelemen, *Making the Invisible Visible*, Munsterschwarzach Abtei: Benedikt Press, 1995, pp. 60–4.
106 W. Gibson, *Agrippa (A Book of the Dead)*, New York: Kevin Begos Publishing, 1992.
http://www.eff.org/pub/Publications/William_Gibson/agrippa_book_of_the_dead.poem.
107 W. Gibson and B. Sterling, *The Difference Engine*, London: Vista, 1996, p. 25.
108 Ibid., p. 25.
109 Ibid., p. 93.
110 Ibid., p. 14.
111 Ibid., p. 21.
112 A. Lovelace, quoted by C. Babbage, in 'Of the analytical engine', in P. Morrison and E. Morrison (eds), *Charles Babbage and His Calculating Engines*, New York: Dover, 1961, p. 250.
113 Ibid.
114 S. Plant, 'The future looms: weaving women and cybernetics', in M. Featherstone and R. Burrows (eds), *Cyberspace/Cyberbodies/Cyberpunk: Cultures of Technological Embodiment*, London: Sage, 1995, p. 49.
115 W. Gibson and B. Sterling, *The Difference Engine*, p. 7 (see note 107).
116 Ibid., p. 94.
117 S. Plant, 'The future looms . . .', p. 51 (see note 113).
118 A. Lovelace, quoted by C. Babbage, in 'Of the analytical engine', p. 264 (see note 112).
119 W. Gibson and B. Sterling, *The Difference Engine*, pp. 36–47 (see note 107).
120 S. Plant, 'The future looms . . .', p. 52 (see note 113).
121 W. Gibson and B. Sterling, *The Difference Engine*, pp. 99–100.
122 Ibid., p. 106.
123 Ibid., p. 21.

EPILOGUE: CYBERPUNK AND MEMORY

1 W. Gibson, quoted in K. Biddick, 'Humanist history and the haunting of virtual worlds: problems of memory and rememoration', *Genders* 18, 1993, p. 48.
2 W. Gibson, quoted in M. Harrison, *Visions of Heaven and Hell*, London: Channel 4 Publications, 1995, p. 21.
3 G. Schwab, 'Cyborgs: postmodern phantasms of body and mind', *Discourse* 9, Spring/Summer 1987, p. 81.
4 K. Biddick, 'Humanist history and the haunting of virtual worlds: problems of memory and rememoration', p. 48.
5 W. Gibson, *Virtual Light*, London: Penguin, [1993] 1994, p. 266.
6 W. Gibson, *Count Zero*, London: HarperCollins, [1986] 1995, p. 62.
7 Ibid., p. 78.
8 N. Clark, 'Rear-view mirrorshades', in M. Featherstone and R. Burrows (eds), *Cyberspace/Cyberbodies/Cyberpunk: Cultures of Technological Embodiment*, London: Sage, 1995, p. 113.
9 W. Benjamin, *Illuminations*, trans. H. Zohn, New York: Schocken, 1969, pp. 257–8.
10 J. Baudrillard, *Selected Writings*, ed. M. Poster, Cambridge: Polity Press, 1988, pp. 145, 121.
11 W. Gibson, *Mona Lisa Overdrive*, London: HarperCollins, [1988] 1995, p. 10.
12 W. Gibson, *Count Zero*, p. 212 (see note 6).
13 Ibid., pp. 311–12.
14 J. Baudrillard, *Simulations*, trans. N. Dufresne, New York: Semiotext(e), 1983.
15 I. Nathan, 'Review of *The Matrix*', *Empire*, July 1999, p. 17.
16 A. Smith, 'Reality bites', *Empire*, July 1999, p. 80.
17 Ibid., p. 81.
18 J. Glover, 'The ultimate Matrix concordance', in S. Goodman (ed.), *Inside Film: The Matrix*, London: Inside Film Limited, 1999, p. 18.

GUIDE TO FURTHER READING

The following entries supply synopses of a selection of theoretical works that address the impact of computer technology on contemporary culture and the role played by cyberpunk in current debates on the relationship between science and society.

Anne Balsamo, *Technologies of the Gendered Body: Reading Cyborg Women*, London and Durham, NC: Duke University Press, 1997.
 The effects of technological development on the human body are here addressed, with an emphasis on the idea that the bodies constructed through practices such as body-building, cosmetic surgery and reproductive medicine are deeply gendered. The book thus counters the claim that technoscience has made material corporeality irrelevant. Analyses of scientific and medical literature are integrated with readings of novels and films.

Michael Benedikt (ed.), *Cyberspace: First Steps*, Cambridge, Mass.: MIT Press, 1991.
 This is a collection of essays presenting various and generally positive interpretations of the term 'cyberspace'. The editor discusses cyberspace in relation to four contexts: language, media technologies, architecture and mathematics. The approach to Internet culture is celebratory and reflects the euphoria typical of early assessments of cyberspace.

Christine Boyer, *Cybercities*, New York: Princeton Architectural Press, 1996.
 This book provides a detailed investigation of the postmodern metropolis based on the idea that contemporary cities are simultaneously dematerialized entities, neatly mapped by cybernetic networks, and highly material spaces, riven by crime, pollution and sickness. Interrelations among the city, the body and the machine are exhaustively investigated with reference to modernist aesthetics, the repercussions of electronic communication and representations of the city in various fictional genres.

Joan Broadhurst Dixon and Eric J. Cassidy (eds), *Virtual Futures: Cyberotics,*

Technology and Post-Human Pragmatism, London and New York: Routledge, 1998.

Contrasting responses to the impact of computer technology, ranging from technophilia to technophobia, constitute this collection's principal theme. One of its leading threads is the concept of 'cyberotics', the idea that technological developments witness the evolution of an erotic relationship between the human and the machine. The book's approach is interdisciplinary and brings together materialist philosophy, feminism, postmodernist literature, science fiction and the performance arts.

James Brook and Iain A. Boal (eds), *Resisting the Virtual Life: The Culture and Politics of Information*, San Francisco: City Lights, 1995.

This collection of essays challenges enthusiastic responses to the age of the Net characteristic of early theorizings of cyberculture. It alerts the reader to the potential dangers of computer technology and to the risk of idealizing cyberspace as a realm of unlimited freedom when, in fact, the options it offers may be rather narrow. It also argues that descriptions of the Net as the embodiment of male myths (conquest, the frontier) may serve to perpetuate negative stereotypes of femininity.

Jonathan Crary and Sanford Kwinter (eds), *Incorporations*, New York: Zone, 1992.

This interdisciplinary anthology combines in thought-provoking ways the written word and the visual image. It contains contributions by major philosophers, literary and film critics, anthropologists, sociologists, scientists, fiction writers and artists. The book focuses on two complementary meanings of 'incorporation': incorporation as the integration of human life into the broad structures of society, science and technology; and incorporation as the state of being embodied and of experiencing the world as physical entities.

Sean Cubitt, *Digital Aesthetics*, London: Sage, 1998.

This book provides a critical overview of the history of digital culture. It asks questions about the relationship between computers and pre-digital technologies, about the impact of computers on notions of creativity and labour, about the origins, functions and aesthetic appeal of electronic networks, and about the implications of global images in the political and economic spheres.

Mike Featherstone and Roger Burrows (eds), *Cyberspace/Cyberbodies/Cyberpunk: Cultures of Technological Embodiment*, London: Sage, 1995.

This anthology assesses the force of electronic mediation in shaping contemporary life, by examining the role it plays in both fiction and social reality. Drawing on cultural studies, sociology, feminist theory, media studies and philosophy, the book highlights various ways in which cyberculture and cyberpunk have affected the relationship between technology and the body.

Chris Hables Gray (ed.), *The Cyborg Handbook*, London and New York: Routledge, 1995.
This is the most comprehensive account so far of different interpretations and uses of the cybernetic organism in the fields of military and astronautical research, medicine, politics, fiction and cinema. It highlights the pervasiveness of cyborg technologies through which bodies are either normalized or reconfigured, by bringing together historical documents and cultural theory. Cyborg films, videos, novels and comics are listed in an especially useful bibliography.

Linda M. Harasim (ed.), *Global Networks: Computers and International Communication*, London: Sage, 1995.
This book postulates that virtual communities offer Net users new meeting-places and alternative opportunities for social interaction. It also raises important questions about the relationship between cyberculture and power: Who controls and censors the Net? What is censored? What is the part played by industry and by governments in the game?

David Holmes (ed.), *Virtual Politics: Identity and Community in Cyberspace*, London: Sage, 1997.
This collection of essays concentrates on the redefinition of notions of identity, agency, community and space compelled by electronic technology. By drawing on sociology, cultural studies and media theory, the book examines the strategies through which virtuality and simulation have affected social relationships and produced anonymous and disembodied consumers.

Steven G. Jones (ed.), *CyberSociety: Computer-Mediated Information and Community*, London: Sage, 1995.
The impact of Net culture on notions of community and identity is the central issue addressed in this text. One of the main questions it poses is whether communities necessarily require the sharing of physical spaces or could in fact exist in their absence. The book also examines the processes through which Net users access their environments, experiment with alternative forms of communication, identities and relationships, and construct group-specific codes and conventions.

Larry McCaffery (ed.), *Storming the Reality Studio: A Casebook of Cyberpunk and Postmodern Fiction*, London and Durham, NC: Duke University Press, 1991.
This is probably the most exhaustive companion to cyberpunk available to date. It contextualizes the genre in relation to science fiction, postmodern narratives and the subculture of punk, as well as to the impact of new technologies and economic formations. The first section of this casebook, headed 'Fiction and Poetry', consists of a selection of short stories, poems and extracts from novels drawn from cyberpunk itself and from postmodern and science-fictional works that have influenced or anticipated cyberpunk. The second section, 'Non-Fiction', provides a selection of critical

evaluations of cyberpunk by major theorists of contemporary culture, literature, music and art.

Rob Shields (ed.), *Cultures of Internet: Virtual Spaces, Real Histories, Living Bodies*, London: Sage, 1996.
  This text investigates the impact of cyberculture on social policies and on people's relation to both history and space. It is concerned with the status of the Net as a decentralized system and with its ability to dismantle traditional cultural boundaries by supplying its users with a playground for the acting out of a potentially solacing sense of control over their surroundings.

Claudia Springer, *Electronic Eros*, Austin: Texas University Press, 1996.
  Focusing on the ways in which virtual technologies and digital simulation have redefined traditional understandings of embodiment and desire, the book explores the relationship between technology and pleasure. Drawing on a broad range of science-fictional novels, films and comics, it argues that cyberculture has not – as many critics contend – rendered the sexual body obsolete but actually created scope for alternative forms of erotic satisfaction.

John Wood (ed.), *The Virtual Embodied: Presence/Practice/Technology*, London and New York: Routledge, 1998.
  This anthology concentrates on the relationship between virtual technologies and the human body. It challenges the idea that virtuality has the power of erasing the physical being by stressing the concept of 'embodiment' – that is, the notion that knowledge, perceptions and actions are produced through material channels. This point is documented by recourse to a wide variety of discourses: ancient philosophy, mystical traditions, colonialism, electronic surveillance, and subcultural phenomena such as the Rave scene.

Benjamin Woolley, *Virtual Worlds*, London: Penguin, 1993.
  This book offers a critical overview of the development of virtual technologies and of their impact on conventional notions of reality. It explores Virtual Reality in relation to concepts such as 'simulation', 'cyberspace', 'hypertext' and 'hyperreality', and with reference to cybernetics, the theories of modern physics, fiction, literary criticism and philosophy. Reader-friendly in its structure and style, this book is likely to prove stimulating for both beginners and experts.

BIBLIOGRAPHY

PRIMARY SOURCES

Acker, K. (1988), *Empire of the Senseless*, New York: Grove.
Atwood, M. (1986), *The Handmaid's Tale*, New York: Ballantine.
Ballard, J.G. [1973] (1995), *Crash*, London: Vintage.
Beckford, W. [1786] (1985) *Vathek*, ed. Roger Lonsdale, Oxford: Oxford University Press.
Bester, A. [1955] (1987), *The Stars My Destination*, New York: Franklin Watts.
Bethke, B. (1983) 'Cyberpunk', *Amazing Science Fiction Stories* 57 (4).
Brunner, J. (1975), *Shockwave Rider*, New York: Harper & Row.
Burgess, A. (1962) *A Clockwork Orange*, London: Heinemann.
Burroughs, W.S. (1959), *Naked Lunch*, New York: Grove.
Cadigan, P. (1987), *Mindplayers*, New York: Bantam.
—— (1998), *Tea from an Empty Cup*, London: Harper Collins.
—— [1984] (1991), 'Rock on', in L. McCaffery (ed.), *Storming the Reality Studio: A Casebook of Cyberpunk and Postmodern Fiction*, London and Durham, NC: Duke University Press, pp. 48–55.
Carter, A. (1979), *Heroes and Villains*, London: Heinemann.
—— [1977] (1982), *The Passion of New Eve*, London: Virago.
Chandler, R. (1939), *The Big Sleep*, New York: Random House.
Delany, S. [1988] (1991), 'Among the Blobs', in L. McCaffery (ed.), *Storming the Reality Studio: A Casebook of Cyberpunk and Postmodern Fiction*, London and Durham, NC: Duke University Press, pp. 56–62.
DeLillo, D. (1984), *White Noise*, New York: Viking.
Dick, P.K. (1972), *Do Androids Dream of Electric Sheep?*, London: Granada.
—— (1994), 'We can remember it for you wholesale', in *We Can Remember It for You Wholesale, The Collected Stories of Philip K. Dick*, Volume V, London: Voyager.
Effinger, G.A. (1987), *When Gravity Fails*, New York: Arbor House.
—— (1990), *A Fire in the Sun*, New York: Arbor House.
—— (1991), *The Exile Kiss*, New York: Arbor House.

Ellis, B.E. (1991), *American Psycho*, London: Picador.

Finney, J. (1955) *The Body Snatchers*, New York: Dell.

Gibson, W. [1984] (1995), *Neuromancer*, London: HarperCollins.

—— [1986] (1995), *Count Zero*, London: HarperCollins.

—— [1988] (1995), *Mona Lisa Overdrive*, London: HarperCollins.

—— (1992), *Agrippa (A Book of the Dead)*, New York: Kevin Begos Publishing.

—— [1993] (1994), *Virtual Light*, London: Penguin.

—— (1995), *Burning Chrome*, London: HarperCollins.

—— [1996] (1997), *Idoru*, London: Penguin.

Gibson, W. and B.Sterling [1990] (1996), *The Difference Engine*, London: Vista.

Hammett, D. (1929), *Red Harvest*, New York: Vintage.

Hardin, R. (1988), 'Fistic Hermaphrodites'; 'Microbes'; 'Penetrabit: Slime-Temples'; 'nerve terminals', *Mississippi Review* 47/48, reprinted in L. McCaffery (ed.), *Storming the Reality Studio: A Casebook of Cyberpunk and Postmodern Fiction*, London and Durham, NC: Duke University Press, pp. 75–9.

Huxley, A. (1932), *Brave New World*, London: Chatto & Windus.

Jaffe, A. [1988] (1991), 'Max Headroom', in L. McCaffery (ed.), *Storming the Reality Studio: A Casebook of Cyberpunk and Postmodern Fiction*, London and Durham, NC: Duke University Press, pp. 80–4.

Kadrey, R. (1988), *Metrophage*, London: Gollancz.

Laidlaw, M. (1984), *Dad's Nuke*, New York: Lorevan.

Lessing, D. (1979–83), *Canopus in Argos: Archives*, London: Grafton.

Lewis, C.S. (1938), *Out of the Silent Planet*, London: John Love (The Bodley Head).

—— (1943), *Perelandra*, London: John Love (The Bodley Head). (Variant title: *Voyage to Venus*.)

—— (1945), *That Hideous Strength*, London: John Love (The Bodley Head).

Leyner, M. (1990), *My Cousin, My Gastroenterologist*, New York: Harmony/Crown.

Miller, F. and B. Sienkiewicz (1986–7), 'Elektra Assassin', New York: Epic Comics.

Mooney, T. (1981), *Easy Travel to Other Planets*, New York: Farrar, Strauss & Giroux.

Mosley, W. (1997), *Gone Fishin'*, London: Serpent's Tail.

O'Barr, J. (1991), 'Frame 137', in L. McCaffery (ed.), *Storming the Reality Studio: A Casebook of Cyberpunk and Postmodern Fiction*, London and Durham, NC: Duke University Press, 118–21.

Orwell, G. (1949), *Nineteen Eighty-Four*, London: Secker & Warburg.

Piercy, M. (1991), *Body of Glass*, London: Penguin.

Pynchon, T. (1966), *The Crying of Lot 49*, New York: Perennial.

Rucker, R. (1982), *Software*, New York: Ace.

Russ, J. (1975), *The Female Man*, Boston: Gregg.

Shelley, M. [1818] (1969), *Frankenstein; or, the Modern Prometheus*, ed. M.K. Joseph, Oxford: Oxford University Press.

Shiner, L. (1988), 'Stoked', *Re: Artes Liberales*, Spring/Fall, 198–202.
Shirley, J. (1985), *Eclipse*, New York: Bluejay.
—— (1987), *Eclipse Penumbra*, New York: Warner.
—— (1988), 'Wolves of the Plateau', in L. McCaffery (ed.), *Storming the Reality Studio: A Casebook of Cyberpunk and Postmodern Fiction*, London and Durham, NC: Duke University Press, 139–53.
—— (1989), *Total Eclipse*, New York: Warner.
Slonczewski, J. (1986), *A Door into Ocean*, New York: Arbor House.
Sterling, B. (1980), *The Artificial Kid*, New York: Ace.
—— (1985), *Schismatrix*, New York: Arbor House.
—— (1988), 'Twenty Evocations', *Mississippi Review* 47/48, 122–9.
Walpole, H. [1765] (1998) *The Castle of Otranto*, ed. W.S. Lewis, Oxford: Oxford University Press.
Wells, H.G. (1895), *The Time Machine*, London: Heinemann.
—— (1898), *The War of the Worlds*, London: Heinemann.
Williams, W.J. (1986), *Hardwired*, New York: T. Doherty Associates.
Winterson, J. (1988), *The Passion*, London: Penguin.
—— (1997), *Gut Symmetries*, London: Granta.
Wolfe, B. [1952] (1985), *Limbo*, New York: Carroll & Graf.
Wood, G. (1998), *The Smallest of All Persons Mentioned in the Records of Littleness*, London: Profile Books.
Wyndham, J. (1952), *The Day of the Triffids*, London: Michael Joseph.
Zamyatin, Y. [1922] (1977), *We*, trans. B.G. Guerney, London: Penguin.

SECONDARY SOURCES

Allen, P.G. (1986), *The Sacred Hoop*, Boston: Beacon Press.
Althusser, L. (1971), *Lenin and Philosophy and Other Essays*, London: New Left Books.
Amis, K. (1960), *New Maps of Hell*, New York: Columbia University Press.
Aronowitz, S., B. Martinsons and M. Menser (eds) (1996), *Technoscience and Cyberculture*, London and New York: Routledge.
Auerbach, N. (1995), *Our Vampires, Ourselves*, Chicago: Chicago University Press.
Ballard, J.G. (1970), 'Interview by Lynn Barber', *Penthouse*, September; reprinted in *Re/Search* 8–9.
Balsamo, A. (1997), *Technologies of the Gendered Body: Reading Cyborg Women*, London and Durham, NC: Duke University Press.
Barlow, J.P. (1994), 'Jack in, young pioneer', HREF 1, Keynote Essay for the 1994 Computerworld College Edition: http://www.eff.org/pub/Publications/John_Perry_Barlow/HTML/jack_in_young_pioneer.html.
Barrow, J.D. (1990), 'Strings' and 'Superstrings', in A. Bullock, O. Stallybrass and S. Trombley (eds), *The Fontana Dictionary of Modern Thought*, 2nd edn, London: Fontana Press.
Barthes, R. (1977), 'The Death of the Author', in *Image, Music, Text*, trans. S. Heath, Glasgow: Fontana.

—— (1990), *A Lover's Discourse: Fragments*, trans. R. Howard, London: Penguin.

Bateson, G. (1972), *Steps to an Ecology of Mind*, New York: Ballantine.

Baudot, F. (1998), *Thierry Mugler*, London: Thames & Hudson.

Baudrillard, J. (1983), *Simulations*, trans. N. Dufresne, New York: Semiotext(e).

—— (1988), *Selected Writings*, ed. M. Poster, Cambridge: Polity Press.

—— (1993), *The Transparency of Evil*, trans. J. Benedict, London: Verso.

Benedikt, M. (ed.) (1991), *Cyberspace: First Steps*, Cambridge, Mass.: MIT Press.

Benford, G. (1988), 'Is something going on?', *Mississippi Review* 47/48: 18–23.

Benjamin, W. (1969), *Illuminations*, trans. H. Zohn, New York: Schocken.

Biddick, K. (1993), 'Humanist history and the haunting of virtual worlds: problems of memory and rememoration', *Genders* 18.

Binion, R. (1993), *Love Beyond Death: the Anatomy of a Myth in the Arts*, New York: New York University Press.

Blake, C. (1993), 'In the shadow of cybernetic minorities: life, death and delirium in the capitalist imaginary', *Angelaki* 1.1.

Blanchot, M. (1982), 'The two versions of the imaginary', in *The Space of Literature*, trans. A. Smock, Nebraska: Nebraska University Press.

Botting, F. (1996), *Gothic*, London: Routledge.

Boyer, M.C. (1996), *CyberCities*, New York: Princeton Architectural Press.

Braidotti, R. (1996), 'Cyberfeminism with a difference', *New Formations* 29 (Autumn): 9–25.

Bright, S. (1992), *Susie Bright's Sexual Reality: A Virtual Sex Reader*, Pittsburgh: Cleis Press.

Broadhurst Dixon, J. and E.J. Cassidy (eds) (1998), *Virtual Futures: Cyberotics, Technology and Post-Human Pragmatism*, London and New York: Routledge.

Bronfen, E. (1992), *Over Her Dead Body*, Manchester: Manchester University Press.

Brook, J. and I.A. Boal (eds) (1995), *Resisting the Virtual Life: The Culture and Politics of Information*, San Francisco: City Lights.

Brooks, P. (1976), *The Melodramatic Imagination*, New Haven and London: Yale University Press.

Bruckman, A. (1996), 'Finding one's own space in cyberspace', *Technology Review* 99.1, January.

Buick, J. and Z. Jevtic (1995), *Cyberspace for Beginners*, Cambridge: Icon.

Bukatman, S. (1993), *Terminal Identity: The Virtual Subject in Postmodern Science Fiction*, London and Durham, NC: Duke University Press.

Caldecott, L. and S. Leland (eds) (1983), *Reclaiming the Earth*, London: The Women's Press.

Calvino, I. (1987), *The Literature Machine*, trans. P. Creagh, London: Secker & Warburg.

—— (1996), *Six Memos for the Next Millennium*, trans. P. Creagh, London: Vintage.

Carpenter, T. (1991), 'Slouching toward cyberspace', *Village Voice*, 12 March.

Clark, K. (1995), *The Gothic Revival*, London: Thames & Hudson.

Cookson, C. (1995), 'A brave new olfactory world', *Financial Times*, 8 June.

Crary, J. and S. Kwinter (eds) (1992), *Incorporations*, New York: Zone.

Cubitt, S. (1998), *Digital Aesthetics*, London: Sage.

Davies, C. (1998), 'On *Osmose*', http://www.softimage.com/Projects/Osmose/notes.htm.

Day, W.P. (1985), *In the Circles of Fear and Desire*, Chicago: Chicago University Press.

Deleuze, G. (1994), *Difference and Repetition*, trans. P. Patton, London: Athlone.

Deleuze, G. and F. Guattari (1984), *Anti-Oedipus: Capitalism and Schizophrenia*, trans. R. Hurley, M. Seem and H.R. Lane, London: Athlone.

—— (1988), *A Thousand Plateaus*, trans. B. Massumi, London: Athlone.

Druckrey, T. (ed.) (1996), *Electronic Culture*, New York: Aperture.

Duzois, G. (1984) Review of new generation of science-fiction writers, *Washington Post*, 30 December.

Dyson, J. (1999), 'Spellbound', *Vogue*, May: 30–3.

Eagleton, T. (1990), *The Ideology of the Aesthetic*, Oxford: Blackwell.

Ewing, W.A. (1996), *Inside Information*, London: Thames & Hudson.

Farrior, R.T. and R.C. Jarchow (1984), 'Surgical principles in face-lift', in P.H. Ward and W.E. Berman (eds), *Aesthetic Surgery*, St Louis, Mo.: C.V. Mosby.

Featherstone, M. and R. Burrows (eds) (1995), *Cyberspace/Cyberbodies/Cyberpunk: Cultures of Technological Embodiment*, London: Sage.

Feher, M. (1987), 'Of bodies and technologies', in H. Foster (ed.), *Discussions in Contemporary Culture*, DIA Art Foundation, Seattle, Wash.: Bay Press.

Fellows, M. (1995), *The Life and Works of Maurits Cornelius Escher*, Bristol: Parragon.

Findlay, A.L.R. (1984), *Reproduction and the Fetus*, London: Edward Arnold.

Fontana, D. (1993), *The Secret Language of Symbols*, London: Pavilion.

Foucault, M. (1979), *Discipline and Punish*, trans. A. Sheridan, New York: Vintage.

Franklin, S. (1991), 'Fetal fascinations', in S. Franklin, C. Lury and J. Stacey (eds), *Off-Centre: Feminism and Cultural Studies*, London: HarperCollins Academic.

Fredericks, C. (1982), *The Future of Eternity*, Bloomington: Indiana University Press.

Freud, S. (1919), 'The uncanny', *The Standard Edition of the Complete Works of Sigmund Freud*, vol.17, trans. J. Strachey, London: Hogarth Press and the Institute of Psychoanalysis.

Gibson, W. (1994), 'Interview by Giuseppe Salza', http://www.sct.fr/cyber/gibson.html.

Gleick, J. (1988), *Chaos*, London: Heinemann.

Goodman, S. (ed.) (1999), *Inside Film: The Matrix*, London: Inside Film Limited.

Gordon, A. (1997), *Ghostly Matters: Haunting and the Sociological*

Imagination, London and Minneapolis: University of Minnesota University Press.

Goy, R. (1998), *Venice: The City and its Architecture*, London: Phaidon.

Gray, C.H. (ed.) (1995), *The Cyborg Handbook*, London and New York: Routledge.

Grolier (1995), 'Science Fiction', *Grolier Multimedia Encyclopedia*, version 7.0, Grolier Electronic Publishing.

Gross, P. and N. Levitt (1995), *Higher Superstition*, Baltimore: Johns Hopkins University Press.

Grunenberg, C. (1997), *Gothic*, Boston: The Institute of Contemporary Art.

Hafner, K. (1997), 'The world's most influential online community', *Wired*, May.

Halberstam, J. (1995), *Skin Shows*, London and Durham, NC: Duke University Press.

Harasim, L.M. (ed.) (1995), *Global Networks: Computers and International Communication*, London: Sage.

Haraway, D. (1985), 'A manifesto for cyborgs', *Socialist Review* 80.2: 65–108.

—— (1991), *Simians, Cyborgs, Women*, London and New York: Routledge.

—— (1992), 'The promise of monsters: a regenerative politics of inappropriate/d others', in L. Grossberg (ed.), *Cultural Studies*, London and New York: Routledge.

—— (1997), *Modest_Witness @ Second_Millennium*, London and New York: Routledge.

Harrison, M. (1995), *Visions of Heaven and Hell*, London: Channel 4 Publications.

Harrison, M.R., M.S. Golbus and R.A. Filly (eds) (1991), *The Unborn Patient*, Philadelphia: W.B. Saunders Company.

Hawkes, T. (1977), *Structuralism and Semiotics*, London and New York: Methuen.

Hayles, K. (1995), *Chaos Unbound: Orderly Disorder in Contemporary Literature and Science*, Ithaca: Cornell University Press.

Hebdige, D. (1988), *Subculture: the Meaning of Style*, London and New York: Methuen.

Heidegger, M. (1977), *Basic Writings*, ed. D.F. Krell, New York: Columbia University Press.

Heim, M. (1993), *The Metaphysics of Virtual Reality*, Oxford: Oxford University Press.

Hewitt, A. (1993), *Fascist Modernism*, Stanford: Stanford University Press.

Holmes, D. (ed.) (1997), *Virtual Politics: Identity and Community in Cyberspace*, London: Sage.

Hoshen, J., J. Sennott and M. Winkler (1995), 'Keeping tabs on criminals', *EEE Spectrum* 32.2, pp. 26–32.

Hughes, T. (1983), *Networks of Power*, Baltimore: Johns Hopkins University Press.

Hume, R.D. (1969), 'Gothic versus Romantic', *PMLA* 84: 282–90.

Irvine, S. (1998), 'Will you?wont't you?', *Vogue*, September: 334–6.

Jacob, F. (1982), *The Possible and the Actual*, New York: Pantheon.

Jacobus, M., E. Fox Keller and S. Shuttleworth (eds) (1990), *Body/ Politics: Women and the Discourse of Science*, London and New York: Routledge.

James, H. [1888] (1970), 'Robert Louis Stevenson', *Partial Portraits by Henry James*, Ann Arbor: University of Michigan Press.

Jameson, F. (1994), *The Seeds of Time*, New York: Columbia University Press.

Johnson, T. (1998), 'When worlds collide', *Guardian*, 19 November.

Jones, S.G. (ed.) (1995), *CyberSociety: Computer-Mediated Information and Community*, London: Sage.

Kelemen, F. (1995), *Making the Invisible Visible*, Munsterschwarzach Abtei: Benedikt Press.

Kemp, M. and K. Arnold (1995), *Materia Medica: A New Cabinet of Medicine and Art*, London: The Wellcome Institute for the History of Medicine.

Kemp, S. and J. Squires (eds) (1997), *Feminisms*, Oxford: Oxford University Press.

Kristeva, J. (1982), *The Powers of Horror*, trans. L. Roudiez, New York: Columbia University Press.

Kroker, A. (1993), *Spasm*, New York: St. Martin's Press.

Kroker, A. and M. Kroker (eds) (1987), *Body Invaders*, New York: St Martin's Press.

Kroker, A. and M. Weinstein (1997), 'The hyper-texted body, or Nietzsche gets a modem', 1997: http://www.aec.at/ctheory/e-hyper-texted.html. From *Data Trash: The Theory of the Virtual Class*, New York: St Martin's Press, and Montreal: New World Perspectives, 1994.

Lacan, J. (1977), *Ecrits: A Selection*, trans. A. Sheridan, London: Tavistock.

Land, N. (1995), 'Travels in cyber-reality', *Guardian*, 18 March.

Lanier, J. and F. Bocca (1992), 'An insider view of the future of virtual reality', *Journal of Communication* 42.4: 150–72.

Laurel, B. (1991), *Computers as Theatre*, Reading, Mass.: Addison-Wesley.

Leary, T. (1989), 'Quark of the decade?', *Mondo 2000* 1: 53–6.

—— (1996), 'Foreword' to *HR Giger ARh=*, Cologne: Taschen.

Lefebvre, H. (1991), *The Production of Space*, Oxford: Blackwell.

Lillington, K. (1998), 'Surfing for Sex', *Guardian ONLINE*, 14 May: 1–3.

Lucic, K. (1991), *Charles Sheeler and the Cult of the Machine*, Cambridge, Mass.: Harvard University Press.

Lyotard, J-F. (1984), *The Postmodern Condition: A Report on Knowledge*, trans. G. Bennington and B. Massumi, Manchester: Manchester University Press.

McCaffery, L. (ed.) (1991), *Storming the Reality Studio: A Casebook of Cyberpunk and Postmodern Fiction*, London and Durham, NC: Duke University Press.

McLuhan, M. (1964), *The Mechanical Bride*, New York: Vanguard Press.

Margolin, V. (1997), 'The politics of the artificial', LEONARDO ON-LINE, world wide web site of Leonardo / the International Society for the Arts, Sciences and Technology: http://mitpress.mit.edu/e-journals/ Leonardo/isast/articles/margolin.html.

Merchant, C. (1980), *The Death of Nature*, San Francisco: Harper & Row.

Meridiani XII, 75 (1999), Milan: Editoriale Domus.

Mies, S. and V. Shiva (1993), *Ecofeminism*, London: Zed Books.

Mitchell, W.J. (1995), *City of Bits: Space, Place, and the Infobahn*, Cambridge, Mass.: MIT Press.

Moravec, H. (1988), *MIND Children: The Future of Robot and Human Intelligence*, Cambridge, Mass.: Harvard University Press.

Morrison, P. and E. Morrison (eds) (1961), *Charles Babbage and His Calculating Engines*, New York: Dover.

Mulvey-Roberts, M. (ed.) (1998), *The Handbook to Gothic Literature*, London: Macmillan.

Nathan, I. (1999), 'Review of *The Matrix*', *Empire*, July: 16–17.

Negroponte, N. (1995), *Being Digital*, New York: Alfred A.Knopf.

Nicholls, P. (ed.) (1978), *Explorations of the Marvellous*, Glasgow: Fontana/Collins.

Nixon, N. (1992), 'Cyberpunk: preparing the ground for revolution or keeping the boys satisfied?', *Science-Fiction Studies* 57 (July): 219–35.

Ousby, I. (1997), *The Crime and Mystery Book: A Reader's Companion*, London: Thames & Hudson.

Park, R.E., E.W. Burgess, R.D. McKenzie and L. Wirth (eds) (1984), *The City: Suggestions for Investigation of Human Behaviour in the Urban Environment*, Chicago and London: Chicago University Press.

Piper, K. (1995), 'The dis-orderly city: a nigger in cyberspace', *Actes: 6e Symposium des arts* electroniques, Montreal, pp. 232–5.

Plant, J. (ed.) (1989), *Healing the Wounds*, Philadelphia: New Society.

Plato (1951), *The Symposium*, trans. W. Hamilton, Harmondsworth: Penguin.

Prigogine, I. and I. Stengers (1984), *Order Out of Chaos*, New York: Bantam Books.

Proctor, R. (1991), *Value Free Science?*, Cambridge, Mass.: Harvard University Press.

Punter, D. (1996), *The Literature of Terror*, Volumes 1 & 2, New York: Longman.

Raban, J. (1974), *Soft City*, London: Hamish Hamilton.

Raven, C. (1998), 'From zero to it-boy', *Guardian*, 14 August.

Rheingold, H. (1991), *Virtual Reality*, New York: Summit.

Rollensteiner, F. (ed.) (1984), *Microworlds: Writings on Science Fiction and Fantasy*, San Diego and New York: Harcourt Brace Jovanovich.

Ross, A. (1991), *Strange Weather: Culture, Science, and Technology in the Age of Limits*, London: Verso.

Sage, V. and A.L. Smith (eds) (1996), *Modern Gothic*, London: Macmillan.

Schwab, G. (1987), 'Cyborgs: postmodern phantasms of body and mind', *Discourse* 9, Spring/Summer.

Shapiro, A.L. (1995), 'Street corners in cyberspace', *The Nation*, 3 July.

Shields, R. (ed.) (1996), *Cultures of Internet: Virtual Spaces, Real Histories, Living Bodies*, London: Sage.

Slusser, G. and T. Shippey (eds) (1992), *Fiction 2000*, Athens, Georgia: University of Georgia Press.

Smith, A. (1999), 'Reality bites', *Empire*, July: 79–84.

Sobchack, V. (1987), *Screening Space*, New York: Ungar.

Sokal, A. and J. Bricmont (1998), *Intellectual Impostures*, London: Profile Books.

Spenser, E. (1978), *The Faerie Queene*, ed. T. Roche Jr., Harmondsworth: Penguin.

Springer, C. (1996), *Electronic Eros*, Austin: Texas University Press.

Stanworth, M. (1987), *Reproductive Technologies*, Cambridge: Polity Press.

Sterling, B. (1986), 'Preface' to *Mirrorshades*, New York: Arbor House.

—— (1991), 'CATscan: cyber-superstition', *Science Fiction Eye* 8, Winter: 11–12.

—— (1993) 'License to Dream', a contribution to the Convocation on Technology and Education, National Academy of Sciences, Washington, DC, 10 May: http://www.uflib.ufl.edu/sterling.license.html.

—— (1995), 'Preface' to *Burning Chrome*, London: HarperCollins.

Stewart, I. (1989), *Does God Play Dice: The Mathematics of Chaos*, Oxford: Blackwell.

Strathern, M. (1992), *After Nature*, Cambridge: Cambridge University Press.

Suvin, D. (1979), *Metamorphoses of Science Fiction*, New Haven and London: Yale University Press.

Taylor, D.R.F. (1989), 'Postmodernism, deconstruction and cartography', *Cartographica* 26 (3–4): 114–17.

Turkle, S. (1996), *Life on the Screen*, London: Weidenfeld & Nicolson.

Turner, B. (1984), *The Body and Society*, Oxford: Blackwell.

Vattimo, G. (1988), *The End of Modernity*, trans. J.R. Snyder, Cambridge: Polity Press.

Vidler, A. (1990), 'The Building in Pain', *AA Files* 19, Spring: 3–10.

Virilio, P. (1991), *The Lost Dimension*, trans. D. Mashenberg, New York: Autonomedia.

Wajcman, J. (1991), *Feminism Confronts Technology*, University Park: Pennsylvania State University Press.

Warner, M. (1996), *The Inner Eye*, London: National Touring Exhibitions/ The South Bank Centre.

West, S. (ed.) (1996), *Guide to Art*, London: Bloomsbury.

Wiener, N. [1948] (1961), *Cybernetics: Control and Communication in Animal and Machine*, Cambridge, Mass.: MIT Press.

Willett, J. (1964), *Brecht on Theatre*, New York: Hill & Wang.

Williams, A. (1995), *Art of Darkness*, London and Chicago: Chicago University Press.

Wood, J. (ed.) (1998), *The Virtual Embodied: Presence/Practice/Technology*, London and New York: Routledge.

Woods, L. (1992), *Anarchitecture*, New York: St Martin's Press.

Woolley, B. (1993), *Virtual Worlds*, London: Penguin.

Wright, J.K. (1947), 'Terrae incognitae: the place of the imagination in geography', *Annals of the Association of American Geographers* 37.1.

Wynne-Davies, M. (ed.) (1989), *Bloomsbury Guide to English Literature*, London: Bloomsbury.

BIBLIOGRAPHY

FILMS

Alien, Ridley Scott, 1979.
Alien 3, David Fincher, 1992.
Blade Runner, Ridley Scott, 1982.
Demon Seed, Donald Cammell, 1977.
The Fly, David Cronenberg, 1986.
Freddy's Dead: The Final Nightmare, Rachel Talalay, 1991.
The Invasion of the Body Snatchers, Don Siegel, 1956.
The Invasion of the Body Snatchers, Philip Kaufman, 1978.
Johnny Mnemonic, Robert Longo, 1995.
Jurassic Park, Steven Spielberg, 1993.
The Lawnmower Man, Brett Leonard, 1992.
Leviathan, George Cosmatos, 1989.
The Matrix, Wachowsky Brothers (1999).
Metropolis, Fritz Lang, 1926.
Robocop, Paul Verhoeven, 1987.
The Silence of the Lambs, Jonathan Demme, 1991.
Strange Days, Kathryn Bigelow, 1996.
The Terminator, James Cameron, 1984.
Terminator 2: Judgment Day, James Cameron, 1991.
Total Recall, Paul Verhoeven, 1990.
2001: A Space Odyssey, Stanley Kubrick, 1968.

INDEX